To my wife (Barbara) and family (Jarrett and Ashlyn) who have supported me over the years. I thank you and know that it has not always been easy.

52-Week Baseball Training

Gene Coleman, EdD
Strength and Conditioning Coach, Houston Astros

Human Kinetics

Library of Congress Cataloging-in-Publication Data

Coleman, A. Eugene.
    52-week baseball training / Gene Coleman.
        p.   cm.
    Includes bibliographical references.
    ISBN 0-7360-0322-3
     1.   Baseball--Training. 2. Physical fitness. I. Title.

  GV875.6 .C63 2000
  613.7'11--dc21   00-021346

ISBN-10: 0-7360-0322-3
ISBN-13: 978-0-7360-0322-3

Developmental Editor: Anne Heiles; Managing Editor: Laurie Stokoe; Assistant Editor: Kim Thoren; Copyeditor: Robert Replinger; Proofreader: Anne Meyer Byler; Permission Manager: Cheri Banks; Photo Manager: Clark Brooks; Cover Designer: Jack W. Davis; Photographer (cover): Ron Vesely; Photographer (interior): Karen Warren; Art Manager: Craig Newsom; Illustrator: Kimberly Maxey; Printer: United Graphics

Human Kinetics books are available at special discounts for bulk purchase. Special editions or book excerpts can also be created to specification. For details, contact the Special Sales Manager at Human Kinetics.

Printed in the United States of America   15   14   13   12   11

Human Kinetics
Web site: www.HumanKinetics.com

United States: Human Kinetics
P.O. Box 5076
Champaign, IL 61825-5076
800-747-4457
e-mail: humank@hkusa.com

Canada: Human Kinetics
475 Devonshire Road, Unit 100
Windsor, ON N8Y 2L5
800-465-7301 (in Canada only)
e-mail: info@hkcanada.com

Europe: Human Kinetics
107 Bradford Road
Stanningley
Leeds LS28 6AT, United Kingdom
+44 (0)113 255 5665
e-mail: hk@hkeurope.com

Australia: Human Kinetics
57A Price Avenue
Lower Mitcham, South Australia 5062
08 8372 0999
e-mail: info@hkaustralia.com

New Zealand: Human Kinetics
Division of Sports Distributors NZ Ltd.
P.O. Box 300 226 Albany
North Shore City, Auckland
0064 9 448 1207
e-mail: info@humankinetics.co.nz

Contents

Foreword

"The decisions you make today determine your performance tomorrow."

The three things that helped me pitch at the major-league level for 27 years were my genetics, mechanics, and conditioning. Your genetic makeup determines the upper limit of how good you will ultimately become. It's not something you can take credit for; it's a gift from God. I was fortunate that God gave me the ability to throw 90 to 100 miles per hour. If you're one of the lucky few with the ability to throw hard, run fast, or hit with power, be thankful, but don't take it for granted. Likewise, if you weren't blessed with exceptional talent, don't be discouraged. Accept the hand you were given and work to achieve your genetic potential. I've seen a lot of players with average talent get to the big leagues with hard work. Likewise, I've seen players with exceptional talent who never made it or never achieved their full potential because they were not willing to make the required sacrifices and commitments. With hard work and the right attitude, you will improve. You may not make it to the major leagues, but you can become the best that you can be.

I didn't have a burning desire to play professional baseball when I signed my first pro contract. Everyone said that I had a lot of natural ability, so I did what people said I should do. People said I could pitch, so I pitched. They said I should be a pro, so I went pro. They saw me as a power pitcher, so I threw as hard as I could. Tom Seaver set a great example for me: he had a plan and a goal. He wanted to be great, to be one of the best. I was only in baseball because I had talent, not because I knew what to do with it. I was not an effective pitcher until I learned how to focus, set realistic goals, and work to maximize my potential.

Regardless of how much talent you have, your ability to hit, run, and throw will, at some point in your career, be limited by your mechanics. You'll run only as fast as your mechanics permit. You'll hit only as far as your mechanics permit, and you'll throw only as accurately as your mechanics permit. Early in my career, I threw hard, but had no clue as to where the ball was going. As Oscar Gamble used to say, "A good day against Nolan Ryan is to go 0 for 4 and not get hit in the head." Inconsistent mechanics was a major problem that I had to learn to overcome.

Although I came into pro ball with a lot of talent, it took me almost four years to approach my potential as a major-league power pitcher. In 1972, my first season with the Angels, I was 19-16, starting 39 games and finishing 20 with an ERA of 2.28, 9 shutouts, and 329 strikeouts in 284 innings. I had 17 games in which I struck out 10 or more batters, including two 14s, a 15, two 16s, and a 17. But something more important happened that year that would affect my performance for the next 23 years: I discovered the weight room in Anaheim Stadium. It hadn't been installed for the Angels, because back then it was believed that weight training made you muscle bound. The weight room must have been there for a soccer team or some other sports team. I started slipping in there and working out, being careful not to overdo it and letting my body tell me how it was responding. In my own way, I learned how to work different areas of my body for balance and flexibility, taking a day off now and then to recover. I also discovered that even if I was somewhat stiff from lifting, it really had no effect on my ability to pitch. And after I began using the weights consistently, my arm bounced back more quickly from one start to the next.

One of the keys to my success with the Angels was that my velocity actually increased in the later innings. Now, this skill certainly could be attributed to establishing a rhythm, finding a good groove, and improving my mechanics as the game progressed. But the conditioning program made this possible by increasing my stamina. Once you fatigue, it affects your mechanics; you can no longer pitch with the precise timing required for a smooth, compact motion. I was so pleased with my results that I bought a Universal gym for my home, and it paid dividends. During my first three years in the American League, I pitched more than 900 innings, a surefire formula for ending up with a strength deficit. There's no way I could have recovered as quickly, or been as durable, without a firm base of strength through weightlifting. My weight routine didn't add velocity to my fastball per se; I think velocity has more to do with rhythm and mechanics. But the weights gave me more consistency.

I had built a sound fitness base with the Angels, but it wasn't until I joined the Astros in 1980 that I met Gene Coleman and learned how to fine-tune my program to better address my needs as a power pitcher. Gene began by adding the Jobe light-dumbbell program to my repertoire. In the earliest days of my trial-and-error lifting, there was little or no information about strengthening the rotator cuff and shoulder capsule through exercise. Gene introduced me to the Jobe program to help prevent some of the serious, career-ending shoulder injuries that were plaguing pitchers at the time. Working with Gene was a turning point in my career. I became more familiar with the principles of throwing a baseball and better equipped to prevent the discomfort and injuries that result from mechanical inefficiency.

Keeping my trunk strong was one of my greatest concerns as a power pitcher. You generate force with your legs and apply it with your arms, but the energy must be transferred through the trunk—it's a three-link chain, and the chain is only as strong as its weakest link. If you don't focus on abdominal training, you'll be unable to transfer the energy efficiently through the midsection and more stress will be placed on the arm. Another reason to work on your midsection is to prevent lower back injuries. A lot of people don't understand how essential the abdominal muscles are in providing support for the lower back. I always knew ab training was important, and Gene helped to reinforce its urgency. He also showed me how riding a bike and running in the water could help me stay in top shape and avoid most of the pounding and residual soreness that comes with running.

As I got older, things began to change. I found that I had to vary my workouts to make up for longer recovery times. I also had to work through injuries and pain. I learned to work around some muscles and concentrate on others. I was fortunate that my genetics allowed me to age more slowly than most, but there's no secret to what it takes to stay in shape— hours and hours of workouts. If that sounds boring or not worth the effort, you feel the same way many big leaguers feel. I can't swear to it, but it may be one of the reasons most big leaguers leave the game in their early thirties. At the end of my career, I really felt the effects of my age. My back bothered me at times. I got stiff more quickly and I needed to spend more time stretching to loosen up. I couldn't run as often, as fast, or as far as I could when I was younger. But I still put myself though the paces of a hard workout nearly every day, because it was worth it to me.

I enjoyed feeling good, strong, and hard. I can't guarantee that a pitcher's fastball will still be with him after 25 years in the big leagues if he works out, but it worked for me. I had to work harder and smarter every year, but the key was deciding to keep with it. Of course, it would have been easier to skip it. But at my age I would have become fat and, for sure, I would have been out of shape.

A lot of people were amazed to see me on an exercise bicycle immediately after a game while my arm was being iced. Did I need to exercise after I'd thrown a complete game? No. I needed to get started on my preparation for the next start. There's no doubt in my mind that if it hadn't been for the weight room, I would have been out of the game many years earlier. Not only did it help me prevent injury, but it also kept me strong so I could continue to hold up over the long grind.

Finally, I believe that you should never lose a game because the opposition is better prepared than you. There are a lot of things you can't control. You can't control the weather, condition of the mound or playing surface, your offensive and defensive support, or the quality of the umpiring. A pitcher can no more control velocity, location, or movement on a given day than a position player can control the quality of pitches he sees or the hops he gets. My philosophy is to focus on the one thing within your control—your preparation—and ignore the things you can't control.

I've had the opportunity to know and work with Gene Coleman since 1980. His knowledge of conditioning, mechanics, and the mental aspects of preparing for baseball are unrivaled. His approach to the game is based on performance research, scientific principles, and 20-plus years of proven major-league practice. He helped me understand that the decisions you make today determine how well you perform tomorrow. I recommend this book to players of all ability levels.

—Nolan Ryan

Introduction—The Physical Demands of the Game

Baseball has a place for players of all sizes and shapes. You don't have to be exceptionally big, fast, or strong to be successful. Big guys like Randy Johnson and Mark McGwire currently dominate the power categories, but a lot of smaller and average-sized players also are successful. Pitching great Sandy Koufax, for example, about average height and 190 pounds in weight, won three Cy Young Awards and threw five no-hitters in only 12 pro seasons. For every Roger Clemens who wins a Cy Young, there is a Randy Jones or Greg Maddux. Nolan Ryan at six feet three inches tall and 212 pounds threw harder than anyone in baseball for over two decades. Today, Billy Wagner throws 95 to 100 miles per hour despite being only 5 feet 10 inches tall and 200 pounds.

Successful players come in all sizes. Hank Aaron set the record for career home runs (755) at 185 pounds. Pete Rose at five feet nine inches tall set the record for most hits. Although Ozzie Smith was the prototype shortstop for the last decade, a much bigger shortstop—Cal Ripken Jr.—set the MLB record for consecutive games played. The Hall of Fame also is a mix of big guys (Willie Stargell, Bob Gibson, and Harmon Killebrew), short guys (Mel Ott and Joe Morgan), stocky fellows (Jackie Robinson, Roberto Clemente, Willie Mays, and Mickey Mantle), and linear guys (Rod Carew, Stan Musial, Ted Williams, Billy Williams, and Ernie Banks). Size has never been, nor will it probably ever be, a prerequisite for success.

Body Composition

Rudy Law, explaining why he can't remember signs: "I got ambrosia."

The average pro player, from class A to the major leagues, is about six feet tall, weighs 190 pounds, and is 11 percent fat. Young players are usually lighter and leaner than older players are. Body weight, muscle mass, and strength increase with age and maturity. Height remains relatively constant. High school players usually gain 30 to 40 pounds between the time they sign and when they reach maturity. College players, because they are older, gain 10 to 20 pounds. Nolan Ryan gained almost 60 pounds between high school and the big leagues. Nolan signed at 155 pounds and played for more than two decades at 212 pounds and 12 percent fat. Ozzie Smith gained about 50 pounds. Ozzie weighed 118 pounds in high school, 145 in college, and finished his career at about 170 pounds. Billy Wagner weighed 135 pounds the day he graduated from high school. Billy gained 30 pounds in college and another 20 pounds before his rookie year. He weighed 195 pounds in his second year of MLB. Darryl Kile grew seven inches in his senior year of high school. He was six feet four inches tall and 145 pounds when he signed out of junior college. Darryl made his MLB debut at 190 pounds and weighs 210 pounds today.

As a group, pitchers (six feet one inch tall) are about two inches taller than catchers and one and a half inches taller than infielders and outfielders. Pitchers and catchers (190 to 200 pounds) are slightly heavier than other players are. Infielders (180 to 185 pounds) are the lightest players and have the least amount of muscle mass. Outfielders on average weigh about 185 to 190 pounds and have the lowest relative body fat. Pitchers are 12.3 percent fat, catchers are 11.5 percent fat, infielders are 9.4 percent fat, and outfielders are 8.4 percent fat. A few players on each team are smaller, lighter, and leaner. Likewise, a few players on each team appear to be bigger and fatter than average.

Pro baseball players, as a group, are not fat. Being fat probably won't affect how you throw or swing, but it will affect your ability to field your position, run the bases, and avoid injury. You must move excess fat every time you take a step, make a throw, or swing a bat. Fat is dead weight that slows you down, makes you tired, and puts extra stress on your joints, especially your back, hips, knees, and ankles. From spring training to the last day of the season, MLB pitchers make nearly twenty thousand pitches in game and practice situations. Position players take about twenty thousand swings, field almost twenty thousand balls, and make over twenty thousand throws. Each of these acts requires strength and energy. They require calories to fuel movement and strength to start, stop, and maintain movement. Body fat, strength, and energy are related. Fat players burn more calories and exert more force than leaner players, which causes them to fatigue in the latter stages of the game and season. With fatigue comes decreased performance and increased risk of injury. Tired muscles can't produce quick movements or protect the joints from stress. As they say in Baltimore, "Fat birds don't fly."

For successful, injury-free performance, watch your weight. Don't exceed 12 percent body fat. If you play a skilled position, try to keep your body fat between 8 and 10 percent. In some situations, being too fat can decrease movement time, agility, flexibility, performance, and playing time. In 1982, the Texas Rangers told Al Oliver that he would have to DH because he was too slow to play in the field. Al was upset. He was a career .300 hitter who came up as first baseman-outfielder with the Pirates and wanted to play defense. When tested, Al was almost twice as fat as outfielders and first basemen. After counseling, he understood that extra fat would not affect his hitting but could affect his play in the field and his ability to run the bases. Al went to work (diet and exercise) and reduced his body fat from 21 percent to 12 percent. The Rangers traded him to Montreal, where he won the NL batting title with a .331 average.

Al Oliver's case was a success. Lamar Johnson's wasn't. Lamar came to the Rangers in 1982 as a free agent from the White Sox. A career .300 hitter with a history of weight problems, he was offered an incentive to stay lean. Lamar was tested for body fat by underwater weighing every month at the Cooper Institute in Dallas and received a cash bonus each time his relative body fat was 12 percent or less. He earned his weight incentives but finished the season hitting only .221. Management and coaches speculated that he spent so much time worrying about his weight and how the organization perceived his appearance that it affected his hitting.

For peak, injury-free performance, stay in shape and keep your body fat at a reasonable level. Pitchers and catchers should be 12 percent fat or less. Position players, especially middle infielders and center fielders should be at 8 to 10 percent.

Don't get confused and think that less is better. There is a minimal level of body fat below which no one should go. A low body fat is good for general health and performance, but you can be too skinny. Minimum fat in adult male athletes is 5 percent. When you drop below this value, your body stops producing testosterone, the hormone responsible for muscle growth and repair. Without adequate testosterone, you lose muscle mass and are more prone to chronic dehydration, muscle weakness, and injury.

A little fat is good. Ask Earl Campbell. The Oilers told him to lose 20 pounds. At 240 pounds and 10 percent fat, he had only 24 pounds of fat, and 5 percent, or 11, of these pounds were essential for health and performance. To lose 20 pounds, he had to drop his fat to 2 percent, an unhealthy proposition, or lose 13 pounds of muscle, a waste of strength and power. Being a team player, Earl lost 20 pounds and spent most of the season nursing leg injuries.

What the Scouts See

About 83 percent of players who sign a pro contract never make it to the big leagues.

Professional baseball scouts see hundreds of games and thousands of players each year. Armed with a stopwatch, radar gun, and clipboard, these men make decisions on talent that will affect both your future and that of their employers. Evaluating current and potential superstars like Barry Bonds, Ken Griffey Jr., Billy Wagner, and Roger Clemens is relatively easy. The great ones really stand out. They have good size, strength, and composure, and they score at the highest levels on most of the items on the scout's checklist.

The fact that most big-league rosters include only one or two superstars indicates that scouts see more average and above-average talent than exceptional talent. When scouting pitchers, they look for velocity, movement, and control. With position players they look for those who can run, hit for average, hit for power, field, and throw but not necessarily in that order.

Each player is evaluated on five different physical attributes, or tools, and given a score of 2 to 8 on each, with 5 being average and 8 being outstanding (see scouting report form on page xii). Scouts evaluate players for both present status and their potential for future development. You don't have to be outstanding in all categories. If you did, no one would have taken a chance on Pete Rose or Mike

Piazza. The table on page xiii prioritizes the essential tools by position. The first two tools at each position are considered the dominant, or carrying, tools. The others are considered secondary. Shortstop has three dominant tools: fielding, throwing, and running. If a player does not rate at least average in the carrying tools for a particular position, it would be difficult to imagine him playing at the major-league level at that position. A catcher, for example, who rates a 4 for both catching and throwing but rates a 7 for batting would fit the profile for first base, not catcher.

Scouting Report—Player Tools

No.   Last Name   First Name   Position

School   City   State

Non-pitchers   Pitchers

	Present	Future		Present	Future
1. Hitting—Average			Fastball velocity		
2. Hitting—Power			Movement		
3. Running speed			Curve		
Base running			Control		
4. Arm strength			Change		
Accuracy			Slider		
5. Fielding			Other		
Range			Fielding		

Games: this year _____

Pull _____   Straight away _____   Innings: this year _____   Total _____
Opposite field _____   Spray _____   Delivery _____   Arm action _____

Physical description:

Abilities:

Weaknesses:

Poise   Aptitude
Instinct   Physical maturity
Aggressiveness   Emotional maturity
Work habits   Off-field habits
Dedication   Married

Summation: Monetary value ($_____)

Tool Priorities by Position

Catcher	First base	Second base	Shortstop
Catch	**Bat**	**Bat**	**Field**
Throw	**Power**	**Field**	**Throw**
Bat	Field	Run	**Run**
Power	Throw	Power	Bat
Run	Run	Throw	Power

Third base	Left field	Center field	Right field
Bat	**Bat**	**Run**	**Bat**
Power	**Power**	**Field**	**Power**
Field	Run	Bat	Field
Throw	Field	Throw	Throw
Run	Throw	Power	Run

Bold type indicates dominant tools at each position.

Scouting for Running Speed

The index of speed in baseball is how fast you can run 60 yards. The faster you run, the more attention you get. An acceptable time is 7.0 seconds or less. Players in skilled positions run a little faster. Catchers, especially big ones, run a little slower. If you run 6.5 to 6.8 seconds, you are considered to have good speed and will get a lot of attention. Run 6.3 to 6.5 and you have exceptional speed.

Only a handful of guys such as Kenny Lofton and Brian Hunter run this fast. Most players are average to above average. Players with exceptional speed are usually placed in center field. Those with average speed tend to play the corners, especially if they have good power at the plate.

Time in the 60 will get you noticed, but it doesn't always translate directly to runs on the scoreboard. Speed in baseball requires more than running a fast 60 yards. Otherwise, there would be many NCAA sprint champions on major-league rosters. Scouts look at base-running ability. They look at how fast you can go from home to first and how fast you run the bases. The average left-handed batter (LHB) reaches first in 4.2 seconds or less. Right-handed batters (RHB) get there in 4.3 seconds or less. Runners with good speed run from home to first in 4.1 (LHB) to 4.2 (RHB) seconds. Those with exceptional speed make it in 4.0 (LHB) to 4.1 (RHB) seconds. Kenny Lofton and Deion Sanders have been clocked at 3.90 to 3.97 seconds. Mickey Mantle went from home to first in 3.35 seconds following a left-handed drag bunt. He was consistently 3.8 to 4.0 seconds from the left side in his early years.

Regardless of your speed, you have to run hard on every play. Hustle is the only act in baseball that requires no special skill. Craig Biggio and Rod Carew are examples of players who ran themselves into extra hits. Craig had 31 infield hits in 1997. Without these hits, he would have hit .258; with them, he hit .309. Biggio's hustle also helped him play the entire 1997 season (619 AB) without hitting into a double play. Carew raised his average by 50 points per year by bunting.

The time you take from first to third and second to home is basically the same. It's usually measured with two outs and the runner breaking on contact. The watch is started on contact and stopped when the runner reaches third or home. A good first-to-third time (or second-to-home time) is 7.0 seconds or less. Players with good speed will run 6.8 to 6.9 seconds. Those with exceptional speed will run 6.7 seconds or less. Jeff Bagwell is an example of a player with average speed in the 60 who has good speed on the bases. He has been clocked at 7.0 seconds in the 60, but goes first to third in 6.80 to 6.85 seconds. What he lacks in speed he makes up for with anticipation, quickness, instinct, and awareness. Jeff has steadily increased his stolen-base total each year and had a 40-30 season in 1997. He seldom makes a base-running mistake because he always knows how many outs there are, who's hitting next, and where the fielders are. He reads the situation as well as any player in the game and, because he always runs hard, gets doubles on balls in the gap and advances on balls to the right side of the infield and pitches in the dirt.

Triples are rare and exciting events in baseball. Since 1930 the number of triples per game has fallen from 1 per game to only 0.38 per game today. Players with average speed run from home to third in 11.4 to 11.7 seconds or less. Those with good speed get there in 10.8 to 11.2 seconds. Players with exceptional speed, like Deion Sanders, get there in 10.4 to 10.7 seconds. Inside-the-park home runs are more rare and more exciting than triples. Players with average speed run the circuit in 15.5 seconds or less. Those with good speed make it in 15.0 seconds and those with exceptional speed run it in 14.0 seconds or less.

Stealing a base requires more than simply running fast. A base stealer needs speed, first-step quickness, and the ability to take a good lead, read the pitcher, get a good jump, and avoid the tag. Most bases are stolen on the pitcher, not the catcher. The average right-handed pitcher releases the ball in about 1.3 seconds. Left-handers take about .10 seconds longer. Pitchers with good release times get the ball out of the glove and started to the plate in 1.2 to 1.3 seconds. Those with exceptional release times get it going in less than 1.2 seconds. Pedro Martinez, at 1.07 to 1.08 seconds, has one of the fastest release times in MLB. Gregg Maddux (1.10 to 1.25 seconds) is also very good. Jeff Juden gave up seven stolen bases in five innings against the Astros in 1997 with release times between 1.44 and 1.71 seconds.

Most catchers have a strong arm and throw hard. A good arm, however, will not make up for a slow release time. The longer it takes the catcher to get rid of the ball, the greater the chance of the runner's being safe. An average release time for catchers is about 2.0 seconds. Catchers with good release times get rid of the ball in 1.9 seconds or less. Those with exceptional release times get it started in 1.8 seconds or less. Johnny Bench was timed consistently at 1.9 seconds; Pudge Rodriguez has been timed at 1.65 to 1.80 seconds.

Few players can outrun the ball. More often than not, a runner with good speed is safe when the total time required for the pitcher to get the ball to the plate and the catcher to get it to second is 3.3 seconds or greater. Ricky Henderson was consistently clocked at 3.0 to 3.1 seconds early in his career. The chances drop to 50-50 when the time is 3.2 to 3.3 seconds. Almost everyone is out when the time falls below 3.2 seconds. Astros pitchers and catchers threw out Kenny Lofton, one of the fastest men in the game, twice in one game with total times of 3.14 to 3.17 seconds. Nolan Ryan, the premier fastball pitcher of his time, had a slow release time (1.50 seconds). Astros catchers had a better chance of throwing runners out with Vern Ruhle (1.35 seconds) pitching than with Nolan, despite the fact that Nolan threw 10 to 15 miles per hour faster than Vern. The total time with Nolan on the mound was 3.4 seconds. With Vern, it was 3.25 seconds.

Scouting for Arm Strength and Accuracy

Outfielders are tested with a stopwatch to determine the time required to throw the ball home from center field. Infielders, catchers, and pitchers are timed with a radar gun. Infielders are evaluated as they throw the ball across the diamond from short to first. Catchers throw from home to second. Pitchers throw from the mound to home. Because there is so much ground to cover, speed, accuracy, and arm strength are essential in the outfield, especially in center. Center fielders usually run the 60 in 6.5 to 6.7 seconds or less and have an average or better-than-average arm. Slower players (6.7 to 7.1) play the corners, with the right fielder having an above-average arm or better. Arm strength is evaluated from the time required for a player to field a ball in center field and throw it to the plate from a distance of about 270 feet. Players charge the ball from a position of about 300 feet and throw it home as fast and accurately as possible. The watch is started on bat contact and stopped when the ball reaches home plate. Because most good runners can score from second base in 7 seconds or less, an outfielder must be able to react, field the ball, set up, and throw it home in 7 seconds or less. Average arms are fairly common in baseball. Above-average arms are scarce and exceptional arms are extremely rare. Dave Parker, Dave Winfield, Raul Mondesi, and Richard Hildago are a few of the players with a 7+ or 8 arm. But a great arm is of little value if you can't make an accurate throw and hit the cutoff man. Tony Gwynn is an example of a below-average outfielder who made himself into a Gold-Glove player. He works on his fielding every day and has learned to make up for his lack of speed and arm strength by always being in proper position, hitting the cutoff man, and making crisp, accurate throws.

Infielders with good arms, agility, body control, and balance will field the ball, set up, and throw it accurately across the diamond at about 82 to 84 miles per hour. Those with excellent arms will throw 85 miles per hour or better. Ozzie Smith had only an average arm and average speed (6.75 seconds over 60 yards), but his knowledge of hitters, positioning, balance, agility, and grace let him get to balls and make plays that seemed almost impossible for other shortstops.

Catchers with good arms, quick feet, and good balance will throw 82 to 83 miles per hour from home to second. Johnny Bench and Benito Santiago were frequently clocked at 83 to 84 miles per hour. Pudge Rodriguez has been clocked at 84 to 85 miles per hour. Footwork, balance, and arm strength are related. Good footwork and balance enhance arm strength; bad footwork and balance reduce it. Bench, Lance Parrish, Tony Pena, and Santiago had quick feet and good balance. Each got his feet under his body quickly and established a solid base from which to throw. Rodriguez and Brad Ausmus have good arms, excellent balance, and quick feet. Each has been clocked at 4.15 to 4.20 from home to first.

Pitchers are harder to evaluate. Although velocity is important, most good hitters will eventually catch up to the best fastballs if there is no movement or deception. A pitcher with an average major-league fastball will throw between 88 and 91 miles per hour (see the table on page xvii). A good fastball will reach 92 to 93 miles per hour, and an exceptional fastball will reach 94 to 97 miles per hour. Few pitchers throw hard enough (98 to 100 miles per hour) to rate an 8 arm (as Billy Wagner and Robb Nen have). Scouts look at a pitcher's mechanics for free movement and good arm action. They look for the ability to command (locate) the fastball and for late movement. Darryl Kile's fastball has late movement and gets many swing and misses (opposing hitters swing and miss 36 percent of Kile's fastballs). Pedro Martinez is deceptively fast, throwing hard with good arm movement, which makes his fastball difficult for hitters to pick up. Nolan Ryan (like Roger Clemens, Randy Johnson, and Kerry Wood) had a fastball that seemed to accelerate and explode as it got to the plate.

A good pitcher must also be able to control an off-speed pitch (curve or slider) and show that he has the potential to develop a change-up. Pitchers must be able to throw all pitches with the same arm action and have a good separation of velocity from the fastball. To be effective, a slider should be about 7 to 8 miles per hour slower than a fastball. Curveballs and change-ups should be 12 to 15 miles per hour slower than fastballs. You don't have to blow away hitters to win. Greg Maddux has won four Cy Young Awards throwing 85- to 88-mile-per-hour fastballs and 78- to 80-mile-per-hour change-ups with good arm action and excellent location.

Don't get discouraged if you have an average or below-average fastball. You will get faster. You probably won't throw 95 miles per hour, but you will get faster. If you have good mechanics and work hard, your fastball will improve in time. Remember, scouts look at both current status and future potential. They know that some of the most successful pitchers in MLB today had an average to below-average fastball in high school. Roger Clemens, Bret Saberhagen, Darryl Kile, Kevin Appier, Justin Thompson, Mark Langston, David Cone, Randy Johnson, Greg Maddux, Danny Darwin, and Nolan Ryan all had an average to below-average fastball and an above-average breaking ball in high school. They all got faster.

Scouts and pitching coaches believe that a young pitcher with a good breaking ball has the potential to throw harder. Why? Because it takes arm speed, a flexible wrist, and a strong hand to impart enough spin on the ball to produce a plus breaking ball. A pitcher with those qualities who is willing to work will improve. Speed will improve with maturity and training. Just because you didn't pitch in high school doesn't mean that you can't pitch professionally. If you have the arm strength, poise, makeup, and desire, you can always change positions. Ricky Botallico, Tim Crabtree, and Troy Percival were catchers. Trevor Hoffman was a shortstop, Todd Worrell was an out-fielder, and Chris Holt and Tim Belcher played third.

MLB Fastball

Rating	Velocity (mph)
8	98–100
7	94–97
6	92–93
5	88–91
4	85–87
3	81–84

Scouting for Fielders

Scouts look for players who can make both routine and difficult plays. They look at fielding skills, positioning, soft hands, footwork, body control, agility, and range. Good players get in front of the ball and set up in a balanced position. They have soft hands that let them catch the ball and transfer it from the glove to the throwing hand quickly. They have the ability to set their feet quickly for a hard, accurate throw. Players up the middle must have more range. Middle infielders have to go in the hole and behind the bag. Center fielders have to be able to come forward, go back, and cover the gaps. First and third basemen have to protect the lines, field bunts, and get to balls in the hole. Pitchers have to field their position, cover first, and back up bases.

Scouting for Hitters

Scouts look for approach, contact, control, bat speed, and power. If you can't make contact, you can't hit. They look for body balance at the plate and a quick, compact swing. Big looping swings may be OK if you're facing bad pitching, but they produce more misses than hits against good pitchers. Good hitters have excellent hand-eye coordination and strong flexible wrists, hands, and forearms. Tony Gwynn, Mark Grace, Dave Justice, Mark McGwire, and Jeff Bagwell are good hitters who swing hard and don't miss very often.

Good hitters don't strike out. With two strikes they make adjustments that increase their chances of making good contact. Players who strike out a lot swing the same way regardless of the count. Good hitters cover the plate with a shorter, quicker swing. Gwynn, for example, strikes out once every 30 to 35 at bats; Grace fans about once every 15 at bats. Joe DiMaggio had more home runs than strikeouts (Ks) seven times in his career and ended his career with only eight more Ks than homers. Power is a plus. Scouts look for guys who make the ball jump off the bat. If you can hit the ball hard, in time you will hit it far. The ball jumped off Joe Morgan's bat when he was young. It flew out of the park when he matured. Good hitters have good balance, leverage, and extension. They keep the bat in the hitting zone longer and have the ability both to pull the ball and drive it to the opposite field. Power hitters such as Jose Canseco, Jeff Bagwell, Mark McGwire, Sammy Sosa, Albert Belle, and Frank Thomas can drive the ball as far to the opposite field as they can pull it.

Scouting for the Intangibles

Pete Rose explaining why he wasn't going to retire from baseball: "The doc says I have the body of a 20-year-old and the mind of a 14-year-old, and that's all it takes to play this game."

Physical tools like strength and speed are relatively easy to see and evaluate. Intangibles like instinct, adaptability, dedication, desire, and the ability and willingness to learn are harder to see but are extremely important. Scouts look for players with a feel for the game. They look for players with good instincts and the ability to think on their feet and make adjustments from pitch to pitch. Many players with good instincts and skills never make it because they are not willing to work or accept coaching.

Because scouts have to rate current status and predict future potential, they are extremely interested in work habits and aptitude. They see which players are first to practice and last to leave. They look for guys with high energy levels who respect the game, run on and off the field, hustle on every play, and have fun. They look at dedication, physical and emotional maturity, poise, instinct, aggressiveness, and off-field habits. You don't have to be a rocket scientist to play the game. There's no place on the scoreboard for IQ, but you must have the aptitude and maturity to learn how to play the game right. Coaches can't teach if players can't learn.

By his own admission, Phil Garner, manager of the Detroit Tigers, was never the best player on any team that he played on, from summer ball to the major leagues. He did, however, have good instincts, the aptitude to learn, and excellent work habits. Phil was the first to arrive each day and the last to leave. His aggressiveness earned him the nickname "Scrap Iron," and he took responsibility for his own success and failure. He understood that "luck occurs when preparation meets opportunity" and that "luck never falls off a trunk and lands on a guy sleeping under a tree."

Nolan Ryan believes that you should never lose because the opposition is better prepared than you are. You can't control many things. You can't control the environment (weather, condition of the mound and playing surface, and so forth), your offensive and defensive support, or the quality of the umpiring. Pitchers can no more control velocity, location, or movement on a given day than position players can control the quality of pitches they see or the hops they get in the field. Nolan's philosophy was to focus on the one thing within his control—his preparation—and ignore those that he couldn't. He never lost a game because the opposition was in better shape, ate better, got more rest, or gave more thought to the game than he did.

When things are going well, it's sometimes hard to motivate yourself to work. Bob Hayes, former Olympic Gold Medalist in the 100-meter race, once said, "Why should I do these drills? I'm already the fastest man in the world. I'll change my approach when someone beats me." Don't wait for someone to beat you to start working. If you're not getting better, you're getting worse. If you're standing still, someone will eventually pass you. Roger Clemens is one of the most talented and hardest workers in the game. Curt Schilling modified his work habits, turned his career around, and won a Cy Young Award after working out with Roger in 1991. The turning point for Curt occurred when he asked Roger what motivated him to work so hard. Roger's response was that he had pride. He is not satisfied with being the best pitcher in the '80s or '90s. He wants to be the best who ever played. He has five Cy Young awards and three American League MVP awards, and he wants at least one more of each. And, when he gets the next one, he will want another one and so on. He also wants Nolan's strikeout record. He may not get it, but it won't be for lack of effort.

"Be All You Can Be"—Reach Your Potential

"There are two types of pain: the pain of discipline and the pain of regret. The choice is yours."—sign in the Cleveland Indians' weight room.

Everyone in baseball has talent. Some have more; others have less. Talent, your genetic potential, is a gift. You can't take credit for it. You didn't earn it—you inherited it. Being born with talent is like winning the lottery. But having talent, even lots of it, is no guarantee of success. Success depends on how you use your gift. If you take it for granted and are content with being on the team and making an occasional contribution, you'll never achieve your true genetic potential. But if you work on your talent, even if it's marginal, you can reach your potential and be successful.

Most scouts look for talent first and skills second. They look for strong arms, soft hands, quick bats, fluid motions, quick feet, good balance, strength, speed, and power. Why? Because they know that you can learn skills, but you can't learn talent. If, for example, you throw 95 miles per hour, you can probably learn to throw some type of off-speed pitch. If you throw in the mid-80s, however, you'll probably never learn to throw 95. The same can be said of speed and power. Talent sets the upper limits for your success. In theory, the more talent you have, the greater your potential for success and vice versa. But, in reality, individuals play the game with markedly different levels of talent. On almost every major-league roster are no more than two or three truly talented, or marquee, players. The remaining spots are filled with players of average to above-average ability.

Skills

Skills are learned. The mechanics of running, sliding, hitting, fielding, and throwing are skills acquired through hard work, repetition, and practice. Skills, like talent, can affect your level of success. Poor skills limit performance. Excellent skills enhance it.

Work Ethic

Bum Phillips: *"Nobody ever drowned himself in his own sweat."*

Talent and skill are important contributors to success, but they're not the only ones. Many successful players are neither gifted nor mechanically perfect. How do they compete? Commitment. They're willing to give whatever it takes—conditioning, drills, diet, and mental preparation—to achieve their full genetic potential. Committed players consistently perform at the upper range of their talent and skill despite the circumstance.

Work and Play

You can get by on talent and skill for a while. Work smart and you'll achieve success and extend your career. To ensure success, limit the time spent in activities not directly related to your development. Surround yourself only with people vital to your success. Avoid those with no goals and negative attitudes. They'll drain your energy and bring you down to their level. Given the choice between work and play, choose work. You'll have the rest of your life to play when you retire. Allow only two things to take priority over your profession—your family and your religion. Take charge of your future. Start closing the gap between where you are and where you want to be.

How you train will affect your success and future. If you're in shape, you can give better effort, avoid injuries, and accomplish more work. There are many factors that you can't control, but you can control how you prepare for the season. You should never get beat because the opposition is better prepared.

To make the team and compete for the championship, it's imperative that you get in shape, stay in shape, and give 100 percent from start to finish. Preparation separates the successful from the could have beens. Look around. You know most of the guys at your position. How hard are they working? If you're competing for the same prize but doing less work, something is wrong. Adjust your priorities.

The choice is really up to you. You can work and be the best you can be, or you can enjoy the moment and do just enough to get by. If you take the easier path, however, someday you might regret what you didn't accomplish. Cal Ripken doesn't plan on having any regrets. He told a reporter from *USA Today* (June 25, 1998), "Along the way, I've watched a number of players retire. And they've always told me, 'I wish I had played more, taken care of myself and taken it more seriously'. I want to be able to say that I took full advantage of the opportunity. I don't want to have any regrets." Cal's approach is relatively simple—when you come to the ballpark, be ready to play. Cal is living proof that the only form of discipline that lasts is self-discipline.

The Year-Round Conditioning Plan

The strength and conditioning program for baseball is designed to improve performance and reduce the risk of injury. To improve performance you have to increase sport-specific strength, speed, endurance, flexibility, and power. To prevent injuries you have to condition the total body to perform the explosive and repetitive tasks encountered in the game.

The baseball season is a marathon, not a sprint. Most college and high school athletes play year-round. Major-league teams play 162 regular-season games in about 180 days; most minor-league teams play 142. The key to effective, injury-free performance is consistency. You have to work on some aspect of your game and fitness every day. You can't play yourself into shape in spring training, and you can't stop working out on Opening Day. You can't have a hit-and-miss program and expect to play your best.

How you train is important. For maximum results and steady gains, use a comprehensive, year-round program based on a periodization model that systematically varies the exercises performed, intensity of the work, and volume of work done from week to week and month to month throughout the year. That plan is what you'll find in the five chapters that make up part I of this book. For specifics on *how* to do the workouts, look to part II.

Periodization Model

The training year has five training phases (see box). Each phase has specific fitness and performance objectives and is more difficult and more sport specific than the previous one. The training year starts in the postseason with a three- to four-week period of active rest. Three to four days of active rest are inserted between training phases to give your body time to recover from the stress of the previous phase and reduce the risk of injury and burnout. Workouts are designed to get you game ready by Opening Day and help you maintain a high level of fitness and performance throughout the season.

Training Phases in the Annual Plan

1. "Active Rest"

Recover and Rehabilitate

Postseason: Fitness Maintenance

2. "Train to Train"

General Fitness

Off-Season: Fitness Training

3. "Train to Compete"

Sport-Specific Fitness

Preseason: Performance Training

4. "Train to Play"

Performance Specific Fitness

Spring Training: Performance Training

5. "Train to Win"

Game-Specific Fitness

In-Season: Performance Training

Fitness training gets you in shape to *train,* not in shape to play. It occurs in the off-season and consists of activities to rehabilitate injuries, correct deficiencies, and improve general fitness. Workouts are designed to improve flexibility, muscular strength, muscular endurance, and aerobic capacity. Performance training, on the other hand, improves performance in game situations. It starts in the preseason, after you are in shape, and continues throughout the year. Your body needs new challenges to stimulate improvement, an opportunity to recover, and time to grow. Lack of new stimulation leads to stagnation, injury, and a loss of fitness and performance. Highly conditioned athletes can maintain peak condition for only four to five months per year. Trying to maintain peak fitness year-round leads to burnout, injuries, fatigue, and illness.

Training Variables

All training plans have basic, unchanging principles as their foundation. Adjusting one or more variables, such as training frequency, intensity, volume, speed, load, or rest time, can help adapt your training plan to your current goals and the stage of the season.

Frequency

Train for general strength and aerobic fitness three times per week in the off-season. Train four to six times per week in spring training and during the season. Alternate upper-body and lower-body workouts so you can lift heavier loads and have more recovery between workouts of the same muscle groups. Run on nonlifting days. Do plyometrics once or twice per week.

Because most gains begin to plateau after about six weeks, divide your workouts into six- to eight-week training phases. Begin each phase with high-volume, low-intensity loads (longer runs and more reps with lighter loads). As phases progress, decrease the volume (distance and reps) and increase the intensity (speed and weight) so that you end each phase with shorter runs, fewer reps, and heavier loads. Use alternate days of moderate and heavy work in each phase. This approach will yield maximum gains and reduce the risk of overtraining.

Intensity and Volume

Periodization lets you work smarter, not harder, to achieve maximum results when needed. Volume and intensity vary from week to week within each phase and from phase to phase. Each phase is harder than the previous one. Volume improves endurance and prepares you for the high-intensity work to come. Intensity produces strength and speed without size and builds a good base for power. Do the number of sets and reps specified for each exercise. Use all the recovery time recommended. Your goal is to improve functional sport-specific strength and speed. You can't work hard or run fast when you're tired.

Aerobic Endurance and Speed

Run the distance suggested in the time allowed. Use all the recovery time recommended. Your goal is to improve functional sport-specific aerobic endurance and speed.

Strength

Use a load that will allow you to complete the recommended number of sets and reps but will be somewhat difficult to finish. When you can do the maximum number of reps specified, add weight in the next workout. Remember, it's better to lift a lighter weight with good form than a heavier weight with bad form.

Choosing Exercises

Vary the type of exercise from phase to phase to ensure maximum gains and prevent boredom. Use alternate days of heavy and lighter work to add variety, ensure adequate recovery between workouts, reduce the risk of injury, and ensure consistent gains throughout the year. Do the exercises suggested, unless prohibited by injury or lack of appropriate equipment. Use free weights or dumbbells (DBs) whenever possible and do functional, closed-chain, multijoint exercises to develop strength, coordination, and balance in the primary and support muscles of each body joint. Do sprints for speed, intervals for endurance, and plyometrics for power.

Arranging Exercise Order

The sequence in which you do the exercises can affect both how you feel during your workout and the training stimulus provided by the workout. Do one warm-up set of each exercise in the circuit, rest two to three minutes, and repeat the circuit two or three times. Work opposing muscle movements—leg press and leg curl, bench press and lat pull, and so on. Do all sets of one exercise before moving to the next.

Workout Order

Use the following sequence when working out each day:

- Warm-up
- Train for skill, speed, and power
- Do lifts, resistance work, endurance
- Do circuit training in the off-season
- Work opposing muscle groups (opposing joint movements)
- Alternate areas
- Work multijoint areas before single-joint areas
- Do split routines in preseason and in-season workouts
- Cool-down

Resting

In periodization training, rest is just as important as training. You must plan for it and understand when and how long to take off between various kinds of workouts.

Rest Between Sets and Exercises

The length of rest between sets and exercises depends on your training goal and training phase. Use long rest periods (three to five minutes) when training for maximum strength, speed, and power and short rest periods (30 to 60 seconds) when training for aerobic endurance. Long rest periods allow the body to recover completely so you can give maximum effort in each set and exercise. Shorter rest periods develop muscular endurance by training the body to tolerate and remove blood lactate. Lactate is a by-product of anaerobic work that causes the muscles to fatigue and burn following strenuous work like running a fast 400 meters or doing six sets of 10RM squats with one minute of rest between sets.

Rest Between Training Sessions

Rest at least 24 hours between workouts to give your body time to recover and grow. Train three times per week in the off-season with alternate days of strength and aerobic work. Use a split routine in preseason and in-season workouts, with 48 hours of rest between workouts of the same muscle group.

Run five or six times per week in the off-season with alternate days of aerobic, speed, interval, and speed-endurance work. Limit plyometrics to no more than three times per week and allow at least 48 hours of rest between workouts. Rest 24 to 48 hours between strength workouts during the season and at least 24 hours between speed and aerobic training.

Chapter 1

Postseason—Active Rest and Recovery

GOAL   *Active rest to recover, rehabilitate, and maintain fitness*

Today's players train year-round and are rarely out of shape. Trying to play yourself into shape is a waste of valuable time and effort. Time spent on conditioning could be better spent on sharpening your skills. Spring training is the time to hone your playing skills and become game ready, not to build a fitness base. If you report in good shape in the spring, you will have a head start, get the most out of the drills, develop good mechanics, avoid injury, and have more success.

Your goal for the first three to four weeks after the season is active rest. Give your body time to recover. Stay just active enough to maintain fitness, but don't start formal training until late October or early November. Work and rest are both important, but neither is beneficial without the other. Postseason is also an ideal time to look at your weight and your diet, and to make necessary changes. Table 1.1 contains an overview of the postseason plan, suitable for high school or college players as well as for major-league or minor-league players. It tells you what fitness and performance variables to work on and when to do them.

College and high school players start the postseason in August. This phase starts the first week in October for major-league teams not involved in the playoffs and one to three weeks later for playoff teams. It starts 1 September for minor leaguers whose teams fail to make the playoffs and those who don't go to instructional league. Minor-league players involved in the playoffs or instructional leagues start the postseason four weeks later.

This is a three- or four-week phase with no formal training that is designed to allow you to recover physically and mentally from the competitive season. It is the bridge from one year to the next, and what you do in this phase will affect how you play next year. You need active rest, not couch-potato rest. Don't stop training completely or you'll lose the gains made in the previous year. Maintaining a general fitness base will help you make quicker improvements when your off-season

Table 1.1 An Overview of the Postseason Active Rest (Weeks 1–4)

Activity	Monday, Wednesday, Friday
Warm-up	General and dynamic
Flexibility	Daily dozen
Strength	Circuit weight-training (CWT) or DB circuit
Trunk	Sit-ups (100)
Aerobic	Cross train (15-20 min)
Cool-down	Daily dozen

conditioning program begins and raise the upper limit on how much you can improve before next spring.

Working the Body

Movement helps your muscles, organs, hormones, and mind unwind, gear down, and recover. Do things that you enjoy but don't have time for during the season. Stretch daily. Stay out of the weight room for two to three weeks.

Work the muscle groups of the trunk, leg, back, shoulder, and arm that provide balance and support by doing push-ups, pull-ups, step-ups, and lunges. Use tubing or dumbbells for the rotator cuff. Use this time to rehabilitate preexisting injuries and correct deficiencies. Don't begin formal weight training until week 5.

Warm-Up, Cool-Down, and Flexibility

Start with general warm-up exercises and then do dynamic warm-up routine #1 to improve strength, endurance, and functional range of motion in the muscles used in running, fielding, hitting, and throwing. Stretch (using the daily dozen) before workouts and cool down after them.

Strength

Concentrate on building strength and endurance in the small muscles that stabilize the shoulder, hip, and legs so that they will be ready to support the larger prime movers in the weeks to come. Use a circuit weight-training (CWT) format (see the plans for weeks 1–4 in table 1.2). Do CWT #1 for the first two weeks using body weight as resistance. Switch to CWT #2 (if you're a position player) or #3 (if you're a pitcher) in week 3, using dumbbells for resistance. For variety, alternate using body weight as resistance (CWT #1) in one workout and dumbbells (CWT #2 or #3) in the next.

Shoulders. Maintain strength in the muscles of the rotator cuff and scapula. Do Jobe-type exercises (see chapter 8) with three- to five-pound dumbbells or surgical tubing for the cuff. Strengthen the muscles of the scapula by doing scarecrows, push-ups plus, push-up and reach backs, scapular dips, and modified pull-ups.

Table 1.2 Postseason (Weeks 1–4)—Fitness Maintenance—"Active Rest"

	Activity	Exercises and Drills	
MONDAY, WEDNESDAY, AND FRIDAY	**WARM-UP**		
		Jog or cycle 5 min General warm-up (do 1 set of 10 reps of each exercise):	Squat, lunge, circle toe touch, good morning, wood chopper, trunk twist, arm circles
		Dynamic warm-up #1 (do 1 set of 10 reps of each exercise):	Leg swings—side/side, leg swings—out/in, leg swings—front/back, leg swings—hip flexion/extension, leg swings—crossover and hold, hurdles—lateral under the bar, hurdles—forward under the bar, hurdles—forward over the bar, hurdles—crawl under the bar
	FLEXIBILITY		
		Daily dozen (do 2-3 reps of each and hold each exercise for 10-15 sec):	Butterfly groin; seated back twist (hook and look); buttocks stretch; standing quadriceps stretch; seated hamstring stretch; lying hamstring stretch Low-back stretch; kneeling hip flexor stretch; standing calf stretch; inclined (inchworm) calf stretch; arm stretch—across the face, across the chest, and down the back; forearm stretch
	STRENGTH/POWER		
	All players **(1-2 × 10-15)**	CWT #1 (body-weight resistance):	Step-up or walking lunge; modified pull-up; squat or split-squat; push-up or incline push-up; lunge or crossover lunge; calf raise; squats and touches (SAT)
	All players **(1-2 × 10-12)**	CWT #2 (dumbbells):	DB step-up or DB split-squat, DB bench press or DB incline press, DB squat or DB lunge, DB row with palm back (palm in), DB calf raise, DB shrug, DB triceps kickback, DB arm curl or DB hammer curl
	Pitchers **(1-2 × 10-12)**	CWT #3 (dumbbells):	DB step-up or DB lunge, DB scapula protraction/retraction or push-up or incline push-up, DB squat or DB split-squat, DB row with palm back or (palm in), DB calf raise, DB shrug, DB triceps kickback, DB arm curl
	Shoulder **(1 × 10)**	Rotator cuff:	Forward raise, lateral raise, shrug, reverse fly, internal rotation, external rotation, supraspinatus, upward rotation, shoulder extension
		Scapula:	Scarecrow, push-up and reach back, scapular dip, modified pull-up
	Sit-ups **100 reps**	Daily core:	Knees up (10 ×), seated leg tuck (10 ×), V-up (10 ×), crunch (10 ×), bicycle (20 ×), lateral crunch (20 ×), reach side to side (20 ×)
	Aerobics **135-150 bpm**	Jog 15-20 min (cycle 15-20 min) Jump rope 10 min	
	COOL-DOWN **AND FLEXIBILITY**	Daily dozen (do 2-3 reps of each and hold each exercise for 10-15 sec)	

Trunk. Maintain trunk strength and range of motion by doing at least 100 sit-ups (daily core) three to five times per week. Work the flexors and oblique muscles each training session.

Running and Conditioning Training

Jog, cycle, use the Stairmaster, swim, or do any combination of these three to four times per week. Work at a comfortable pace for 15 to 20 minutes per session. Your goal is to maintain, not improve, aerobic fitness. Jump rope for 10 minutes three times per week for balance and fitness.

Fueling the Body

"That makes me a Jelly-Nellie, Ding Dong, and Big Gulp."—**Mike Scott,** *when asked if he had ever heard the statement, "You are what you eat."*

For good health and maximum performance, you need to eat well year-round. There are no valid reasons for poor food choices, only excuses. Sleeping through breakfast, missing meals, eating just before bedtime, and pounding candy bars and soft drinks are not sound nutritional practices.

Take control of your diet, and your health and performance will improve. The choice is yours. You can start eating better today or keep on making excuses for why you're tired, sluggish, and overweight. The essential things that you need to know about sport nutrition, health, and performance are in this chapter. Read the information, try the options, and determine what works best for you.

The three most important factors for athletic performance are genetics, training, and diet. You can't do anything about heredity, but you can control training and diet. Although a balanced diet won't guarantee success, an unbalanced diet can undermine even the best training program. Most popular diets and supplements won't provide the results you want, and some are actually harmful. The best-tuned car can't win the Indianapolis 500 on half a tank of gas, and the best-trained athlete can't go nine innings on a Twinkie and Coke. To be successful, you must eat the right foods, at the right times, and in the right amounts.

Nutrients—Building Blocks for Performance

Nutrients are life-sustaining substances obtained from food. They work together to give you the energy you need to compete, build muscle, and maintain health. There are at least 50 nutrients in food that can be classified (by chemical structure or function) into six major groups: carbohydrates, fats, proteins, vitamins, minerals, and water. Three of these—carbohydrates, fats, and proteins—provide energy (calories). Consuming extra vitamins and minerals will not give you more energy, and losing water weight will not make you leaner. Vitamins and minerals help convert the carbohydrate, protein, and fat in food into usable energy for work, metabolism, growth, and repair. Water is the medium in which nutrients are suspended within the body.

Calories

Your car runs on gas; your body runs on food. Energy is measured as heat and expressed as calories. A calorie is not a nutrient but a unit of measure expressing the energy value of foods.

Fat has the most calories, about 9 calories per gram. Carbohydrate and protein contain about 4 calories per gram. By knowing the exact amount of each (grams of each), you can estimate the total caloric content of the food. An Egg McMuffin, for example, has 31 grams of carbohydrate, 18 grams of protein, and 15 grams of fat. If you multiply the grams of carbohydrate (31 grams) and protein (18 grams) by 4 and the grams of fat (15 grams) by 9, you find that an Egg McMuffin contains approximately 331 calories. Read the labels: if a product has a lot of grams of fat, it will have a lot of calories.

Energy Needs

The trick in any diet is to match your caloric intake to your caloric needs. If you consume more than you need, you will gain weight. Consume less than you need, and you will lose weight. Active people need more calories; inactive people need fewer calories.

The caloric cost of playing baseball varies by position. Infielders and outfielders expend fewer calories per minute in game situations than catchers or pitchers. In a typical nine-inning game, fielders will burn about 1,000 calories, catchers will expend 1,100 calories, and pitchers will use 1,440 calories. To estimate your postseason caloric needs, multiply your body weight in pounds by 15. A 200-pounder, for example, will need about 3,000 calories to keep from gaining or losing weight in the postseason. Once you start working out, multiply your weight by 18. The same 200-pounder will need 3,600 calories to fuel training. When games start, multiply weight by 23 if you're in the starting lineup and by 20 if you're an extra man. A starting 200-pounder will need about 4,600 calories on game days. Between appearances, relievers and starting pitchers should multiply weight by 20. Sample caloric needs for players of different weights and activity levels are presented in table 1.3.

Carbohydrates

Todd Jones, *after a five-minute lecture on the role of fiber in the diet: "Now, what's roughage?"*

Carbohydrates, the body's preferred energy source, are generally high in fiber and low in fat. They contain many vitamins and minerals. They come in two basic forms, starch and simple sugar. Sugars are the primary ingredient in foods like fruit juice, soft drinks, desserts, processed foods, honey, and table sugar. They provide quick, but short, bursts of energy. Starch or complex carbs contain many vitamins and minerals as well as protein. They are relatively fat-free, unless you add butter and fatty sauces. The starch found in whole grains, breads, pasta, rice, potatoes, beans, cereals, fruits, and vegetables provides a significant amount of fiber and a sustained source of energy.

Table 1.3 Caloric Needs by Body Weight and Activity Level

Weight (pounds)	Postseason (cal)	Off-season (cal)	In-season (cal) Non-starter	Starter
150	2,100	2,550	3,000	3,450
160	2,240	2,720	3,200	3,680
170	2,380	2,890	3,400	3,910
180	2,520	3,060	3,600	4,140
190	2,660	3,230	3,800	4,370
200	2,800	3,400	4,000	4,600
210	2,949	3,570	4,200	4,830
220	3,080	3,740	4,400	5,060
230	3,220	3,910	4,600	5,290
240	3,360	4,080	4,800	5,520

Your performance, to a large extent, depends on the quantity of glycogen (stored carbohydrate) in your muscles before and during exercise. If you want to have a lot of energy for practice, games, and workouts, make sure that 50 to 70 percent of your total calories come from carbohydrates, most as complex carbs. Build your diet around carbohydrates so your body can spare protein for building and repairing tissue.

Protein

Protein is a major structural component of all body tissues and is essential for tissue growth and repair. It is not a major source of energy under normal circumstances. If your diet is unbalanced or low in total calories (carbohydrate and fat), your body will use protein as fuel instead of for its intended job of tissue building. The body uses only as much protein as it needs. Excess protein does not build muscle; it becomes an expensive source of fat.

You should obtain about 15 percent of your total calories from protein, about six ounces per day. Animal protein, meat, eggs, and dairy products are complete or high-quality proteins and contain all the essential amino acids needed by the body. Plant sources are incomplete proteins, meaning that one or several of the essential amino acids are missing. You can, however, combine incomplete proteins to form complete proteins. Mixing beans and rice, combining beans and corn, and spreading peanut butter on bread are good, complete sources of protein.

A *meat serving* is three ounces, about the size of a deck of cards. Meat is an excellent source of protein, and you need two to three servings of protein per day. Poultry and fish are low in calories and fat. Beef and pork are higher in calories and fat. Eat baked and broiled poultry. Select white meat and remove the skin and visible fat beneath it. Removing the skin from chicken can cut the fat content by 75 percent and the total calories by half. Some well-trimmed, lean cuts of beef or pork (loin or round) have no more fat, ounce for ounce, than skinless dark-meat chicken. Frying adds two to six grams of fat per serving. Eat beef in moderation and go for the leanest cuts like eye of round, London broil, top loin, tenderloin, and filet mignon. The fatter cuts are prime rib, ribs, and ground beef; go easy on these! Limit pork to center-cut ham.

Dairy products have more calories (about 90 calories per serving) and more fat. Pour a cup of low-fat milk (1 percent or less) on your cereal, add a slice of low-fat cheese to your sandwich, and have a glass of low-fat milk with dinner. This will satisfy your daily needs for dairy products with less than 300 total calories.

Fruits and Vegetables

Fruits (60 calories per serving) and vegetables (25 calories per serving) are nutritious, low calorie, and fat-free. A fruit serving is one small apple, orange, banana, or other fruit. Large oranges, apples, or bananas count as 2 servings. Drink a small glass of juice and drop a handful of berries on your cereal at breakfast and you'll get 3 servings before you finish the sports page. Put a small box of raisins and a banana in your backpack and you'll get 5 or 6 total servings before dinner. Put lettuce, tomatoes, and pickles on your sandwich at lunch for 1 serving. Eat a small potato (2 servings), cup of green beans (2 servings), and mixed salad (2 servings) at dinner and you'll end the day with 8 to 10 servings of fruits and vegetables.

Fat

Despite their bad press, fats are essential in the athlete's diet. They are the most concentrated source of food energy, containing about twice as many calories per gram as either carbohydrate or protein. Carbohydrates provide the energy needed to hit, run, and throw. Fats provide the energy you need to stay out there for nine innings. Dietary fat can be liquid or solid. Most liquid forms of fat (oils) come from plant sources (vegetable oils) and are unsaturated. Unsaturated fats are healthier than saturated fats. Most saturated fats come from animal sources, tend to be solid at room temperature, and are considered to be less healthy.

No more than 20 to 30 percent of your total calories should come from fat. Fat calories should be equally distributed among saturated, monounsaturated, and polyunsaturated fats. Sources of saturated fat include beef, pork, eggs, and dairy products. Monounsaturated fats include chicken, canola oil, olive oil, and peanuts. Polyunsaturated fats include fish and margarine made from corn, safflower, soybean, and sunflower oil. Two oils, coconut and palm, are rich in saturated fat. Processed foods are made with transfatty acids, which have the same effects on your health as saturated fat.

It's OK to put a pat of margarine and a spoon of jelly on your toast. You can also use a little mayo on your sandwich when you tire of mustard or put a little dressing on your salad. But remember that every spoon of dressing or gravy and every pat of margarine is 45 empty calories. Avoid fast foods—they're high in fat and calories, and low in vitamins, minerals, and fiber. A three-piece dinner at Kentucky Fried Chicken, for example, contains over 900 calories and 46 grams of fat. A Big Mac has about 550 calories and 30 grams of fat. Avoid the pizza buffets. Two slices of a medium pizza give you almost 600 calories and 20 grams of fat.

Vitamins and Minerals

Vitamins are compounds that have no calories, provide no energy, and build no structure. They are metabolic regulators that help govern the processes of energy production, growth, maintenance, and repair. Thirteen vitamins, each with a specific function in the body, have been identified. Vitamins are either water soluble (B and C) or fat soluble (A, D, E, and K). Excess water-soluble vitamins are eliminated in the urine, so you need to replace those vitamins daily. Fat-soluble vitamins are stored in body fat, primarily in the liver, so you can replenish them less often. Taking too many fat-soluble vitamins can, over time, produce serious toxic effects. Vitamins are essential, but we need them in small amounts. If you eat the maximum recommended servings in the food pyramid, you will consume 100 percent of the recommended daily allowance for most vitamins. For peace of mind take a single multivitamin supplement with meals. Don't spend more than $10 or $20 per month on vitamins. Avoid "athletic formula" vitamins, which tend to be more marketing than science. Synthetic vitamins are as good as natural vitamins, and generic brands are as good as pharmaceutical brands. Price is not a guarantee of quality. For optimal health, consider taking 500 milligrams of vitamin C daily with breakfast and 500 milligrams with your evening meal. Take a single 200 to 400 IU (International Unit) dose of vitamin E with breakfast.

Minerals are compounds that help build structures and regulate systems. Calcium and phosphorus, for example, help build strong bones and teeth. Iodine is a component of the hormone thyroxin, and iron is essential for the formation of hemoglobin, the oxygen carrier within red blood cells. Others help with muscle contractions, nerve impulses, blood clotting, fluid balance, and heart rhythm. Minerals are classified as major (more than five grams) or minor (less than five grams) based on their availability in food and in the body. Major minerals, like calcium and potassium, are needed in large amounts; trace minerals, like iron and iodine, are needed in lesser amounts.

Water

Water is the most essential—and most neglected—nutrient for sport performance. All the body's important chemical reactions occur in water. Sixty percent of body weight and 70 percent of muscle weight is water. Adequate fluid intake is critical for muscular function, energy production, waste elimination, and temperature control. Inadequate water causes dehydration, elevated body temperature, fatigue, decreased performance, and increased risk of heat illness.

Drink a lot of water and drink it often. You need at least one-half ounce of water per pound of body weight each day, or about 15 eight-ounce glasses per day. Drink 2 or 3 cups of water, the colder the better, one hour before workouts to superhydrate the body. Drink another cup every 15 or 20 minutes throughout workouts to maintain fluid balance. Replace each pound of fluid loss with 16 ounces of water immediately after workouts to restore body-fluid balance and then drink 1 or 2 cups every hour between workouts.

Weight Management

Don't use the bathroom scales or height-weight tables to determine how much you should weigh. They can't differentiate between fat weight and muscle weight. Have your body composition checked by skinfolds or underwater weighing to determine your best weight.

If you need to lose weight, the best time to lose body fat is in the off-season. If you cut calories and increase off-field activity during the season, you might not have enough energy to maintain lean body mass and play at a winning level.

The secret to safe, sensible weight loss is mild caloric restriction, aerobic exercise, and strength training. You have to eat at least 1,500 to 2,000 calories per day to meet the body's nutritional needs and provide the energy needed to fuel exercise. Do 20 to 30 minutes of aerobic exercise three to five times per week to burn calories and lift weights three or four times per week to maintain muscle mass and elevate resting metabolic rate. Plan to lose no more than one or two pounds per week.

For maximum nutrition and good results, eat a variety of foods from each of the groups in the food pyramid. Eat enough carbohydrates to fuel your workouts and reduce fat and sugar intake to cut calories. Eat five or six regular meals rather than two or three large meals a day. Eating smaller, more frequent meals. keeps metabolism high, spreads the energy intake evenly throughout the day, and makes energy readily available for training. Crash diets and fad diets are not suitable for athletes. They limit your performance, damage your health, and do not produce significant, long-term reductions in fat. You can take control of your diet, but there are no shortcuts. Adopt a low-fat eating plan so simple that it becomes a way of life.

You can't add muscle by eating. Strength training is required to stimulate the body to increase lean body weight, and extra food is needed to fuel the training and building processes.

Muscle grows slowly. Don't fall for the claims made in many of the bodybuilding magazines that you can gain 25 pounds in 12 weeks. Under ideal dietary conditions, it is impossible for even the most motivated and highly trained athlete to gain more than about half an ounce of muscle per day. With proper diet and training, most athletes will gain about a pound of new muscle per month, or 10 to 12 pounds per year.

Chapter 2

Off-Season— Fitness Training

GOAL *Prepare a general fitness base, especially for the neuromuscular and cardiorespiratory systems*

This is the first formal training phase of your annual training program. It starts in week 5 and could extend from 8 to 12 weeks. Designed to produce a sound, general fitness base, the off-season phase you'll find here consists of plans for two 4-week blocks. In the first block you'll do a total fitness program to prepare the neuromuscular and cardiorespiratory systems for the harder work to come in the weeks that follow.

You will be "training to train," doing high-volume, low-intensity, general fitness workouts (running longer distances and doing many reps with light to moderate loads). Don't immediately overload the body. Gradually build functional strength and endurance in the major muscle groups, tendons, ligaments, and joints so they can adapt and handle the more stressful work to come in later phases.

Working the Body (Weeks 5–8)

Players with less than one year of training background should spend at least four weeks on general fitness training. Advanced players should do at least two weeks of general fitness training. Be sure to warm up and stretch before workouts and cool down afterward. Work especially on your running mechanics and trunk strength. Use dumbbells, tubing, and body-weight exercises for the rotator cuff and scapula. Do basic plyometric drills to learn how to land, stabilize, and jump. Do many reps with light to moderate loads for strength and endurance. Cross-train for aerobics.

Do a little skill work but not a lot. Volume (many reps and longer distance) causes fatigue, and fatigue inhibits skill development. Play catch and swing the bat two or three times per week for 5 to 10 minutes per day. Increase the amount and quality of skill training from week to week.

Whatever you do, don't skip this phase! You can't do high-intensity training without first building a sound base. High-intensity, year-round training increases your risk of overtraining injury and reduces your ability to achieve maximum gains and peak performance. Players with less than one year of training background need at least four weeks of general fitness training to allow the body time to get in shape and prepare for the more intense work to follow. Advanced athletes need at least two weeks of general fitness training.

Warm-Up and Flexibility

Start with the general warm-up exercises and the first dynamic warm-up routine. Stretch (using the daily dozen) before you get into the workout and cool down afterward.

Running and Conditioning Training

Emphasize mechanics early in the workout, when you are fresh. For at least two weeks, you should work three times per week on the three basic techniques: posture, arm action, and leg action (PAL). Do aerobics and interval runs at the end of the workout for cardiovascular fitness. Do intervals on Monday, Wednesday, and Friday. Jog, cycle, and jump rope on Tuesday and Thursday.

Mechanics

Learn one PAL technique at a time. Practice the first technique at half speed. Walk back and run again. Do five reps over 20 to 30 yards at half speed, rest two to three minutes, and then do five more reps at three-quarters speed. Rest and repeat the technique at full speed. Then try the next technique.

After learning each technique in isolation, put them together in a single 20- to 30-yard run at half speed. Walk back and run again. Do five reps at half speed, rest, and do five reps at three-quarters speed. Rest and repeat at full speed. Stop when you become tired and start to slow down.

Quickness

Start working on agility, balance, and first-step quickness. Use the wheel drill to learn how to move in all directions. Step in the direction of each spoke and hold for three to five seconds. Then do X-jumps and hops for quickness. Jump side to side as quickly as you can. Rest and jump front to back. Repeat the drill using one foot (hops). Notice whether you jump or hop farther in one direction than the other. Try to move the same distance in each direction. Now jump and hop in four directions (side to side and front and back). Finish with the dot drill. Try to reduce time from set to set and week to week. Add ladder drills in week 7.

Strength

Do the circuit weight-training program outlined in table 2.1 for the first two weeks (weeks 5 and 6) to develop a sound base of strength and endurance. Train three

Table 2.1 Off-Season (Weeks 5–6)—Fitness Training—"Train to Train"

	Activity	Exercises and Drills
MONDAY	**WARM-UP AND FLEXIBILITY**	Jog or cycle 5 min, general warm-up (1 × 10), dynamic warm-up #1 (1 × 10) Daily dozen (do 3 sets and hold each stretch for 10-15 sec)
	SPEED/QUICKNESS	
	Mechanics	Leg cycles (3 sets); eye focus (3 sets over 20-30 yd at half, three-quarters, and full speed); cheek to cheek (3 sets over 20-30 yd at half, three-quarters, and full speed); rise, fall, and run (3 sets over 20-30 yd at half, three-quarters, and full speed); seated arm runs (3 sets); ins and outs (3 sets); "A" skip (3 sets over 20-30 yd); arm runs (3 sets over 20-30 yd)
	First-step quickness	Wheel drill (3 sets to each spoke), X-jumps front/back (3 × 10), X-jumps side/side (3 × 10), X-jumps front/back-side/side (3 × 10), X-hops front/back (3 × 10), X-hops side/side (3 × 10), X-hops front/back-side/side (3 × 10), dot drill (3 sets)
	STRENGTH/POWER	
	Position players and pitchers	Position players: CWT (3 × 10): DB step-up—core, DB bench—core, lat pull (overhand)—core, DB squat—core, standing calf raise, DB shrug, seated long row, EZ triceps press, DB arm curl, leg curl, EZ-bar curl, rope triceps press Pitchers: CWT (3 × 10): DB step-up—core, DB bench—core, or push-up/DB squat—core, lat pull (overhand)—core, standing calf raise, DB shrug, seated long row, triceps press-down, DB arm curl, leg curl, triceps kickback
	Shoulder	Rotator cuff and scapula (1 × 10)
	Trunk	Sit-ups, daily core (100 reps), drop series (2 × 10), 50 series (2 × 50) MD ball drills (1 × 10): MD twist (3 positions), back to back (3 positions), figure 8 (3 positions), off-center (3 positions), seated toss-over
	Wrist and hand	Wrist—superset (1 × 10): wrist flexion and extension, wrist radial flexion and ulnar flexion Hand (1 × 10): rice drill #3, hand grip
	Intervals	10 × 100 yd in 10 min
	COOL-DOWN AND FLEXIBILITY	Jog and walk 5 min Daily dozen (3 × 10-15 sec)

times per week and do three circuits of each exercise. Don't change the resistance until you can complete all reps in each circuit with good form. Then switch to a sets-and-reps program (table 2.2) in week 7 and do all sets of one exercise before doing the next exercise. Find your training loads by trial and error (you can find information in chapter 7 on how to do this). Your goal is to do all the reps of each exercise in each set, so choose a load that allows you to

Table 2.1 Off-Season (Weeks 5–6)—Fitness Training—"Train to Train"

	Activity	Exercises and Drills
TUESDAY	**WARM-UP AND FLEXIBILITY**	Jog or cycle 5 min, general warm-up (1 × 10), dynamic warm-up #1 (1 × 10) Daily dozen (do 3 sets and hold each stretch for 10-15 sec)
	SPEED/QUICKNESS	
	Mechanics	Leg cycles (3 sets); eye focus (3 sets over 20-30 yd at half, three-quarters, and full speed); cheek to cheek (3 sets over 20-30 yd at half, three-quarters, and full speed); rise, fall, and run (3 sets over 20-30 yd at half, three-quarters, and full speed); seated arm runs (3 sets); ins and outs (3 sets); "A" skip (3 sets over 20-30 yd); arm runs (3 sets over 20-30 yd)
	First-step quickness	Wheel drill (3 sets to each spoke), X-jumps front/back (3 × 10), X-jumps side/side (3 × 10), X-jumps front/back-side/side (3 × 10), X-hops front/back (3 × 10), X-hops side/side (3 × 10), X-hops front/back-side/side (3 × 10), dot drill (3 sets)
	STRENGTH/POWER	
	Plyometrics	
	Week 5	Landing drills (5 ×): standing long jump—two-foot landing, standing long jump—one-foot landing, 3 consecutive SL jumps—two-foot landing, 3 consecutive SL jumps—one-foot landing Stabilization drills (2 × 5): step off 6-inch box—two foot landing, step off 6-inch box—one-foot landing, jump on 12-inch box—two foot landing, jump on 12-inch box—one-foot landing
	Week 6	Jump-ups (2 × 5): jump on 12-inch box—two foot landing, jump on 12-inch box—one foot landing, and ankle bounce (2 × 5), ice skater (2 × 5), squat jump (2 × 5), tuck jump (2 × 5), split jump (2 × 5), scissors jump (2 × 5)
	Aerobics (135-150 bpm)	Jog, stairclimb, or cycle 15-20 min Jump rope 5-10 min
	COOL-DOWN AND FLEXIBILITY	Jog and walk 5 min Daily dozen (3 × 10-15 sec)

Table 2.1 Off-Season (Weeks 5–6)—Fitness Training—"Train to Train"

	Activity	Exercises and Drills
WEDNESDAY	**WARM-UP AND FLEXIBILITY**	Jog or cycle 5 min, general warm-up (1 × 10), dynamic warm-up #1 (1 × 10) Daily dozen (do 3 sets and hold each stretch for 10-15 sec)
	SPEED/QUICKNESS	
	Mechanics	Leg cycles (3 sets); eye focus (3 sets over 20-30 yd at half, three-quarters, and full speed); cheek to cheek (3 sets over 20-30 yd at half, three-quarters, and full speed); rise, fall, and run (3 sets over 20-30 yd at half, three-quarters, and full speed); seated arm runs (3 sets); ins and outs (3 sets); "A" skip (3 sets over 20-30 yd); arm runs (3 sets over 20-30 yd)

Table 2.1 Off-Season (Weeks 5–6)—Fitness Training—"Train to Train"

	Activity	Exercises and Drills
WEDNESDAY	**SPEED/QUICKNESS**	
	First-step quckness	Wheel drill (3 sets to each spoke), X-jumps front/back (3 × 10), X-jumps side/side (3 × 10), X-jumps front/back-side/side (3 × 10), X-hops front/back (3 × 10), X-hops side/side (3 × 10), X-hops front/back-side/side (3 × 10), dot drill (3 sets)
	STRENGTH/POWER	
	Position players and pitchers	Position players: CWT (3 × 10): DB split-squat—core, DB incline press—core, lat pull (underhand)—core, DB lunge—core, seated calf raise, DB shrug Pitchers: CWT (3 × 10): DB split-squat—core, DB incline or push-up—core, DB lunge—core, lat pull (underhand)—core, seated calf raise, DB shrug, DB row (palm in), rope triceps press, DB hammer curl, multihip, triceps press-down
	Shoulder	Rotator cuff and scapula (1 × 10)
	Trunk	Sit-ups, daily core (100 reps), drop series (2 × 10), 50 series (2 × 50) MD ball drills (1 × 10): MD twist (3 positions), back to back (3 positions), figure 8 (3 positions), off-center (3 positions), seated toss-over
	Wrist and hand	Wrist (1 × 10): rice drill #1, rice drill #2 Hand (1 × 10): towel pull-up, plate squeeze
	Intervals	10 × 100 yd @ 18:18
	COOL-DOWN AND FLEXIBILITY	Jog and walk 5 min Daily dozen (3 × 10-15 sec)

Table 2.1 Off-Season (Weeks 5–6)—Fitness Training—"Train to Train"

	Activity	Exercises and Drills
THURSDAY	**WARM-UP AND FLEXIBILITY**	Jog or cycle 5 min, general warm-up (1 × 10), dynamic warm-up #1 (1 × 10) Daily dozen (do 3 sets and hold each stretch for 10-15 sec)
	SPEED/QUICKNESS	
	Mechanics	Leg cycles (3 sets); eye focus (3 sets over 20-30 yd at half, three-quarters, and full speed); cheek to cheek (3 sets over 20-30 yd at half, three-quarters, and full speed); rise, fall, and run (3 sets over 20-30 yd at half, three-quarters, and full speed); seated arm runs (3 sets), ins and outs (3 sets); "A" skip (3 sets over 20-30 yd); arm runs (3 sets over 20-30 yd)
	First step quickness	Wheel drill (3 sets to each spoke), X-jumps front/back (3 × 10), X-jumps side/side (3 × 10), X-jumps front/back-side/side (3 × 10), X-hops, front/back (3 × 10), X-hops side/side (3 × 10), X-hops front/back-side/side (3 × 10), dot drill (3 sets)

(continued)

Table 2.1 Off-Season *(Weeks 5–6, continued)*

	Activity	Exercises and Drills
THURSDAY	**STRENGTH/POWER**	
	Plyometrics	
	Week 5	Landing drills (5 ×): standing long jump—two-foot landing, standing long jump —one-foot landing, 3 consecutive SL jumps—two-foot landing, 3 consecutive SL jumps—one-foot landing
		Stabilization drills (2 × 5): step off 6-inch box—two-foot landing, step off 6-inch box—one-foot landing, jump on 12-inch box—two-foot landing, jump on 12-inch box—one-foot landing
		In-place jumps (2 × 5): ankle flips, split jump, scissors jump, tuck jump
	Week 6	Jump-ups (2 × 5): jump on 12-inch box—two-foot landing, jump on 12-inch box—one-foot landing, and leg bounce (2 × 5), ice skater (2 × 5), squat jump (2 × 5), tuck jump (2 × 5), split jump (2 × 5), scissors jump (2 × 5)
	Aerobics (135-150 bpm)	Jog, stairclimb, or cycle 15-20 min; jump rope 5-10 min
	COOL-DOWN AND FLEXIBILITY	Jog and walk 5 min Daily dozen (3 × 10-15 sec)

Table 2.1 Off-Season (Weeks 5–6)—Fitness Training—"Train to Train"

	Activity	Exercises and Drills
FRIDAY	**WARM-UP AND FLEXIBILITY**	Jog or cycle 5 min, general warm-up (1 × 10), dynamic warm-up #1 (1 × 10) Daily dozen (do 3 sets and hold each stretch for 10-15 sec)
	SPEED/QUICKNESS	
	Mechanics	Leg cycles (3 sets); eye focus (3 sets over 20-30 yd at half, three-quarters, and full speed); cheek to cheek (3 sets over 20-30 yd at half, three-quarters, and full speed); rise, fall, and run (3 sets over 20-30 yd at half, three-quarters, and full speed); seated arm runs (3 sets); ins and outs (3 sets); "A" skip (3 sets over 20-30 yd); arm runs (3 sets over 20-30 yd)
	First-step quickness	Wheel drill (3 sets to each spoke), X-jumps front/back (3 × 10), X-jumps side/side (3 × 10), X-jumps front/back-side/side (3 × 10), X-hops front/back (3 × 10), X-hops side/side (3 × 10), X-hops front/back-side/side (3 × 10), dot drill (3 sets)
	STRENGTH/POWER	
	Position players and pitchers	Position players: CWT (3 × 10): DB step-up—core, DB bench press—core, lat pull (overhand)—core, DB squat—core, standing calf raise, DB shrug, seated long row, EZ triceps press, DB arm curl, leg curl, EZ-bar curl, rope triceps press

Table 2.1 Off-Season (Weeks 5–6)—Fitness Training—"Train to Train"

	Activity	Exercises and Drills
FRIDAY	**STRENGTH/POWER**	
	Position players and pitchers	Pitchers: CWT (3 × 10): DB step-up—core, DB bench or push-up—core, DB squat—core, lat pull (overhand)—core, standing calf raise, DB shrug, seated long row, triceps press-down, DB arm curl, leg curl, triceps kickback
	Shoulder	Rotator cuff and scapula (1 × 10)
	Trunk	Sit-ups, daily core (100 reps), drop series (2 × 10), 50 series (2 × 50) MD ball drills (1 × 10): MD twist (3 positions), back to back (3 positions), figure 8 (3 positions), off-center (3 positions), seated toss-over
	Wrist and hand	Wrist—superset (1 × 10): wrist flexion and extension, wrist radial flexion and ulnar flexion Hand (1 × 10): rice drill #3, hand grip
	Intervals	2 × 200 yd @ 40:120, jog 10 min
	COOL-DOWN AND FLEXIBILITY	Jog and walk 5 min Daily dozen (3 × 10-15 sec)

do the specified number of reps in all sets with good form. If, for example, the first workout in week 7 calls for 3 × 8, select a load that allows you to do the full number of reps (8) in each set. The load is too light if you can do all reps in each set. Increase it by 5 or 10 pounds in the next workout. The load is too heavy if you can't do the full number of reps in the first set. Reduce it by 5 or 10 pounds and continue the workout. If you complete the full number of reps in the first set, but can't do all the reps in the remaining sets, the load is adequate. Continue to use this load until you can do all reps in all sets.

Shoulders.   Pitchers and position players with a history of shoulder problems may want to substitute push-ups and incline push-ups for bench and incline presses. They may also want to substitute kickbacks, press-downs, and DB curls for EZ-bar triceps presses, EZ-bar curls, and bench dips. Do exercises for the rotator cuff and scapula three to four times per week.

Trunk.   Do sit-ups three or four times per week. Use a six-pound medicine (MD) ball and do MD ball twisting drills from three positions (standing, kneeling, and sitting) each workout. Finish with seated back toss-overs for the low back. Add the North Carolina and rocky twist drills in week 7.

Wrist and Hand.   Superset three to five exercises for the wrist and do two drills for the hand each workout. A superset alternates agonists and antagonists of a joint with minimal rest between exercises. Examples are wrist flexion and extension, wrist abduction and adduction, and wrist pronation and supination. Work the wrist first and the hand last.

Plyometrics

Do plyometrics twice per week. Use the first week (week 5) to learn proper landing technique, stabilization, and body control. Your first drill on day 1 is a standing long jump. Jump forward off both feet, land on two feet, and hold for five seconds for balance and control. Do two sets of five reps and then jump off both feet and land on one foot for more balance and control. Make five landings on each foot. Next, do three consecutive standing long jumps. Repeat the drill landing on one foot after the third jump. Make five landings on each foot.

When you can jump and stabilize, develop eccentric strength by stepping off a 6-inch box and landing on two feet, and then repeat the drill, landing on one foot. End the session by jumping up onto a 12-inch box. Land on two feet and then land on one foot.

Start workouts 2 and 3 by reviewing the drills learned on day 1 and then do ankle flips, tuck jumps, split jumps, and scissors jumps to learn how to get off the ground quickly. Add box jumps in week 6. Use a 12-inch box and learn how to do two- and one-foot landings.

Deficiencies and Cooling Down

In the off-season it is important to continue to rehab any injuries you might have had and correct deficiencies in your skills or condition. Do more aerobic work if you need to lose weight. Cross-train for 30 to 60 minutes per day. Jog for 10 minutes, use the StairMaster, or jump rope for 10 minutes and finish with 10 minutes on a bike or slideboard. Start with 30 minutes of work. Increase total work time by 10 percent per week and build to 45 to 60 minutes per workout.

Working the Body (Weeks 9–12)

This is the second half of your general fitness phase. Work on total fitness (see tables 2.2–2.6) each training session to prepare your body for the more intense work to come.

Warm-Up and Flexibility

Do the general warm-up exercises and dynamic warm-up routine #1 before each workout. Stretch (daily dozen) before and cool down after workouts.

Running

Work on stamina three to four times per week and pick up the pace. Run 10×100 yards in 10 minutes on Monday, do interval sprints on Wednesday and Friday, and do aerobics on Tuesday and Thursday.

First-Step Quickness

Sprint forward after the last rep of each spoke of the wheel drill to learn how to sprint in all directions. Then do down-the-line jumps and hops for quickness while

Table 2.2 Off-Season (Weeks 7–8)—Fitness Training—"Train to Train"

	Activity	Exercises and Drills
MONDAY	**WARM-UP AND FLEXIBILITY**	Jog or cycle 5 min, general warm-up (1 × 10), dynamic warm-up #1, (1 × 10) Daily dozen (do 3 sets and hold each stretch for 10-15 sec)
	STRENGTH/POWER	
		All players—sets × reps (all reps in all sets) Total-body workout Core—4 × 10 Assist—3 × 8
	Shoulder	Rotator cuff and scapula (1 × 10)
	Trunk	Sit-ups, daily core (100 reps), drop series (3 × 10), 50 series (2 × 50) MD ball drills (1 × 10): MD twist (3 positions), back to back (3 positions), figure 8 (3 positions), off-center (3 positions), rocky twist (feet up and down), North Carolina (feet up and down), seated toss-over
	Wrist and hand	Wrist—superset (2 × 10): wrist flexion and extension, wrist radial flexion and ulnar flexion Hand (1 × 10): rice drill #3, hand grip
	Intervals	10 × 100 yd in 10 min
	COOL-DOWN AND FLEXIBILITY	Jog and walk 5 min Daily dozen (3 × 10-15 sec)

Table 2.2 Off-Season (Weeks 7–8)—Fitness Training—"Train to Train"

	Activity	Exercises and Drills
TUESDAY	**WARM-UP AND FLEXIBILITY**	Jog or cycle 5 min, general warm-up (1 × 10), dynamic warm-up #1, (1 × 10) Daily dozen (do 3 sets and hold each stretch for 10-15 sec)
	SPEED/QUICKNESS	
	Mechanics	Leg cycles (3 sets), ins and outs (3 sets), "A" skip (3 sets over 20-30 yd), arm runs (3 sets over 20-30 yd)
	First-step quickness	Wheel drill (3 sets to each spoke), X-jumps front/back (3 × 10), X-jumps side/side (3 × 10), X-jumps front/back-side/side (3 × 10), X-hops front/back (3 × 10), X-hops side/side (3 × 10), X-hops front/back-side/side (3 × 10), dot drill (3 sets)
	LSA (Lateral speed agility)	Ladder drills (2 sets of each drill): forward wide skip, backward wide skip, forward crossover skip, backward crossover skip Microhurdle drills (3 sets of 4; over and back is one): high step with 4 hurdles, high step with 3 hurdles, high step with 2 hurdles

(continued)

Table 2.2 Off-Season *(Weeks 7–8, continued)*

	Activity	Exercises and Drills
TUESDAY	**STRENGH/POWER**	
	Plyometrics	Box drills (2 × 10): box pop-up, box crossover, supported jump-ups Resisted (tubing) drills (2 × 10): shuffle crossover, over the shoulder MD ball drills (2 × 5): thigh kick, donkey kick (2 feet), donkey kick (1 foot), soccer kick-up
	Trunk	Sit-ups, daily core (100 reps), drop series (3 × 10), 50 series (2 × 50) MD ball drills (1 × 10): MD twist (3 positions), back to back (3 positions), figure 8 (3 positions), off-center (3 positions), rocky twist (feet up and down), North Carolina (feet up and down), seated toss-over
	Aerobics **(135-150 bpm)**	Jog, stairclimb, or cycle 15-20 min; jump rope 5-10 min
	COOL-DOWN **AND FLEXIBILITY**	Jog and walk 5 min Daily dozen (3 × 10-15 sec)

Table 2.2 Off-Season (Weeks 7–8)—Fitness Training—"Train to Train"

	Activity	Exercises and Drills
WEDNESDAY	**WARM-UP** **AND FLEXIBILITY**	Jog or cycle 5 min, general warm-up (1 × 10), dynamic warm-up #1 (1 × 10) Daily dozen (do 3 sets and hold each stretch for 10-15 sec)
	STRENGTH/POWER	
		All players—sets × reps (all reps in all sets) Total-body workout Core—4 × 10 Assist—3 × 8
	Shoulder	Rotator cuff and scapula (1 × 10)
	Trunk	Sit-ups, daily core (100 reps), drop series (3 × 10), 50 series (2 × 50) MD ball drills (1 × 10): MD twist (3 positions), back to back (3 positions), figure 8 (3 positions), off-center (3 positions), rocky twist (feet up and down), North Carolina (feet up and down), seated toss-over
	Wrist and hand	Wrist—superset (2 × 10): rice drill #1, rice drill #2 Hand (1 × 10): towel pull-up, plate squeeze
	Intervals	2 × 8 × 100 yd @ 22:22
	COOL-DOWN **AND FLEXIBILITY**	Jog and walk 5 min Daily dozen (3 × 10-15 sec)

Table 2.2 Off-Season (Weeks 7–8)—Fitness Training—"Train to Train"

	Activity	Exercises and Drills
THURSDAY	**WARM-UP AND FLEXIBILITY**	Jog or cycle 5 min, general warm-up (1 × 10), dynamic warm-up #1, (1 × 10) Daily dozen (do 3 sets and hold each stretch for 10-15 sec)
	SPEED/QUICKNESS	
	Mechanics	Leg cycles (3 sets), ins and outs (3 sets), "A" skip (3 sets over 20-30 yd), arm runs (3 sets over 20-30 yd)
	First-step quickness	Wheel drill (3 sets to each spoke), X-jumps front/back (3 × 10), X-jumps side/side (3 × 10), X-jumps front/back-side/side (3 × 10), X-hops front/back (3 × 10), X-hops side/side (3 × 10), X-hops front/back-side/side (3 × 10), dot drill (3 sets)
	LSA (Lateral speed agility)	Ladder drills (2 sets of each drill): forward wide skip, backward wide skip, forward crossover skip, backward crossover skip Microhurdle drills (3 sets of 4; over and back is one): high step with 4 hurdles, high step with 3 hurdles, high step with 2 hurdles
	STRENGTH/POWER	
	Plyometrics	Cone jumps (2 × 10): front/back, side/side Cone hops (2 × 10): front/back, side/side MD throwing drills (2 × 5): squat and chest throw, underhand throw, backward (over-the-head) throw, discus throw
	Trunk	Sit-ups, daily core (100 reps), drop series (3 × 10), 50 series (2 × 50) MD ball drills (1 × 10): MD twist (3 positions), back to back (3 positions), figure 8 (3 positions), off-center (3 positions), rocky twist (feet up and down), North Carolina (feet up and down), seated toss-over
	Aerobics (135-150 bpm)	Jog, stairclimb, or cycle 15-20 min; jump rope 5-10 min
	COOL-DOWN AND FLEXIBILITY	Jog and walk 5 min Daily dozen (3 × 10-15 sec)

Table 2.2 Off-Season (Weeks 7–8)—Fitness Training—"Train to Train"

	Activity	Exercises and Drills
FRIDAY	**WARM-UP AND FLEXIBILITY**	Jog or cycle 5 min, general warm-up (1 × 10), dynamic warm-up #1 (1 × 10) Daily dozen (do 3 sets and hold each stretch for 10-15 sec)
	STRENGTH/POWER	
		All players—sets 3 reps (all reps in all sets) Total-body workout Core—4 × 10 Assist—3 × 8

(continued)

Table 2.2 Off-Season *(Weeks 7–8, continued)*

	Activity	Exercises and Drills
FRIDAY	**STRENGTH/POWER**	
	Shoulder	Rotator cuff and scapula (1 × 10)
	Trunk	Sit-ups, daily core (100 reps), drop series (3 × 10), 50 series (2 × 50)
		MD ball drills (1 × 10): MD twist (3 positions), back to back (3 positions), figure 8 (3 positions), off-center (3 positions), rocky twist (feet up and down), North Carolina (feet up and down), seated toss-over
	Wrist and hand	Wrist—superset (2 × 10): wrist flexion and extension, wrist radial flexion and ulnar flexion Hand (1 × 10): rice drill #3, hand grip
	Intervals	3 × 200 yd @ 40:120, jog 10 min
	COOL-DOWN AND FLEXIBILITY	Jog and walk 5 min Daily dozen (3 × 10-15 sec)

moving. Jump side to side as you go forward down a line five feet long. Make quick low jumps to the end and then come back jumping backward. Repeat the drill (jump front and back) going sideways down the line and then repeat the sequence hopping on one foot. Next, do the dot drill and ladder drills for foot speed, hurdle drills for lateral speed and agility, and ball pick-ups for game-specific quickness.

Add a 10-yard forward sprint to the down-the-line drills. Sprint forward after the last jump or hop. Add lateral sprints (run to the right or left after the last jump or hop) and wall runs. Start wall runs by leaning forward with both hands extended against a wall for support. Pump your knees at a moderate pace for 5 steps (right-left is one step). Increase speed for 5 steps after the fifth step. Sprint after the 10th step. Do quicks on a four- to six-inch high box. Cycle your feet on and off the box as fast as you can for 10 contacts with each foot.

Speed-Strength

Start doing squat-and-touch (SAT) drills. Squat down (in place) on one leg and touch the ground with the opposite hand. Stand and repeat 10 times on each leg. Then step forward on one foot before doing an SAT. Repeat the drill stepping backward before each SAT. Then step sideways before doing an SAT.

Strength

Continue to use the sets-and-reps program. Do all sets of one exercise before doing the second exercise. Beginners use a load that permits them to do all reps in each set. Advanced players switch to a pyramid training system.

Shoulders. Train the rotator cuff and scapula three or four times per week.

Trunk. Do sit-ups, leg drops, and MD ball drills each workout. Do the MD ball rotations from three positions and rocky twist and North Carolina (NC) with both feet on the ground. Then repeat the drills with both feet off the ground. Always finish with back toss-overs.

Wrist and Hand. Superset three or four exercises for the wrist and do two drills for the hand.

Plyometrics

Use box drills, resisted (tubing) movements, and MD ball kicks on Tuesdays. Jump, hop, and do MD ball throws on Thursdays.

Position-Specific Conditioning

For players at all positions, it is crucial to continue to rehabilitate injuries, correct deficiencies, and do extra aerobic work for weight control. You should also play catch and swing the bat for 10 to 15 minutes, two to three times per week.

Catchers

In games, catchers make more throws, get up and down more, and run farther than any player on the field. The catcher should be the best-conditioned player on the field. Use this time to get your hips and legs in shape. Do a second set of hurdle and under-the-bar exercises to maximize hip flexibility. Do lateral box crossovers and ice skaters for lateral quickness and rhythm.

Start box crossovers by standing two to three feet to the right of a six-inch box with a dumbbell in each hand. Lunge sideways onto the middle of the box with your right foot. Pause for one or two seconds, extend your right leg, and step onto the box with your left foot. Lunge off the box with your right foot, pause, extend your right leg, and step off the box with your left foot. Alternate lunging right and left across the box until you do 10 lunges in each direction. Finish with ice skaters. Start slowly and increase speed each set.

Infielders

Third basemen and second basemen move at least two or three steps on almost 30 percent of all ground balls. The shortstop, the most active infielder, moves on almost 40 percent of all ground balls. The first baseman moves on 25 percent. Because infielders get into and out of the ready, or fielding, position 135 to 150 times per game, are involved in almost half of all balls hit, and move on 25 to 40 percent of all ground balls, they need to be in position and ready to move on every pitch. Use this phase of training to build strength in the muscles used to get into and maintain a fielding position. Do box crossovers and MD ball passes from a squat position for posture and shuttles for lateral speed and agility (LSA) and first-step quickness.

Start with box crossovers and then do MD ball squat passes. Stand with your feet in a fielding position and hold a six-pound MD ball at chest height. Squat until your thighs are parallel to the ground. Hold this position for one or two seconds and make a chest pass to a partner standing five or six feet away. Stand, receive a return pass, and repeat the sequence to simulate getting into and out of the fielding position. Start the 5-10-5 drill by standing at the middle cone. Use a crossover step and sprint 5 yards to the right. Stop and touch your glove hand to the ground just inside the end cone. Use a crossover step and sprint 10 yards to the left. Stop and touch your glove hand to the ground inside the first cone. Use a crossover step and sprint back to the right and touch the middle cone with your glove hand. Rest and repeat going to the left.

Outfielders

Outfielders are involved in more than half of all balls hit and move five feet or more on 75 to 80 percent of all fly balls and line drives. On every pitch they need to be in position and ready to move to catch the ball or cut it off to prevent extra bases. Do the wheel drill with sprints to simulate the moves required in the outfield. Start with straight-ahead movements. Step forward with one foot and sprint 10 to 30 yards to catch a line drive. Then go diagonally. Step at a 45-degree angle to one side and sprint to catch a sinking liner. Now go side to side. Use a crossover step and sprint to one side. Next, turn, use a drop step, and sprint to catch a ball over your shoulder. Finish by turning and running to catch a ball hit directly over your head. Start with 10-yard sprints in each direction and build to 30-yard sprints.

Pitchers

Pitchers are important and may have special needs, but they are not made of glass. Coaches, they will not break if you work them. In fact, the reverse is true. If you treat them like glass, they will, in time, break. If you expect them to break down, they will break down.

A pitcher must work the total body, not just his rotator cuff and legs. Do some form of upper-body training. You don't have to lift weights. Try push-ups or incline push-ups for the chest and shoulder. Do shoulder protractions and retractions with dumbbells, or on a chest-press machine and a lat-pull device, to help stabilize the shoulder. Do DB rows, curls, and kickbacks for the back and elbow. Pound the trunk and legs. Do 300 to 500 sit-ups and 100 to 200 MD ball trunk rotations per day. Add two extra leg lifts per workout. Choose from split-squats, walking lunges, lateral lunges, crossover lunges, and step-ups. Train the wrist and hand. Remember, the fingers are the last thing to touch the ball, and you need strong hands to impart good spin. Do a lot of aerobic work in the off-season. Cross-train within and between workouts. Jump rope and do slideboard exercises for balance and coordination.

Fueling the Body to Train

Eat smart to get the most out of your training program. Don't go to the gym on an empty stomach or expect a cup of coffee and a Pop Tart to get you through the morning. Breakfast is the most important meal of the day. It breaks the fast that started when you went to bed the night before. When you wake up, your energy level is rock bottom. Eat a breakfast that will get you through your workout with energy to spare. A cup of coffee and a donut will give you a quick

Table 2.3 Off-Season (Week 9)—Fitness Training—"Train to Train"

	Activity	Exercises and Drills
MONDAY	**WARM-UP AND FLEXIBILITY**	Jog or cycle 5 min, general warm-up (1 × 10), dynamic warm-up #1 (1 × 10) Daily dozen (do 3 sets and hold each stretch for 10-15 sec)
	STRENGTH/POWER	
	Strength	Beginners: Sets × reps (all reps in all sets): Total-body workout Core—4 × 8 Assist—3 × 8 Advanced: Pyramid program Total-body workout Core—heavy = 1 × 8; 5 × 5 × 75% Core—moderate = 1 × 8; 5 × 5 × 70% Assist—heavy = 2 × 10; 1 × 8 × 75% Assist—moderate = 2 × 10; 1 × 8 × 70%
	Shoulder	Rotator cuff and scapula (1 × 10)
	Trunk	Sit-ups, daily core (100 reps), drop series (2 × 15), 50 series (2 × 50) MD ball drills (1 × 10): MD twist (3 positions), back to back (3 positions), figure 8 (3 positions), off-center (3 positions), rocky twist (feet up and down), North Carolina (feet up and down), seated toss-over
	Wrist and hand	Wrist—superset (3 × 10): wrist flexion and extension, wrist radial flexion and ulnar flexion Hand (1 × 10): rice drill #3, hand grip
	Intervals	10 × 100 yd in 10 min
	COOL-DOWN AND FLEXIBILITY	Jog and walk 5 min Daily dozen (3 × 10-15 sec)

Table 2.3 Off-Season (Week 9)—Fitness Training—"Train to Train"

	Activity	Exercises and Drills
TUESDAY	**WARM-UP AND FLEXIBILITY**	Jog or cycle 5 min, general warm-up (1 × 10), dynamic warm-up #1 (1 × 10) Daily dozen (do 3 sets and hold each stretch for 10-15 sec)
	SPEED/QUICKNESS	
	Mechanics	"A" skip (3 sets over 20-30 yd at half, three-quarters, and full speed), arm runs (3 sets over 20-30 yd)
	First-step quickness	Wheel drill and sprint forward 5-10 yd (3 sets to each spoke), dot drill (3 sets) Ladder drills (2 sets of each drill): forward wide skip, backward wide skip, forward crossover skip, backward crossover skip, Icky shuffle, backward Icky shuffle, crossover, backward crossover
	Agility	Microhurdle drills (3 sets of 4; over and back is one): high step with 4 hurdles, high step with 3 hurdles, high step with 2 hurdles Jumps and hops (2 ×): down-the-line jumps, down-the-line hops, ball pick-ups (1 × 20)

(continued)

Table 2.3 Off-Season *(Week 9, continued)*

	Activity	Exercises and Drills
TUESDAY	**Speed-Strength**	SAT: backward then forward (2 × 10), side/side (2 × 10)
	STRENGTH/POWER	
	Plyometrics	Box drills (18-inch box, 2 × 10): box pop-up, box crossover, supported jump-up; resisted (tubing) drills (2 ×): shuffle, crossover, over the shoulder MD ball drills (2 × 10): thigh kick, donkey kick (two legs), donkey kick (one leg), soccer kick-up
	Trunk	Sit-ups, daily core (100 reps), drop series (2 × 15), 50 series (2 × 50) MD ball drills (1 × 10): MD twist (3 positions), back to back (3 positions), figure 8 (3 positions), off-center (3 positions), rocky twist (feet up and down), North Carolina (feet up and down), seated toss-over
	Aerobics	Jog, stairclimb, or cycle 15-20 min; jump rope 5-10 min
	COOL-DOWN AND FLEXIBILITY	Jog and walk 5 min Daily dozen (3 × 10-15 sec)

Table 2.3 Off-Season (Week 9)—Fitness Training—"Train to Train"

	Activity	Exercises and Drills	
WEDNESDAY	**WARM-UP AND FLEXIBILITY**	Jog or cycle 5 min, general warm-up (1 × 10), dynamic warm-up #1(1 × 10) Daily dozen (do 3 sets and hold each stretch for 10-15 sec)	
	STRENGTH/POWER		
	Strength	Beginners: Sets × reps (all reps in all sets): Total-body workout Core—4 × 8 Assist—3 × 8	Advanced: Pyramid program Total-body workout Core—moderate = 1 × 8; 5 × 5 × 70% Assist—moderate = 2 × 10; 1 × 8 × 70%
	Shoulder	Rotator cuff and scapula (1 × 10)	
	Trunk	Sit-ups, daily core (100 reps), drop series (2 × 15), 50 series (2 × 50) MD ball drills (1 × 10): MD twist (3 positions), back to back (3 positions), figure 8 (3 positions), off-center (3 positions, rocky twist (feet up and down), North Carolina (feet up and down), seated toss-over	
	Wrist and hand	Wrist (3 × 10): rice drill #1, rice drill #2 Hand (1 × 10): towel pull-up, plate squeeze	
	Intervals	2 × 10 × 100 yd @ 22:22	
	COOL-DOWN AND FLEXIBILITY	Jog and walk 5 min Daily dozen (3 × 10-15 sec)	

Table 2.3 Off-Season (Week 9)—Fitness Training—"Train to Train"

Activity	Exercises and Drills
WARM-UP AND FLEXIBILITY	Jog or cycle 5 min, general warm-up (1 × 10), dynamic warm-up #1(1 × 10) Daily dozen (do 3 sets and hold each stretch for 10-15 sec)
SPEED/QUICKNESS	
Mechanics	"A" skip (3 sets over 20-30 yd at half, three-quarters, and full speed), arm runs (3 sets over 20-30 yd)
First-step quickness	Wheel drill and sprint forward 5-10 yd (3 sets to each spoke), dot drill (3 sets) Ladder drills (2 sets of each drill): forward wide skip, backward wide skip, forward crossover skip, backward crossover skip, Icky shuffle, backward Icky shuffle, crossover, backward crossover
Agility	Microhurdle drills (3 sets of 4; over and back is one): high step with 4 hurdles, high step with 3 hurdles, high step with 2 hurdles Jumps and hops (2 ×): down-the-line jumps, down-the-line hops, ball pick-ups (1 × 20)
Speed-Strength	SAT: backward then forward (2 × 10), side/side (2 × 10)
STRENGTH/POWER	
Plyometrics	Box drills (18-inch box, 2 × 10): box jump, box crossover jump; Cone jumps (2 × 10): front/back, side/side; Cone hops (2 × 10): front/back, side/side MD ball throws (5 ×): squat and chest throw, underhand throw, backward (over-the-head) throw, discus throw
Trunk	Sit-ups, daily core (100 reps), drop series (2 × 15), 50 series (2 × 50) MD ball drills (1 × 10): MD twist (3 positions), back to back (3 positions), figure 8 (3 positions), off-center (3 positions, rocky twist (feet up and down), North Carolina (feet up and down), seated toss-over
Aerobics	Jog, stairclimb, or cycle 15-20 min; jump rope 5-10 min
COOL-DOWN AND FLEXIBILITY	Jog and walk 5 min Daily dozen (3 × 10-15 sec)

The entire table is labeled **THURSDAY** (vertical text at left).

Table 2.3 Off-Season (Week 9)—Fitness Training—"Train to Train"

	Activity	Exercises and Drills
FRIDAY	**WARM-UP AND FLEXIBILITY**	Jog or cycle 5 min, general warm-up (1 × 10), dynamic warm-up #1 (1 × 10) Daily dozen (do 3 sets and hold each stretch for 10-15 sec)
	STRENGTH/POWER	
	Strength	Beginners: Sets × reps (all reps in all sets) Total-body workout Core—4 × 8 Assist—3 × 8 Advanced pyramid: Total-body workout Core—heavy = 1 × 8; 5 × 5 × 75% Assist—heavy = 2 × 10; 1 × 8 × 75%
	Shoulder	Rotator cuff and scapula (1 × 10)
	Trunk	Sit-ups, daily core (100 reps), drop series (2 × 15), 50 series (2 × 50) MD ball drills (1 × 10): MD twist (3 positions), back to back (3 positions), figure 8 (3 positions), off-center (3 positions), rocky twist (feet up and down), North Carolina (feet up and down), seated toss-over
	Wrist and hand	Wrist—superset (3 × 10): wrist flexion and extension, wrist radial flexion and ulnar flexion Hand (1 × 10): rice drill #3, hand grip
	Intervals	4 × 200 yd @ 40:120; jog 10 min
	COOL-DOWN AND FLEXIBILITY	Jog and walk 5 min Daily dozen (3 × 10-15 sec)

Table 2.4 Off-Season (Week 10)—Fitness Training—"Train to Train"

	Activity	Exercises and Drills
MONDAY	**WARM-UP AND FLEXIBILITY**	Jog or cycle 5 min, general warm-up (1 × 10), dynamic warm-up #1(1 × 10) Daily dozen (do 3 sets and hold each stretch for 10-15 sec)
	STRENGTH/POWER	
		Beginners: Sets × reps (all reps in all sets): Total-body workout Core—4 × 8 Assist—3 × 8 Advanced pyramid: Total-body workout Core—heavy = 1 × 8; 2 × 5; 3 × 3 × 85% Core—moderate = 1 × 8; 2 × 5; 3 × 3 × 75% Assist—heavy = 1 × 10; 2 × 8 × 75% Assist—moderate = 1 × 10; 2 × 8 × 70%
	Shoulder	Rotator cuff and scapula (1 × 10)
	Trunk	Sit-ups, daily core (100 reps), drop series (3 × 15), 50 series (2 × 50) MD ball drills (1 × 10): MD twist (3 positions), lateral twist (3 positions), rocky twist (feet up and down), North Carolina (feet up and down), seated toss-over
	Wrist and hand	Wrist—superset (2 × 15): wrist flexion and extension, wrist radial flexion and ulnar flexion Hand (1 × 10): rice drill #3, hand grip
	Intervals	10 × 100 yd in 10 min
	COOL-DOWN AND FLEXIBILITY	Jog and walk 5 min Daily dozen (3 × 10-15 sec)

Table 2.4 Off-Season (Week 10)—Fitness Training—"Train to Train"

	Activity	Exercises and Drills
TUESDAY	**WARM-UP AND FLEXIBILITY**	Jog or cycle 5 min, general warm-up (1 × 10), dynamic warm-up #1 (1 × 10) Daily dozen (do 3 sets and hold each stretch for 10-15 sec)
	SPEED/QUICKNESS	
	Mechanics	"A" skip (3 sets over 20-30 yd), arm runs (3 sets over 20-30 yd)
	First-step quickness	Wheel drill and lateral sprint 5-10 yd (3 sets to each spoke), dot drill (3 sets) Ladder drills (2 sets of each drill): forward wide skip, forward crossover skip, Icky shuffle, crossover, two-foot hopscotch, one-foot hopscotch
	Agility	Microhurdle drills (3 sets of 4; over and back is one): high step with 4 hurdles, high step with 3 hurdles, high step with 2 hurdles, high-step crossover with 2 hurdles Jumps and hops (2 ×): down-the-line jumps and sprint forward 5-10 yd, down-the-line hops and sprint forward 5-10 yd, ball pick-ups (1 × 25)
	Speed-Strength	SAT: diagonal (2 × 10), side/side (2 × 10)
	STRENGTH/POWER	
	Plyometrics	Box drills (18-inch box, 2 × 10): box pop-up, box crossover, supported jump-up Resisted (tubing) drills (2 ×): shuffle Crossover, over the shoulder, resisted W—forward/backward, resisted W—lateral MD ball drills (2 × 10): thigh kick, donkey kick (2 legs), donkey kick (1 leg), soccer kick-up
	Trunk	Sit-ups, daily core (100 reps), drop series (3 × 15), 50 series (2 × 50) MD ball drills (1 × 10): MD twist (3 positions), lateral twist (3 positions), rocky twist (feet up and down), North Carolina (feet up and down), seated toss-over
	Aerobics	Jog, stairclimb, or cycle 15-20 min; jump rope 5-10 min
	COOL-DOWN AND FLEXIBILITY	Jog and walk 5 min Daily dozen (3 × 10-15 sec)

Table 2.4 Off-Season (Week 10)—Fitness Training—"Train to Train"

	Activity	Exercises and Drills	
WEDNESDAY	**WARM-UP AND FLEXIBILITY**	Jog or cycle 5 min, general warm-up (1 × 10), dynamic warm-up #1 (1 × 10) Daily dozen (do 3 sets and hold each stretch for 10-15 sec)	
	STRENGTH/POWER		
		Beginners: Sets × reps (all reps in all sets): Total-body workout Core—4 × 8 Assist—3 × 8	Advanced pyramid: Total-body workout Core—moderate = 1 × 8; 2 × 5; 3 × 3 × 75% Assist—moderate = 1 × 10; 2 × 8 × 70%

(continued)

Table 2.4 Off-Season *(Week 10, continued)*

<table>
<tr><th></th><th>Activity</th><th>Exercises and Drills</th></tr>
<tr><td rowspan="6">WEDNESDAY</td><td>Shoulder</td><td>Rotator cuff and scapula (1 × 10)</td></tr>
<tr><td rowspan="2">Trunk</td><td>Sit-ups, daily core (100 reps), drop series (3 × 15), 50 series (2 × 50)</td></tr>
<tr><td>MD ball drills (1 × 10): MD twist (3 positions), lateral twist (3 positions), rocky twist (feet up and down), North Carolina (feet up and down), seated toss-over</td></tr>
<tr><td>Wrist and hand</td><td>Wrist—superset (2 × 15): rice drill #1, rice drill #2
Hand (1 × 10): towel pull-up, plate squeeze</td></tr>
<tr><td>Intervals</td><td>2 × 8 × 100 yd @ 20:20</td></tr>
<tr><td>COOL-DOWN AND FLEXIBILITY</td><td>Jog and walk 5 min
Daily dozen (3 × 10-15 sec)</td></tr>
</table>

Table 2.4 Off-Season (Week 10)—Fitness Training—"Train to Train"

<table>
<tr><th></th><th>Activity</th><th>Exercises and Drills</th></tr>
<tr><td rowspan="14">THURSDAY</td><td>WARM-UP AND FLEXIBILITY</td><td>Jog or cycle 5 min, general warm-up (1 × 10), dynamic warm-up #1 (1 × 10)
Daily dozen (do 3 sets and hold each stretch for 10-15 sec)</td></tr>
<tr><td colspan="2">SPEED/QUICKNESS</td></tr>
<tr><td>Mechanics</td><td>"A" skip (3 sets over 20-30 yd), arm runs (3 sets over 20-30 yd)</td></tr>
<tr><td rowspan="2">First-step quickness</td><td>Wheel drill and lateral sprint 5-10 yd (3 sets to each spoke), dot drill (3 sets)</td></tr>
<tr><td>Ladder drills (2 sets of each drill): forward wide skip, forward crossover skip, Icky shuffle, crossover, two-foot hopscotch, one-foot hopscotch</td></tr>
<tr><td rowspan="2">Agility</td><td>Microhurdle drills (3 sets of 4; over and back is one): high step with 4 hurdles, high step with 3 hurdles, high step with 2 hurdles, high-step crossover with 2 hurdles</td></tr>
<tr><td>Jumps and hops (2 ×): down-the-line jumps and sprint forward 5-10 yd, down-the-line hops and sprint forward 5-10 yd, ball pick-ups (1 × 25)</td></tr>
<tr><td>Speed-Strength</td><td>SAT: diagonal (2 × 10), side/side (2 × 10)</td></tr>
<tr><td colspan="2">STRENGTH/POWER</td></tr>
<tr><td rowspan="2">Plyometrics</td><td>Box drills (18-inch box, 2 × 10): box jump, box crossover; cone jumps (2 × 10): front/back, side/side; cone hops (2 × 10): front/back, side/side</td></tr>
<tr><td>MD ball throws (5 ×): squat and chest throw, underhand throw, backward (over-the-head) throw, discus throw</td></tr>
<tr><td rowspan="2">Trunk</td><td>Sit-ups, daily core (100 reps), drop series (3 × 15), 50 series (2 × 50)</td></tr>
<tr><td>MD ball drills (1 × 10): MD twist (3 positions), lateral twist (3 positions), rocky twist (feet up and down), North Carolina (feet up and down), seated toss-over</td></tr>
<tr><td>Aerobics</td><td>Jog, stairclimb, or cycle 15-20 min; jump rope 5-10 min</td></tr>
</table>

| | COOL-DOWN AND FLEXIBILITY | Jog and walk 5 min
Daily dozen (3 × 10-15 sec) |

Table 2.4 Off-Season (Week 10)—Fitness Training—"Train to Train"

	Activity	Exercises and Drills
FRIDAY	**WARM-UP AND FLEXIBILITY**	Jog or cycle 5 min, general warm-up (1 × 10), dynamic warm-up #1 (1 × 10) Daily dozen (do 3 sets and hold each stretch for 10-15 sec)
	STRENGTH/POWER	
		Beginners: Sets × reps (all reps in all sets): Total-body workout Core—4 × 8 Assist—3 × 8 Advanced pyramid: Total-body workout Core—heavy = 1 × 8; 2 × 5; 3 × 3 × 85% Assist—heavy = 1 × 10; 2 × 8 × 75%
	Shoulder	Rotator cuff and scapula (1 × 10)
	Trunk	Sit-ups, daily core (100 reps), drop series (3 × 15), 50 series (2 × 50) MD ball drills (1 × 10): MD twist (3 positions), lateral twist (3 positions), rocky twist (feet up and down), North Carolina (feet up and down), seated toss-over
	Wrist and hand	Wrist—superset (2 × 15): wrist flexion and extension, wrist radial flexion and ulnar flexion Hand (1 × 10): rice drill #3, hand grip
	Intervals	2 × 300 yd @ 60:180
	COOL-DOWN AND FLEXIBILITY	Jog and walk 5 min Daily dozen (3 × 10-15 sec)

Table 2.5 Off-Season (Week 11)—Fitness Training—"Train to Train"

	Activity	Exercises and Drills
MONDAY	**WARM-UP AND FLEXIBILITY**	Jog or cycle 5 min, general warm-up (1 × 10), dynamic warm-up #1 (1 × 10) Daily dozen (do 3 sets and hold each stretch for 10-15 sec)
	STRENGTH/POWER	
		Beginners: Sets × reps (all reps in all sets): Total-body workout Core—4 × 10 Assist—3 × 10 Advanced pyramid: Total-body workout Core—heavy = 1 × 8; 2 × 5; 2 × 2 × 90% Assist—heavy = 3 × 8 × 80%
	Shoulder	Rotator cuff and scapula (1 × 10)
	Trunk	Sit-ups, daily core (100 reps), drop series (2 × 20), 50 series (3 × 50) MD ball drills (1 × 10): good morning, wood chopper, MD twist (3 positions), lateral twist (3 positions), rocky twist (feet up and down), North Carolina (feet up and down), seated toss-over

(continued)

Table 2.5 Off-Season *(Week 11, continued)*

	Activity	Exercises and Drills
MONDAY	**STRENGTH/POWER**	
	Wrist and hand	Wrist—superset (2 × 20): wrist flexion and extension, wrist radial flexion and ulnar flexion Hand (1 × 10): rice drill #3, hand grip
	Intervals	10 × 100 yd in 10 min
	COOL-DOWN AND FLEXIBILITY	Jog and walk 5 min Daily dozen (3 × 10-15 sec)

Table 2.5 Off-Season (Week 11)—Fitness Training—"Train to Train"

	Activity	Exercises and Drills
TUESDAY	**WARM-UP AND FLEXIBILITY**	Jog or cycle 5 min, general warm-up (1 × 10), dynamic warm-up #1 (1 × 10) Daily dozen (do 3 sets and hold each stretch for 10-15 sec)
	SPEED/QUICKNESS	
	First-step quickness	Dot drill (3 sets) Ladder drills (2 sets of each drill): forward wide skip, forward crossover skip, two-foot hopscotch, one-foot hopscotch, alternate-foot hopscotch
	Agility	Microhurdle drills (3 sets of 4; over and back is one): high step with 4 hurdles, high step with 3 hurdles, high step with 2 hurdles, high-step crossover with 2 hurdles Jumps and hops (2 ×): down-the-line jumps and lateral sprint 5-10 yd, down-the-line hops and lateral sprint 5-10 yd, ball pick-ups (2 × 20)
	Speed-Strength	SAT: combo (2 × 10)
	STRENGTH/POWER	
	Plyometrics	Box drills (18-inch box, 2 × 10): box pop-up, box crossover, supported jump-up Resisted (tubing) drills (2 ×): shuffle, crossover, over the shoulder, resisted W—forward/backward, resisted W—lateral MD ball drills (2 × 10): thigh kick, donkey kick (2 legs), donkey kick (1 leg), soccer kick-up
	Trunk	Sit-ups, daily core (100 reps), drop series (2 × 20), 50 series (3 × 50) MD ball drills (1 × 10): good morning, wood chopper, MD twist (3 positions), lateral twist (3 positions), rocky twist (feet up and down), North Carolina (feet up and down), seated toss-over
	Aerobics	Jog, stairclimb, or cycle 15-20 min; jump rope 5-10 min
	COOL-DOWN AND FLEXIBILITY	Jog and walk 5 min Daily dozen (3 × 10-15 sec)

Table 2.5 Off-Season (Week 11)—Fitness Training—"Train to Train"

	Activity	Exercises and Drills
WEDNESDAY	**WARM-UP AND FLEXIBILITY**	Jog or cycle 5 min, general warm-up (1 × 10), dynamic warm-up #1 (1 × 10) Daily dozen (do 3 sets and hold each stretch for 10-15 sec)
	STRENGTH/POWER	
		Beginners: Sets × reps (all reps in all sets): Total-body workout Core—4 × 10 Assist—3 × 10 Advanced pyramid: Total-body workout Core—moderate = 1 × 8; 2 × 5; 2 × 2 × 80% Assist—moderate = 3 × 8 × 75%
	Shoulder	Rotator cuff and scapula (1 × 10)
	Trunk	Sit-ups, daily core (100 reps), drop series (2 × 20), 50 series (3 × 50) MD ball drills (1 × 10): good morning, wood chopper, MD twist (3 positions), lateral twist (3 positions), rocky twist (feet up and down), North Carolina (feet up and down), seated toss-over
	Wrist and hand	Wrist—superset (2 × 20): rice drill #1, rice drill #2 Hand (1 × 10): towel pull-up, plate squeeze
	Intervals	2 × 10 × 100 yd @ 20:20
	COOL-DOWN AND FLEXIBILITY	Jog and walk 5 min Daily dozen (3 × 10-15 sec)

Table 2.5 Off-Season (Week 11)—Fitness Training—"Train to Train"

	Activity	Exercises and Drills
THURSDAY	**WARM-UP AND FLEXIBILITY**	Jog or cycle 5 min, general warm-up (1 × 10), dynamic warm-up #1 (1 × 10) Daily dozen (do 3 sets and hold each stretch for 10-15 sec)
	SPEED/QUICKNESS	
	First-step quickness	Dot drill (3 sets) Ladder drills (2 sets of each drill): forward wide skip, forward crossover skip, two-foot hopscotch, one-foot hopscotch, alternate-foot hopscotch
	Agility	Microhurdle drills (3 sets of 4; over and back is one): high step with 4 hurdles, high step with 3 hurdles, high step with 2 hurdles, high-step crossover with 2 hurdles Jumps and hops (2 ×): down-the-line jumps and lateral sprint 5-10 yd, down-the-line hops and lateral sprint 5-10 yd, ball pick-ups (2 × 20)

(continued)

Table 2.5 Off-Season (*Week 11, continued*)

	Activity	Exercises and Drills
THURSDAY	**SPEED/QUICKNESS**	
	Speed-Strength	SAT: combo (2 × 10)
	STRENGTH/POWER	
	Plyometrics	Box drills (18-inch box, 2 × 10): box jump, box crossover Cone jumps (2 × 10): front/back, side/side Cone hops (2 × 10): front/back, side/side MD ball throws (2 × 5): squat and chest throw, underhand throw, backward (over-the-head) throw, discus throw
	Trunk	Sit-ups, daily core (100 reps), drop series (2 × 20), 50 series (3 × 50) MD ball drills (1 × 10): good morning, wood chopper, MD twist (3 positions), lateral twist (3 positions), rocky twist (feet up and down), North Carolina (feet up and down), seated toss-over
	Aerobics	Jog, stairclimb, or cycle 15-20 min; jump rope 5-10 min
	COOL-DOWN AND FLEXIBILITY	Jog and walk 5 min Daily dozen (3 × 10-15 sec)

Table 2.5 Off-Season (Week 11)—Fitness Training—"Train to Train"

	Activity	Exercises and Drills	
FRIDAY	**WARM-UP AND FLEXIBILITY**	Jog or cycle 5 min, general warm-up (1 × 10), dynamic warm-up #1 (1 × 10) Daily dozen (do 3 sets and hold each stretch for 10-15 sec)	
	STRENGTH/POWER		
		Beginners: Sets × reps (all reps in all sets): Total-body workout Core—4 × 10 Assist—3 × 10	Advanced pyramid: Total-body workout Core—heavy = 1 × 8; 2 × 5; 2 × 2 × 90% Assist—heavy = 3 × 8 × 80%
	Shoulder	Rotator cuff and scapula (1 × 10)	
	Trunk	Sit-ups, daily core (100 reps), drop series (2 × 20), 50 series (3 × 50) MD ball drills (1 × 10): good morning, wood chopper, MD twist (3 positions), lateral twist (3 positions), rocky twist (feet up and down), North Carolina (feet up and down), seated toss-over	
	Wrist and hand	Wrist—superset (2 × 20): wrist flexion and extension, wrist radial flexion and ulnar flexion Hand (1 × 10): rice drill #3, hand grip	
	Intervals	3 × 300 yd @ 60:180, jog 10 min	
	COOL-DOWN AND FLEXIBILITY	Jog and walk 5 min Daily dozen (3 × 10-15 sec)	

Table 2.6 Off-Season (Week 12)—Fitness Training—"Train to Train"

<table>
<tr><td></td><th>Activity</th><th>Exercises and Drills</th></tr>
<tr><td rowspan="8">MONDAY</td><td>WARM-UP AND FLEXIBILITY</td><td>Jog or cycle 5 min, general warm-up (1 × 10), dynamic warm-up #1 (1 × 10)
Daily dozen (do 3 sets and hold each stretch for 10-15 sec)</td></tr>
<tr><td colspan="2">STRENGTH/POWER</td></tr>
<tr><td></td><td>Beginners:
Sets × reps)
(all reps in all sets):
Total-body workout
Core—4 × 10
Assist—3 × 10

Advanced pyramid:
Total-body workout
Core—heavy = 1 × 8; 1 × 5; 1 × 3; 2 × 2 × 100%
Assist—heavy = 3 × 8 × 85%</td></tr>
<tr><td>Shoulder</td><td>Rotator cuff and scapula (1 × 10)</td></tr>
<tr><td>Trunk</td><td>Sit-ups, daily core (100 reps), drop series (3 × 20), 50 series (3 × 50)

MD ball drills (1 × 10): good morning, wood chopper, MD twist (3 positions), lateral twist (3 positions), rocky twist (feet up and down), North Carolina (feet up and down), seated toss-over</td></tr>
<tr><td>Wrist and hand</td><td>Wrist—superset (3 × 20): wrist flexion and extension, wrist radial flexion and ulnar flexion
Hand (1 × 10): rice drill #3, hand grip</td></tr>
<tr><td>Intervals</td><td>10 × 100 yd in 10 min</td></tr>
<tr><td>COOL-DOWN AND FLEXIBILITY</td><td>Jog and walk 5 min
Daily dozen (3 × 10-15 sec)</td></tr>
</table>

Table 2.6 Off-Season (Week 12)—Fitness Training—"Train to Train"

<table>
<tr><td></td><th>Activity</th><th>Exercises and Drills</th></tr>
<tr><td rowspan="7">TUESDAY</td><td>WARM-UP AND FLEXIBILITY</td><td>Jog or cycle 5 min, general warm-up (1 × 10), dynamic warm-up #1 (1 × 10)
Daily dozen (do 3 sets and hold each stretch for 10-15 sec)</td></tr>
<tr><td colspan="2">SPEED/QUICKNESS</td></tr>
<tr><td>First-step quickness</td><td>Dot drill (3 sets), quicks (3 sets), wall runs (3 sets)

Ladder drills (2 sets of each drill): forward wide skip, forward crossover skip, two-foot hopscotch, one-foot hopscotch, alternate-foot hopscotch</td></tr>
<tr><td>Agility</td><td>Microhurdle drills (3 sets of 4; over and back is one): high step with 4 hurdles, high step with 3 hurdles, high step with 2 hurdles, high-step crossover with 2 hurdles, ball pick-ups (3 × 20)</td></tr>
<tr><td>Speed-Strength</td><td>SAT: combo (3 × 10)</td></tr>
<tr><td colspan="2">STRENGTH/POWER</td></tr>
<tr><td>Plyometrics</td><td>Box drills (18-inch box, 2 × 10): box pop-up, box crossover, supported jump-up

Resisted (tubing) drills (2 ×): shuffle, crossover, over the shoulder, resisted W—forward/backward, resisted W—lateral</td></tr>
</table>

(continued)

Table 2.6 Off-Season *(Week 12, continued)*

	Activity	Exercises and Drills
TUESDAY	**Plyometrics** *(continued)*	MD ball drills (2 × 10): thigh kick, donkey kick (2 legs), donkey kick (1 leg), soccer kick-up
	Trunk	Sit-ups, daily core (100 reps), drop series (3 × 20), 50 series (3 × 50) MD ball drills (1 × 10): good morning, wood chopper, MD twist (3 positions), lateral twist (3 positions), rocky twist (feet up and down), North Carolina (feet up and down), seated toss-over
	Aerobics	Jog, stairclimb, or cycle 15-20 min; jump rope 5-10 min
	COOL-DOWN AND FLEXIBILITY	Jog and walk 5 min Daily dozen (3 × 10-15 sec)

Table 2.6 Off-Season (Week 12)—Fitness Training—"Train to Train"

	Activity	Exercises and Drills	
WEDNESDAY	**WARM-UP AND FLEXIBILITY**	Jog or cycle 5 min, general warm-up (1 × 10), dynamic warm-up #1 (1 × 10) Daily dozen (do 3 sets and hold each stretch for 10-15 sec)	
	STRENGTH/POWER		
		Beginners: Sets × reps (all reps in all sets): Core—4 × 10 Total-body workout Assist—3 × 10	Advanced pyramid: Total-body workout Core—moderate = 1 × 8; 1 × 5; 1 × 3 2 × 2 × 85% Assist—moderate = 3 × 8 × 80%
	Shoulder	Rotator cuff and scapula (1 × 10)	
	Trunk	Sit-ups, daily core (100 reps), drop series (3 × 20), 50 series (3 × 50) MD ball drills (1 × 10): good morning, wood chopper, MD twist (3 positions), lateral twist (3 positions), rocky twist (feet up and down), North Carolina (feet up and down), seated toss-over	
	Wrist and hand	Wrist (3 × 20): rice drill #1, rice drill #2 Hand (1 × 10): towel pull-up, plate squeeze	
	Intervals	3 × 6 × 100 yd @ 18:18	
	COOL-DOWN AND FLEXIBILITY	Jog and walk 5 min Daily dozen (3 × 10-15 sec)	

Table 2.6 Off-Season (Week 12)—Fitness Training—"Train to Train"

	Activity	Exercises and Drills
THURSDAY	**WARM-UP AND FLEXIBILITY**	Jog or cycle 5 min, general warm-up (1 × 10), dynamic warm-up #1 (1 × 10) Daily dozen (do 3 sets and hold each stretch for 10-15 sec)
	SPEED/QUICKNESS	
	First-step quickness	Dot drill (3 sets), quicks (3 sets), wall runs (3 sets) Ladder drills (2 sets of each drill): forward wide skip, forward crossover skip, two-foot hopscotch, one-foot hopscotch, alternate-foot hopscotch
	Agility	Microhurdle drills (3 sets of 4; over and back is one): high step with 4 hurdles, high step with 3 hurdles, high step with 2 hurdles, high step crossover with 2 hurdles, ball pick-ups (3 × 20)
	Speed-Strength	SAT: combo (3 × 10)
	STRENGTH/POWER	
	Plyometrics	Box drills (18-inch box, 2 × 10): box jump, box crossover Cone jumps and sprints (2 × 10): front/back and sprint forward, side/side and sprint lateral Cone hops (2 × 10): front/back and sprint forward, side/side and sprint lateral MD ball throws after 2 jumps forward (2 × 5): squat and chest throw, underhand throw, backward (over-the-head) throw, discus throw
	Trunk	Sit-ups, daily core (100 reps), drop series (3 × 20), 50 series (3 × 50) MD ball drills (1 × 10): good morning, wood chopper, MD twist (3 positions), lateral twist (3 positions), rocky twist (feet up and down), North Carolina (feet up and down), seated toss-over
	Aerobics	Jog, stairclimb, or cycle 15-20 min; jump rope 5-10 min
	COOL-DOWN AND FLEXIBILITY	Jog and walk 5 min Daily dozen (3 × 10-15 sec)

Table 2.6 Off-Season (Week 12)—Fitness Training—"Train to Train"

	Activity	Exercises and Drills	
FRIDAY	**WARM-UP AND FLEXIBILITY**	Jog or cycle 5 min, general warm-up (1 × 10), dynamic warm-up #1 (1 × 10) Daily dozen (do 3 sets and hold each stretch for 10-15 sec)	
	STRENGTH/POWER		
		Beginners: Sets × reps (all reps in all sets): Core—4 × 10 Total-body workout Assist—3 × 10	Advanced pyramid: Total-body workout Core—moderate = 1 × 8; 1 × 5; 1 × 3; 2 × 2 × 90% Assist—moderate = 3 × 8 × 85%
	Shoulder	Rotator cuff and scapula (1 × 10)	

(continued)

Table 2.6 Off-Season *(Week 12, continued)*

	Activity	Exercises and Drills
	STRENGTH/POWER	
FRIDAY	Trunk	Sit-ups, daily core (100 reps), drop series (3 × 20), 50 series (3 × 50)
		MD ball drills (1 × 10): good morning, wood chopper, MD twist (3 positions), lateral twist (3 positions), rocky twist (feet up and down), North Carolina (feet up and down), seated toss-over
	Wrist and hand	Wrist: wrist flexion and extension, wrist radial flexar and ulnar flexion Hand (1 × 10): rice drill #3, hand grip (3 × 20)
	Intervals	4 × 300 yd @ 60:180, jog 10 min
	COOL-DOWN AND FLEXIBILITY	Jog and walk 5 min Daily dozen (3 × 10-15 sec)

spark of energy, but about 30 minutes into your workout, the spark goes out and you crash. The work that was relatively easy a few minutes earlier becomes very hard. You waste the day—if you push through, you're usually too tired to enjoy the afternoon and don't look forward to the next day's workout. If you quit, you'll miss a workout that you'll never get back.

By eating the right foods at the right time, you'll get the most out of your workout, have energy to enjoy the rest of the day, and be physically and mentally ready for the next workout. What you eat before and during workouts gives you the energy to get through the workout. When you eat determines how hard you train and how fast and much you grow.

Breakfast

Bob Knepper, on why he ate 27 bowls of Sugar Frosted Flakes in seven days: *"I heard breakfast was the most important meal of the day."*

You need three things for breakfast: complex carbohydrates for quick energy, protein for sustained energy, and vitamin C for growth and repair. Start with whole-grain cereal and whole-wheat toast. Your body digests whole grains much more slowly than it does sugar; whole grains thus provide a steady flow of energy. Eat cold cereal, pancakes, waffles, oatmeal or Cream of Wheat, and some protein. Protein is digested more slowly than carbs, providing energy to finish the workout. Drink low-fat or skim milk and put a piece of low-fat cheese, lean ham, turkey, or chicken on a piece of toast, bagel, or English muffin for protein. Other good sources of protein are low-fat yogurt, cheese, cottage cheese, boiled egg whites (throw the yolk away), and omelets made with two egg whites and one yolk. Put fresh fruits on cereal and drink a glass of juice. Eat about 500 calories. The best cereals are Shredded Wheat, Raisin Bran, Total, Wheaties, Special K, Cheerios, oatmeal, Cream of Wheat, and grits. Frosted cereals have more sugar than most candy bars. Table 2.7 contains seven balanced options for a power breakfast.

Table 2.7 Balanced 300-700 cal Power Breakfast Options

Breakfast Foods	Major Nutrients	Energy
1 1.5 cups of shredded wheat	carbohydrate, fiber, iron	570 cal
	protein, sodium	17% protein
1.5 cups low-fat milk	calcium, protein	85% carbo
1 banana	carbohydrate, fiber, potassium, vitamin C	6% fat
2 1 bagel	vitamin E, carbohydrate, fiber	400 cal
2 slices mozzarella cheese	calcium, protein	22% protein
1 cup berries	vitamin A, vitamin C, fiber	54% carbo
3 1 cup oatmeal	carbohydrate, fiber, protein	300 cal
1 cup low-fat milk	calcium, protein	18% protein
1/4 cup raisins	fiber, vitamin C, iron	79% carbo, 7% fat
4 2 oatbran waffles	carbohydrate, protein, fiber	550 cal
2 tbsp peanut butter	carbohydrate, vitamin E, protein	16% protein
1 cup low-fat milk	calcium, protein	52% carbo
1 cup OJ	vitamin C	39% fat
5 4 boiled eggs (whites only)	protein	620 cal
2 slices whole wheat toast	vitamin E, carbohydrate, fiber	22% protein
1 cup fat-free yogurt	calcium, potassium	67% carbo
1/2 grapefruit	fiber, vitamin C	12% fat
6 3 pancakes & 6 oz syrup	carbohydrate	700 cal
1 orange	fiber, vitamin C	9% protein
1 cup low-fat milk	calcium, protein	91% carbo, 4% fat
7 2 slices French toast	carbohydrate, protein	465 cal
1 cup berries	vitamin A, vitamin C, fiber	17% protein
1 cup low-fat milk	calcium, protein	56% carbo, 29% fat

If you're trying to lose weight, eat breakfast. Skipping breakfast lowers your metabolic rate, causing you to burn fewer calories. Eating raises your metabolic rate, making it easier to burn calories. When you skip breakfast, you miss an opportunity to take in nutrients. If you don't like traditional breakfast foods, try yogurt, graham crackers, fruit, bagels, raisins, peanuts, toaster pastries, instant breakfasts, and energy bars.

Workout Snacks

Have a high carbo drink or snack during or after each workout. Use Cytomax, PowerAde, or some other carbo drink during workouts. The fluid will keep you hydrated, and the carbs will provide the energy to get you through the workout. Take some fruit (banana, orange, raisins, or grapes), Fig Newtons, low-fat yogurt, a bagel, granola, or energy bar and a second carbo drink for your postworkout snack. Getting a high carbo source into your body within 30 minutes after a workout will increase the rate at which you put energy back into your muscles. The faster you refuel your muscles, the better prepared you will be for the next workout. Try to eat or drink 200 to 300 calories during workouts and another 200 to 300 calories afterward. Ultramet, MET-Rx, Myoplex, and others are good sources of calories (300 calories) and protein (42 grams). Use them to supplement your diet, not as an excuse for skipping breakfast. Mix them with bananas or strawberries for extra carbs, fiber, vitamins, and minerals. Drink them during or after workouts.

Lunch

Curt Schilling, calling the Astros clubhouse to explain why he will be late for an off-season workout: "I'm stuck in the drive-through line at McDonald's."

If you eat a good breakfast and snacks, you shouldn't need a big lunch. Eat a sandwich, soup, or both with low-fat milk and a piece of fruit for a 500-kilocalorie lunch. Use whole-wheat or pita bread, lean meat (turkey, chicken, tuna, or ham), low-fat cheese, lettuce, tomato, and mustard. Choose chicken, turkey, or vegetable soup. Skip cream and cheese soups—they're too fat. Limit hamburgers and pizza (50 percent fat) to once per week and hot dogs to once per month (85 percent fat). Hold the fries and skip the appetizers. Get your hamburger on whole-wheat bread with mustard and no cheese. Eat fruit in place of dessert.

Afternoon Snack

Eat about 200 calories between 2 and 3 P.M. to keep your metabolism and energy level high. Good high-performance fast foods for those too busy, too lazy, or unable to prepare food include fresh fruit, fruit juice, raw carrots, dried fruit (apricots or pineapple), bagels, low-fat muffins, peanut butter, cashew nuts, dry cereals, water-packed tuna on pita bread, low-fat yogurt, cheese or pudding, graham crackers, pretzels, energy bars, MET-Rx-type drinks, and carbo drinks. Avoid cookies and candy, which contain too much sugar and fat and too little nutrients.

Dinner

Ted "the Chicken" Giannoulas responding to a reporter who asked if he expected to be elected to the Baseball Hall of Fame: "Who knows? They've got a broadcaster's wing, and they've got a writer's wing. Maybe one day they'll have a chicken wing."

Eat about 1,000 calories. Have a salad with low-fat dressing on the side, lean meat, fish or poultry, a complex carb (pasta, potatoes, rice, corn), two to three veggies, and a couple of slices of whole-wheat bread or rolls. Eat lean beef and pork once per week. Eat more skinless chicken and turkey (half the fat is in the skin). Eat broiled fish at least once per week. Have pasta without meat sauce, rice without gravy, and potatoes without butter or other fats. Consume a lot of green, yellow, and orange vegetables without butter or cheese. Limit desserts to fat-free varieties or fresh fruit with low-fat topping.

Evening Snack

Eat 100 to 200 calories about two hours after dinner to keep your metabolism and energy level high. Snack on fresh or dried fruit, low-fat cheese, yogurt or puddings, pretzels, air-popped popcorn, graham crackers, granola bar, or fat-free cookies.

DO YOU DRINK ENOUGH WATER?

Your body is like your car's engine; if you can't cool it off, it won't perform. Overheat your body and you run the risk of breaking down entirely. That is why it's so important to monitor your fluid intake during workouts and games to avoid dehydration and heat exhaustion. Be especially watchful on hot and humid days. To make sure that you stay hydrated, drink before and during games, and drink often. Remember, if you're thirsty, you're already dehydrated.

Your body is approximately 65 percent water. During games, drills, and workouts, you lose body fluids through sweating. It's not unusual for some pitchers and catchers to lose 4 pounds of body weight (about two quarts of sweat) each hour. At this rate, you could lose 10 to 12 pounds in a three-hour game. You will feel tired and drained. You can't train or compete at your best and you significantly increase your risk of heat illness.

Drink at least 8 to 24 ounces of water one hour or more before pregame drills to superhydrate the body. If you lose as little as 2 or 3 percent of your body weight (4 to 5 pounds), you'll decrease your work capacity by 10 to 15 percent. If you don't get enough water, you'll finish your workouts feeling tired and drained. Weigh yourself before and after workouts. Replace each pound of weight lost with two cups of fluid.

Coffee and alcohol are diuretics, which means they cause you to lose water. Drink each in moderation. Beer also contains carbonation, which gives you a sense of fullness and limits fluid consumption at a time when fluid consumption should be high. Downing a six-pack after a game will not allow you to rehydrate completely before the next day's game.

Monitor your urine. If it's light or clear, you're probably OK. If it's dark or smells like ammonia, hit the water. You don't have to be gasping for water to be dried out. One of the earliest signs of dehydration is fatigue. Other signs include red skin, loss of appetite, dizziness, muscle cramps, or spasms. The bottom line is that you should drink at least two or three quarts of water a day for optimal health and performance. Water is essential not only to prevent dehydration but to achieve weight loss, proper bowel function, and optimal performance of all body systems.

Fruit Juice

Except for the fiber, fruit juice has the same advantages of fruit. But all fruit juices are not created equal. Some contain many nutrients, and some contain almost none. For good health and nutrition, read the label. If it says anything less than "contains 100 percent fruit juice," put it down—it's probably diluted with sugar water. Avoid fruit juice drinks that list apple, grape, or pear juice as the first ingredient; they are usually low in essential vitamins and minerals. Your best buy is orange juice. If you're trying to lose body fat, eat more fresh fruit and drink less juice. Juice is higher in calories than fruit. Eight ounces of OJ, for example, contains nearly twice as many calories (112 calories) as an orange (60 calories). Drinking three or four glasses of juice per day will add 2,100 to 2,800 extra calories and nearly two-thirds of a pound of added weight in a one-week period.

Preseason I— Training to Compete

GOAL	*Transfer off-season training to the playing field—developing functional speed, strength, and power*

Preseason training should be sport specific. You'll use it to harness the physical tools you developed in the off-season and transfer them onto the field to support performance in game situations. Your goal for the next six to eight weeks is to develop maximal functional strength, speed, and power.

Working the Body

Train five times per week for the next six weeks to achieve maximum fitness before spring training. Inexperienced players do total-body workouts three times per week using the required reps method and a load that allows them to do all reps in the first set. Advanced players switch to a four-day split and train the upper and lower body twice per week with training loads based on a percentage of max. Both groups should do all sets of one exercise before doing the next.

Your objective is to lift heavier weights for more sets and fewer reps to teach your body and central nervous system (CNS) to turn on more fast-twitch fibers. Reduce the number of lifts and concentrate on movements specific to baseball.

Do intervals for aerobic fitness, sprint for speed and acceleration, and run shuttles for lateral speed and agility. Do plyometrics twice a week. Warm up and stretch before workouts; cool down after them. Play catch, and swing the bat three to five times per week.

Remember that your goal is to arrive at spring training ready to compete for a job, not to get in shape. Use the program outlined in tables 3.1 through 3.8. High school students train for eight weeks, repeating weeks 13 and 14. After four weeks, take the readiness test at the end of the chapter to see what areas you need to concentrate on for spring training.

Warm-Up and Flexibility

Alternate days using the dynamic warm-ups, routines #1 and #2, before each workout. Routine #1 increases hip strength and flexibility, and routine #2 prepares you for game-related running. Stretch (using the daily dozen) before the workout and cool down afterward.

Running Speed

Train five times per week. Work on speed, acceleration, lateral speed and direction, and speed-endurance on alternate days. Take weekends off or jog 15 to 20 minutes, once per weekend.

Reaction Time

Keep the drills short (five seconds or less) and quick. Do ball drops from a fielding position. Spring forward as your partner drops the ball and catch it before it bounces twice. You have to make a throw after you catch the ball, so don't dive. Repeat the drill using a crossover step, then do the drill with your back to your partner. Turn, find the ball, and catch it before it bounces twice. Repeat all drills with two balls. Do reaction ball drills with a "crazy" ball or a tennis ball off a wall.

Quickness

Do quicks, dot drill, X-jumps, X-hops, and ladder drills for foot speed. Use hurdles and lateral speed and agility (LSA) drills for agility. Do ball pick-ups for game-specific speed.

Aerobics

Pitchers jog 20 to 30 minutes every day at a 7:00- to 7:30-per-mile pace. Position players jog three or four times per week. All players jump rope two or three times per week.

Speed-Strength

Do squat and touch (SAT) drills in all planes of motion. When you can do them while standing in one place, sprint 5 or 10 yards after the last rep. Start by sprinting forward. Then sprint laterally and diagonally to the right and left.

BUILDING SPEED-STRENGTH

Strong legs increase speed by pushing you farther through the air with each step. Concentrate on the hip joint. The hip muscles generate about seven times more force in sprinting than the muscles of the thigh and calf. Work the buttocks, quads, hams, and calves. Step-ups, lunges, and squats are core exercises for speed because they use the same muscles, same movement patterns, same energy sources, and same neural pathways used in sprinting. Don't worry about doing a lot of leg extensions for the quads; they'll get plenty of work from step-ups, lunges, and squats. Do leg curls to keep a balance between quad and ham strength but recognize that the hamstrings are more active as hip extensors than as a knee flexors during sprinting and should be trained as such. Do multihip exercises and straight-leg curls with a low pulley for the upper hams. Also do straight-leg dead lifts to stretch and strengthen the buttocks and hamstrings at the same time. Don't forget the calf muscles; they generate 25 to 40 percent of the forces used in running and jumping. Do standing and seated calf raises. Do lateral lunges, split-squats, and squat and touches to increase hip flexibility, develop balance, and strengthen the muscles of the hip, knee, and ankle used in starting, stopping, and changing direction.

A strong upper body helps you maintain a good running posture, especially when trying to score from first. Don't neglect the back, abdomen, chest, and arms. You'll need these to maintain posture and drive the arms. Have you ever rounded third and had your back become so tight that you felt as if your shoulders had moved up to your ears? When this happens, your arms slow down, your stride gets shorter, and you look as if you're running in sand. Do shrugs, inclines, lat pulls, and rows to help maintain a good running posture. Do bench presses, curls, and kickbacks to help pump your arms. Don't forget your abs. Without a strong trunk, you can't maintain a firm central core from which the arms and legs can move like pistons. If you round third with a weak trunk, your belly will sag, your butt will rise, and your low back will get very tight. Weak abs can't support a good upright running posture. Do sit-ups and work the lower abs—they help lift the legs.

Strength

Lift heavier weights for more sets and fewer reps to teach the central nervous system (CNS) to turn on more fast-twitch fibers. Reduce the number of lifts and concentrate on movements specific to baseball. Use the program outlined in table 3.1 for beginners and table 3.2 for advanced athletes.

Beginners should use the required rep method with a load that will allow them to do all reps in the first set. If, for example, the first workout calls for 3 × 10, select a load that allows you to do the full number of reps (10) in the first set. If you can do all reps in the first set, the load is too light. Increase it by 5 or 10 pounds on the next workout day. If you can't do the full number of reps in the first set, continue to use the same load in subsequent workouts until you can do all reps in the first set. If you fail to get within one rep of the target on the first set, the load is too heavy. Reduce it by 5 to 10 pounds for the next workout.

Advanced athletes should use a pyramid system in which they increase the load each set and base training loads on a percentage of maximum. You can find the specifications in table 3.2, the plan for advanced athletes.

Shoulder. Train the rotator cuff and scapula three or four times per week.

Trunk. Work the trunk five times per week. Do 200 to 300 sit-ups per day and MD ball twists from three positions, Rocky, and NC passes. End workouts with seated back toss-overs.

Wrist and Hand. Train the wrist and hands three times per week.

Table 3.1 Preseason Strength Training Workouts for Beginner Athletes

Week	Exercise	Set × rep	Exercise	Set × rep
13–14	Core	4 - 5 × 10	Assist	3 × 10
15–16		5 × 8		3 × 8
17–18		5 × 8; 5 × 6		3 × 8

Table 3.2 Preseason Strength Training Workouts for Advanced Athletes

Week	Exercise	Set × rep × % max	Exercise	Set × rep × % max
13	Core	1 × 8; 4 × 6 × 75%	Assist	3 × 10 × 70%
14		1 × 8; 4 × 4 × 80%		2 × 10; 1 × 8 × 75%
15		1 × 8; 1 × 5; 4 × 4 × 85%		1 × 10; 2 × 8 × 75%
16		1 × 8; 1 × 5; 4 × 4 × 85%		3 × 8 × 80%
17		1 × 8: 1 × 5; 4 × 3 × 90%		1 × 10; 1 × 8; 1 × 6 × 85%
18		1 × 8; 1 × 5; 4 × 2 × 95%		1 × 8; 2 × 6 × 85%

Plyometrics

Work on plyometrics twice per week. Do box drills, supported jumps, and MD ball throws for speed-power for the first two weeks. Alternate days of box jumps and jump or hops into a run in weeks 15 and 16. Start by jumping (standing long jump) off both feet. Land with one foot forward and one foot back and sprint forward 5 to 10 yards. Then hop forward three times on one foot and sprint after the third hop. Finish by hopping to the right on your right foot three times. Sprint to the right after the third hop. Repeat going left on the left foot. Bound in the last two weeks. Start with a run-bound-run. Accelerate for about 10 yards and then sprint (run) for 4 steps (right-left-right-left). After the fourth step, bound for 4 steps and then run again for 4 steps. Start the bound-run-bound by bounding for 4 steps. After the 4th step, run for 4 steps and then bound again for 4 steps. Finish by bounding continuously for 30 yards. Start slowly and gradually accelerate until you are bounding full speed after 20 yards.

Deficiencies and Cool-down

Continue to rehabilitate injuries, correct deficiencies, or do extra aerobic work for weight control.

Position-Specific Conditioning

Catchers

Make drills more sport specific. Do squats, low box crossovers, and ice skaters. Add walking lunges and one-leg squats on leg days. Get your hips, legs, and back ready to catch by doing low box crossovers. Build a low box two feet square and two inches high. Cover the top with carpet or turf. Start from a receiving position on the right side of the box. Step right on the middle of the box with your right foot. Then bring your left foot into position next to the right foot, so you are in a receiving position on top of the box. Continue across the box first with your right foot and then your left foot. Finish in a receiving position with both feet on the right side of the box. Maintain a receiving position and cross back and forth over the top of the box.

Table 3.3   Preseason (Week 13) – Performance Training – "Train to Compete"

	Activity	Exercises and Drills
MONDAY	**WARM-UP AND FLEXIBILITY**	Jog 5 min, general (1 × 10), dynamic warm-up #1 (1 × 10) Daily dozen (1 × 10)
	SPEED/QUICKNESS	
	Reaction time	Ball drops (2 × 5): forward, lateral Reaction ball (2 × 5)
	First-step quickness	Ladder drills (2 sets of each drill): wide skip, crossover skip, Icky shuffle, backward Icky, crossover, and backward crossover Pick-ups (1 × 25)
	Speed	100s: 2 × 10 × 100 yd @ 20:20 sec
	Aerobics	Pitchers and position players: jog 20 min @ 7:00-7:30-per-mile pace, jump rope 10 min
	Speed-Strength (sprint 10 yd after last rep in each set)	SAT: forward/back (4 × 5), side/side (4 × 5)
	STRENGTH/POWER	
	Position players and pitchers 4-day split	**Workloads:** Beginners: do all reps in the first set Advanced players: do a pyramid Core–5 × 10 Core–1 × 8; 4 × 6 × 75% Assist–3 × 10 Assist–3 × 10 × 70% **Exercises:** Position players: DB lunge-core, calf raise, leg press-core, leg curl, multihip, leg extension, back extension, DB lateral lunge Pitchers: Lunge or DB lunge-core, calf raise, leg press—core, leg curl, multihip, leg extension, back extension, DB lateral lunge
	Shoulders	Cuff and scapula (1 × 10)
	Trunk	Daily core 2 × 50 series, leg drops (1 × 20), 2 × 100 series MD drills (1 × 10): off-center (3 positions), rocky twist feet up, rocky twist feet down, seated tossover
	Wrist and hand	Wrist (3 × 20): superset 3 exercises Hand (3 × 20): rice drill #2, plate squeeze
	Plyometrics	Box pop-up (1 × 10), box crossover (1 × 10), supported jump (1 × 10), 12-inch box jump (1 × 5), 18-inch box jump (1 × 5), 24-inch box jump (1 × 5), 36-inch box jump (1 × 5)
	COOL-DOWN AND FLEXIBILITY	Jog and walk 5 min Daily dozen (do 3 sets of each exercise and hold for 10-15 sec)

(continued)

Table 3.3 Preseason (Week 13) – Performance Training – "Train to Compete"

	Activity	Exercises and Drills
TUESDAY	**WARM-UP AND FLEXIBILITY**	Jog 5 min, general warm-up (1 × 10), dynamic warm-up #2 (1 × 10) Daily dozen (1 × 10)
	SPEED/QUICKNESS	
	Speed	Hollow sprint, 10 × 30 yd
	Aerobics	Pitchers: jog 30 min @ 7:00-7:30-per-mile pace
	STRENGTH/POWER	
	Position players and pitchers	**Workloads:** Beginners: do all reps in the first set Advanced players: do a pyramid Core–5 × 10 Core–1 × 8; 4 x 6 × 75% Assist–3 × 10 Assist–3 × 10 × 70% **Exercises:** Position players: Bench press or DB bench–core, lat pull wide–core, incline DB fly+, seated row–core, triceps press-down, DB curl, EZ triceps press, straight bar or machine curl Pitchers: DB bench–core*, lat pull wide–core, DB incline, DB fly+, seated row–core, triceps press-down, DB curl, triceps kickback, DB shrug *Substitutions for DB bench and DB incline: push-up, incline push-up, DB shoulder protraction and retraction
	Trunk	Daily core 2 × 50 series, 2 × 100 series, leg drops (1 × 20) MD drills (1 × 10): lateral twist (3 positions), NC feet up, NC feet down, seated toss-over
	COOL-DOWN AND FLEXIBILITY	Jog and walk 5 min Daily dozen (do 3 sets of each exercise and hold for 10-15 sec)

Table 3.3 Preseason (Week 13) – Performance Training – "Train to Compete"

	Activity	Exercises and Drills
WEDNESDAY	**WARM-UP AND FLEXIBILITY**	Jog 5 min, general warm-up (1 × 10), dynamic warm-up #1 (1 × 10) Daily dozen (1 × 10)
	SPEED/QUICKNESS	
	Reaction time	Ball drops (2 × 5): forward, lateral Reaction ball (2 × 5)
	First-step quickness	Hurdle drills: high step with 4 hurdles, high step with 3 hurdles, high step with 2 hurdles, high step crossover with 2 hurdles, pick-ups (1 × 25)
	Speed	10 × 100 yd in 10 min
	Aerobics	Position players and pitchers: jog 20 min @ 7:00-7:30-per-mile pace, jump rope 10 min

Table 3.3 Preseason (Week 13) – Performance Training – "Train to Compete"

	Activity	Exercises and Drills
WEDNESDAY	**STRENGTH/POWER**	
	Shoulders	Cuff and scapula (1 × 10)
	Trunk	Daily core 2 × 50 series, 2 × 100 series, leg drops (1 × 20) MD drills (1 × 10): off-center (3 positions), rocky twist feet up, rocky twist feet down, seated toss-over
	Wrist and hand	Wrist (3 × 20): superset 3 exercises Hand (3 × 20): rice drill #2, plate squeeze
	COOL-DOWN AND FLEXIBILITY	Jog and walk 5 min Daily dozen (do 3 sets of each exercise and hold for 10-15 sec)

Table 3.3 Preseason (Week 13) – Performance Training – "Train to Compete"

	Activity	Exercises and Drills	
THURSDAY	**WARM-UP AND FLEXIBILITY**	Jog 5 min, general warm-up (1 × 10), dynamic warm-up #2 (1 × 10) Daily dozen (1 × 10)	
	SPEED/QUICKNESS		
	Speed	LSA, 10 × (5-10-5)	
	Aerobics	Position players and pitchers: jog 30 min @ 7:00-7:30-per-mile pace	
	Speed-Strength (sprint 10 yd after last rep in each set)	SAT: forward/back (4 × 5), side/side (4 × 5)	
	STRENGTH/POWER		
	Position players and pitchers	**Workloads:** Beginners: do all reps in the first set Core–5 × 10 Assist–3 × 10	Advanced players: do a pyramid Core–1 × 8; 4 × 6 × 75% Assist–3 × 10 × 70%
		Exercises:	
		Position players:	Squat or DB squat–core, calf raise, DB step-up–core, leg curl, DB split-squat, back extension, DB walking lunge, DB crossover lunge
		Pitchers:	Squat or DB squat–core, calf raise, DB step-up–core, leg curl, DB split–squat, back extension, DB walking lunge, DB crossover lunge
	Trunk	Daily core 2 × 50 series, 2 × 100 series, leg drops (1 × 20) MD drills (1 × 10): lateral twist (3 positions), NC feet up, NC feet down, seated toss-over	
	Plyometrics	Box pop-up (1 × 10), box crossover (1 × 10), supported jump up (1 × 10), discus throw (1 × 5), two jumps and throw (1 × 5), squat chest throw, under hand throw, overhead throw	
	COOL-DOWN AND FLEXIBILITY	Jog and walk 5 min Daily dozen (do 3 sets of each exercise and hold for 10-15 sec)	

(continued)

Table 3.3 Preseason (Week 13) – Performance Training – "Train to Compete"

	Activity	Exercises and Drills
FRIDAY	**WARM-UP AND FLEXIBILITY**	Jog 5 min, general warm-up (1 × 10), dynamic warm-up #1 (1 × 10) Daily dozen (1 × 10)
	SPEED/QUICKNESS	
	Reaction time	Ball drops (2 × 5): forward, lateral Reaction ball (2 × 5)
	First-step quickness	Ladder drills (2 sets of each drill): wide skip, crossover skip, Icky shuffle, backward Icky, crossover, backward crossover Pick-ups (1 × 25)
	Speed	Speed-endurance 3 × 200 @ 40:120
	Aerobics	Position players and pitchers: jog 20 min @ 7:00-7:30 per mile pace, jump rope 10 min
	Speed-Strength (sprint 10 yd after last rep in each set)	SAT: forward/back (4 × 5), side/side (4 × 5)
	STRENGTH/POWER	
	Position players and pitchers	**Workloads:** Beginners: do all reps in the first set Advanced players: do a pyramid Core–5 × 10 Core–1 × 8; 4 × 6 × 75% Assist–3 × 10 Assist–3 × 10 × 70% **Exercises:** Position players: Incline press or DB incline press–core, lat pull underhand–core, DB fly+, DB row, rope triceps press, hammer curl, triceps kickback, EZ-bar curl Pitchers: DB incline press–core*, lat pull underhand–core, DB fly+, DB row, rope triceps press, machine or DB pullover, triceps kickback, DB shrug *Substitutions for DB bench and DB incline: push-up, incline push-up, DB shoulder protraction and retraction
	Shoulders	Cuff and scapula (1 × 10)
	Trunk	Daily core 2 × 50 series, leg drops (1 × 20), 2 × 100 series MD drills (1 × 10): off-center (3 positions), rocky twist feet up, rocky twist feet down, seated tossover
	Wrist and hand	Wrist (3 × 20): superset 3 exercises Hand (3 × 20): rice drill #2, plate squeeze
	COOL-DOWN AND FLEXIBILITY	Jog and walk 5 min Daily dozen (do 3 sets of each exercise and hold for 10-15 sec)

Table 3.4 Preseason (Week 14) – Performance Training – "Train to Compete"

	Activity	Exercises and Drills
MONDAY	**WARM-UP AND FLEXIBILITY**	Jog 5 min, general warm-up (1 × 10), dynamic warm-up #1 (1 × 10) Daily dozen (1 × 10)
	SPEED/QUICKNESS	
	Reaction time	Two-ball drops: forward, lateral (2 × 5) X-jump (1 × 10): forward/backward, side/side, X-hop (1 × 10): forward/backward, side/side
	First-step quickness (do 2 sets of each)	Hurdle drills: high step with 4 hurdles, high step with 3 hurdles, high step with 2 hurdles, high step crossover with 2 hurdles Pick-ups (2 × 25)
	Speed	100s, 2 × 10 × 100 yd @ 18:18 sec
	Speed-Strength (sprint forward 10 yd after last rep in each set)	SAT: diagonal (4 × 5), side/side (4 × 5)
	STRENGTH/POWER	
	Position players and pitchers **4-day split**	**Workloads: Position players** Beginners: do all reps in the first set Advanced players: do a pyramid Core–4 × 10 Core–1 × 8; 4 × 4 × 80% Assist–3 × 10 Assist–2 × 10; 1 × 8 × 75% See table 3.3 for specific exercises **Workloads: Pitchers** Beginners: do all reps in the first set Advanced players: do a pyramid Core–4 × 10 Core–1 × 8; 4 × 4 × 80% Assist–3 × 10 Assist–2 × 10; 1 × 8 × 75% See table 3.3 for specific exercises
	Aerobics	Position players and pitchers: jog 20 min @ 7:00-7:30-per-mile pace, jump rope 10 min
	Shoulders	Cuff and scapula (1 × 10)
	Trunk	Daily core: 2 × 50 series, 2 × 100 series, leg drops (1 × 20) MD drills (1 × 10): off-center (3 positions), rocky twist feet down, seated toss-over
	Wrist and hand	Wrist (3 × 20): superset 3 exercises Hand (3 × 20): rice drill #2, plate squeeze
	Plyometrics	Box pop-up (1 × 10), box crossover (1 × 10), supported jump (1 × 10), 12-inch box jump (1 × 5), 18-inch box jump (1 × 5), 24-inch box jump (1 × 5), 36-inch box jump (1 × 5)
	COOL-DOWN AND FLEXIBILITY	Jog and walk 5 min Daily dozen (do 3 sets of each exercise and hold for 10-15 sec)

(continued)

Table 3.4   Preseason (Week 14) – Performance Training – "Train to Compete"

	Activity	Exercises and Drills
TUESDAY	**WARM-UP AND FLEXIBILITY**	Jog 5 min, general warm-up (1 × 10), dynamic warm-up #2 (1 × 10) Daily dozen (1 × 10)
	SPEED/QUICKNESS	
	Speed	Hollow sprint, 10 × 30 yd
	Aerobics	Position players and pitchers: jog 20 min @ 7:00-7:30-per-mile pace, jump rope 10 min
	STRENGTH/POWER	
	Position players and pitchers **4-day split**	**Workloads:** Position players Beginners: do all reps in the first set / Advanced players: do a pyramid Core–4 × 10 / Core–1 × 8; 4 × 4 × 80% Assist–3 × 10 / Assist–2 × 10; 1 × 8 × 75% See table 3.3 for specific exercises **Workloads:** Pitchers Beginners: do all reps in the first set / Advanced players: do a pyramid Core–4 × 10 / Core–1 × 8; 4 × 4 × 80% Assist–3 × 10 / Assist–2 × 10; 1 × 8 × 75% See table 3.3 for specific exercises
	Trunk	Daily core 2 × 50 series, 2 × 100 series, 4 × 4 MD drills (1 × 10): lateral twist (3 positions), NC feet up, NC feet down, seated toss-over
	COOL-DOWN AND FLEXIBILITY	Jog and walk 5 min Daily dozen (do 3 sets of each exercise and hold for 10-15 sec)

Table 3.4   Preseason (Week 14) – Performance Training – "Train to Compete"

	Activity	Exercises and Drills
WEDNESDAY	**WARM-UP AND FLEXIBILITY**	Jog 5 min, general warm-up (1 × 10), dynamic warm-up #1 (1 × 10) Daily dozen (1 × 10)
	SPEED/QUICKNESS	
	Reaction time	Ball drops: forward (2 × 5), lateral (2 × 5) Dot drill (3 sets)
	First-step quickness (do 2 sets of each)	Ladder drills: wide skip, crossover skip, Icky shuffle, backward Icky, crossover, backward crossover, Pick-ups (2 × 25)
	Speed	10 × 100 in 10 min
	STRENGTH/POWER	
	Aerobics	Position players and pitchers: jog 20 min @ 7:00-7:30-per-mile pace, jump rope 10 min

Table 3.4   Preseason (Week 14) – Performance Training – "Train to Compete"

	Activity	Exercises and Drills
WEDNESDAY	**STRENGTH/POWER** *(continued)*	
	Shoulders	Cuff and scapula (1 × 10)
	Trunk	Daily core 2 × 50 series, 2 × 100 series, leg drops 1 × 20
		MD drills (1 × 10): off-center (3 positions), rocky twist feet down, seated toss-over
	Wrist and hand	Wrist (3 × 20): superset 3 exercises
		Hand (3 × 20): rice drill #2, plate squeeze
	COOL-DOWN AND FLEXIBILITY	Jog and walk 5 min
		Daily dozen (do 3 sets of each exercise and hold for 10-15 sec)

Table 3.4   Preseason (Week 14) – Performance Training – "Train to Compete"

	Activity	Exercises and Drills	
THURSDAY	**WARM-UP AND FLEXIBILITY**	Jog 5 min, general warm-up (1 × 10), dynamic warm-up #2 (1 × 10)	
		Daily dozen (1 × 10)	
	SPEED/QUICKNESS		
	Speed	LSA, 10 × (5-10-5)	
	Aerobics	Pitchers: jog 30 min @ 7:00-7:30-per-mile pace	
	Speed-Strength (sprint forward 10 yd after last rep in each set)	SAT: diagonal (4 × 5), side/side (4 × 5)	
	STRENGTH/POWER		
	Position players and pitchers **4-day split**	**Workloads:** Position players	
		Beginners: do all reps in the first set	Advanced players: do a pyramid
		Core–4 × 10	Core–1 × 8; 4 × 4 × 80%
		Assist–3 × 10	Assist–2 × 10; 1 × 8 × 75%
		See table 3.3 for specific exercises	
		Workloads: Pitchers	
		Beginners: do all reps in the first set	Advanced players: do a pyramid
		Core–4 × 10	Core–1 × 8; 4 × 4 × 80%
		Assist–3 × 10	Assist–2 × 10; 1 × 8 × 75%
		See table 3.3 for specific exercises	
	Trunk	Daily core 2 × 50 series, 2 × 100 series, 4 × 4	
		MD drills (1 × 10): lateral twist (3 positions), NC feet up, NC feet down, seated toss-over	
	Plyometrics	Box pop-up (1 × 10), box crossover (1 × 10), supported jump up (1 × 10), discus throw (1 × 5), two jumps and throw (1 × 5), squat chest throw, over-head throw	
	COOL-DOWN AND FLEXIBILITY	Jog and walk 5 min	
		Daily dozen (do 3 sets of each exercise and hold for 10-15 sec)	

(continued)

Table 3.4 Preseason (Week 14) – Performance Training – "Train to Compete"

	Activity	Exercises and Drills
FRIDAY	**WARM-UP AND FLEXIBILITY**	Jog 5 min, general warm-up (1 × 10), dynamic warm-up #1 (1 × 10) Daily dozen (1 × 10)
	SPEED/QUICKNESS	
	Reaction time	Two-ball drops: forward (2 × 5), lateral (2 × 5) X-jump (1 × 10): forward/backward, side/side X-hop (1 × 10): forward/backward, side/side
	First-step quickness (do 2 sets of each)	Hurdle drills: high step with 4 hurdles, high step with 3 hurdles, high step with 2 hurdles, high step crossover with 2 hurdles Pick-ups (2 × 25)
	Speed	Speed-endurance, 4 × 200 @ 40:120
	STRENGTH/POWER	
	Position players and pitchers **4-day split**	**Workloads:** Position players Beginners: do all reps in the first set Advanced players: do a pyramid Core–4 × 10 Core–1 × 8; 4 × 4 × 80% Assist–3 × 10 Assist–2 × 10; 1 × 8 × 75% See table 3.3 for specific exercises **Workloads:** Pitchers Beginners: do all reps in the first set Advanced players: do a pyramid Core–4 × 10 Core–1 × 8; 4 × 4 × 80% Assist–3 × 10 Assist–2 × 10; 1 × 8 × 75% See table 3.3 for specific exercises
	Aerobics	Position players and pitchers: jog 20 min @ 7:00-7:30-per-mile pace, jump rope 10 min
	Shoulders	Cuff and scapula (1 × 10)
	Trunk	Daily core 2 × 50 series, 2 × 100 series, leg drops 1 × 20 MD drills (1 × 10): off-center (3 positions), rocky twist feet up, rocky twist feet down, seated toss-over
	Wrist and hand	Wrist (3 × 20): superset 3 exercises Hand (3 × 20): rice drill #2, plate squeeze
	COOL-DOWN AND FLEXIBILITY	Jog and walk 5 min Daily dozen (do 3 sets of each exercise and hold for 10-15 sec)

Table 3.5 Preseason (Week 15) – Performance Training – "Train to Compete"

Activity	Exercises and Drills
WARM-UP AND FLEXIBILITY	Jog 5 min, general warm-up (1 × 10), dynamic warm-up #1 (1 × 10) Daily dozen (1 × 10)
SPEED/QUICKNESS	
Reaction time	One-ball drops: forward (2 × 5), lateral (2 × 5) Two-ball drops: forward (2 × 5), lateral (2 × 5) Reaction ball (2 × 10)
First-step quickness (do 2 sets of each)	Ladder drills: wide skip, crossover skip, two-foot hopscotch, alternate-foot hopscotch Pick-ups (3 × 25)
Speed	100s, 3 × 8 × 100 yd @ 18:18 sec
Aerobics	Pitchers and position players: jog 20 min @ 7:00-7:30 per mile pace, jump rope 10 min
Speed-Strength (lateral sprint 10 yd after last rep in each set)	SAT: forward (4 × 5), side/side (4 × 5)
STRENGTH/POWER	
Position players and pitchers 4-day split	**Workloads:** Position players Beginners: do all reps in the first set · Advanced players: do a pyramid Core–5 × 8 · Core–1 × 8; 1 × 5; 4 × 4 × 85% Assist–3 × 8 · Assist–1 × 10; 2 × 8 × 75% See table 3.3 for specific exercises **Workloads:** Pitchers Beginners: do all reps in the first set · Advanced players: do a pyramid Core–5 × 8 · Core–1 × 8; 1 × 5; 4 × 4 × 85% Assist–3 × 8 · Assist–1 × 10; 2 × 8 × 75% See table 3.3 for specific exercises
Shoulders	Cuff and scapula (1 × 10)
Trunk	Daily core 2 × 50 series, 2 × 100 series, 4 × 4, leg drops (1 × 20) MD drills (1 × 10): off-center (3 positions), rocky twist feet up, rocky twist feet down, seated toss-over
Wrist and hand	Wrist (3 × 20): superset 3 exercises Hand (3 × 20): rice drill #2, plate squeeze
Plyometrics	Box crossover (3 × 10), 12-inch box jump (3 × 5), 18-inch box jump (3 × 5), 24-inch box jump (3 × 5), 36-inch box jump (3 × 5)
COOL-DOWN AND FLEXIBILITY	Jog and walk 5 min Daily dozen (do 3 sets of each exercise and hold for 10-15 sec)

MONDAY

(continued)

Table 3.5 Preseason (Week 15) – Performance Training – "Train to Compete"

	Activity	Exercises and Drills
TUESDAY	**WARM-UP AND FLEXIBILITY**	Jog 5 min, general warm-up (1 × 10), dynamic warm-up #2 (1 × 10) Daily dozen (1 × 10)
	SPEED/QUICKNESS	
	Speed	Starts: 3 × 10 × 10 yd, 3 × 10 × 15 yd
	Aerobics	Pitchers: jog 30 min @ 7:00-7:30-per-mile pace
	STRENGTH/POWER	
	Position players and pitchers 4-day split	**Workloads:** Position players Beginners: do all reps in the first set Advanced players: do a pyramid Core–5 × 8 Core–1 × 8; 1 × 5; 4 × 4 × 85% Assist–3 × 8 Assist–1 × 10; 2 × 8 × 75% See table 3.3 for specific exercises **Workloads:** Pitchers Beginners: do all reps in the first set Advanced players: do a pyramid Core–5 × 8 Core–1 × 8; 1 × 5; 4 × 4 × 85% Assist–3 × 8 Assist–1 × 10; 2 × 8 × 75% See table 3.3 for specific exercises
	Trunk	Daily core 3 × 50 series, 3 × 100 series, 4 × 4, leg drops (1 × 20) MD drills (1 × 10): lateral twist (3 positions), NC feet up, NC feet down, seated toss-over
	COOL-DOWN AND FLEXIBILITY	Jog and walk 5 min Daily dozen (do 3 sets of each exercise and hold for 10-15 sec)

Table 3.5 Preseason (Week 15) – Performance Training – "Train to Compete"

	Activity	Exercises and Drills
WEDNESDAY	**WARM-UP AND FLEXIBILITY**	Jog 5 min, general warm-up (1 × 10), dynamic warm-up #1 (1 × 10) Daily dozen (1 × 10)
	SPEED/QUICKNESS	
	Reaction time	One-ball drops: forward (2 × 5), lateral (2 × 5) Two-ball drops: forward (2 × 5), lateral (2 × 5) Reaction ball (2 × 10)
	First-step quickness (do 2 sets of each)	Hurdle drills: high step with 4 hurdles, high step with 3 hurdles, high step crossover with 2 hurdles, cone jumps: side/side (2 × 10), front/back (2 × 10) Pick-ups (3 × 25)
	Speed	10 × 100 yd in 10 min
	Aerobics	Position players and pitchers: jog 20 min @ 7:00-7:30-per-mile pace, jump rope 10 min

Table 3.5 Preseason (Week 15) – Performance Training – "Train to Compete"

	Activity	Exercises and Drills
WEDNESDAY	**STRENGTH/POWER**	
	Shoulders	Cuff and scapula (1 × 10)
	Trunk	Daily core 2 × 50 series, 2 × 100 series, 4 × 4, leg drops (1 × 20) MD drills (1 × 10): off-center (3 positions), rocky twist feet up, rocky twist feet down, seated toss-over
	Wrist and hand	Wrist (3 × 20): superset 3 exercises Hand (3 × 20): rice drill #2, plate squeeze
	COOL-DOWN AND FLEXIBILITY	Jog and walk 5 min Daily dozen (do 3 sets of each exercise and hold for 10-15 sec)

Table 3.5 Preseason (Week 15) – Performance Training – "Train to Compete"

	Activity	Exercises and Drills	
THURSDAY	**WARM-UP AND FLEXIBILITY**	Jog 5 min, general warm-up (1 × 10), dynamic warm-up #2 (1 × 10) Daily dozen (1 × 10)	
	SPEED/QUICKNESS		
	Speed	LSA, 10 × (5-10-5)	
	STRENGTH/POWER		
	Position players and pitchers **4-day split**	**Workloads:** Position players Beginners: do all reps in the first set Core–5 × 8 Assist–3 × 8 See table 3.3 for specific exercises	Advanced players: do a pyramid Core–1 × 8; 1 × 5; 4 × 4 × 85% Assist–1 × 10; 2 × 8 × 75%
		Workloads: Pitchers Beginners: do all reps in the first set Core–5 × 8 Assist–3 × 8 See table 3.3 for specific exercises	Advanced players: do a pyramid Core–1 × 8; 1 × 5; 4 × 4 × 85% Assist–1 × 10; 2 × 8 × 75%
	Aerobics	Pitchers: jog 30 min @ 7:00-7:30-per-mile pace, jump rope 10 min	
	Trunk	Daily core 3 × 50 series, 3 × 100 series, 4 × 4 leg drops (1 × 20) MD drills (1 × 10): lateral twist (3 positions), NC feet up, NC feet down, seated toss-over	
	Plyometrics	Jumps, hops, and sprints (5 yd): cone jump and sprint forward (1 × 5); cone lateral hop and sprint forward (1 × 5); lateral hop, open hips, and lateral sprint (1 × 5); lateral hop, crossover, and lateral sprint (1 × 5)	
	COOL-DOWN AND FLEXIBILITY	Jog and walk 5 min Daily dozen (do 3 sets of each exercise and hold for 10-15 sec)	

(continued)

Table 3.5 Preseason (Week 15) – Performance Training – "Train to Compete"

	Activity	Exercises and Drills
FRIDAY	**WARM-UP AND FLEXIBILITY**	Jog 5 min, general warm-up (1 × 10), dynamic warm-up #1 (1 × 10) Daily dozen (1 × 10)
	SPEED/QUICKNESS	
	Reaction time	One-ball drops: forward (2 × 5) lateral (2 × 5) Two-ball drops: forward (2 × 5), lateral (2 × 5) Reaction ball (2 × 10)
	First-step quickness (do 2 sets of each)	Ladder drills: wide skip, crossover skip, two-foot hopscotch, alternate-foot hopscotch Pick-ups (3 × 25)
	Speed	Speed-endurance, 3 × 300 @ 60:180
	STRENGTH/POWER	
	Position players and pitchers **4-day split**	**Workloads:** Position players Beginners: do all reps in the first set Advanced players: do a pyramid Core–5 × 8 Core–1 × 8; 1 × 5; 4 × 4 × 85% Assist–3 × 8 Assist–1 × 10; 2 × 8 × 75% See table 3.3 for specific exercises **Workloads:** Pitchers Beginners: do all reps in the first set Advanced players: do a pyramid Core–5 × 8 Core–1 × 8; 1 × 5; 4 × 4 × 85% Assist–3 × 8 Assist–1 × 10; 2 × 8 × 75% See table 3.3 for specific exercises
	Aerobics	Position players and pitchers: jog 20 min @ 7:00-7:30-per-mile pace, jump rope 10 min
	Shoulders	Cuff and scapula (1 × 10)
	Trunk	Daily core 3 × 50 series, 3 × 100 series, 4 × 4 leg drops 1 × 20 MD drills (1 × 10): lateral twist (3 positions), NC feet up, NC feet down, seated toss-over
	Wrist and hand	Wrist (3 × 20): superset 3 exercises Hand (3 × 20): rice drill #2, plate squeeze
	COOL-DOWN AND FLEXIBILITY	Jog and walk 5 min Daily dozen (do 3 sets of each exercise and hold for 10-15 sec)

Table 3.6 Preseason (Week 16) – Performance Training – "Train to Compete"

	Activity	Exercises and Drills
MONDAY	**WARM-UP AND FLEXIBILITY**	Jog 5 min, general warm-up (1 × 10), dynamic warm-up #1 (1 × 10) Daily dozen (1 × 10)
	SPEED/QUICKNESS	
	Reaction time	Two-ball drops: forward (2 × 5), lateral (2 × 5)
	First-step quickness (do 2 sets of each)	Hurdle drills: high step with 4 hurdles, high step with 2 hurdles, high step crossover with 2 hurdles, cone jumps with 5-yd forward sprint: side/side (2 × 5), front/back Pick-ups (3 × 25)
	Speed	Sprints, 3 × 6 × 60 yd and walk back
	Aerobics	Position players and pitchers: jog 20 min @ 7:00-7:30-per-mile pace, jump rope 10 min
	STRENGTH/POWER	
	Position players and pitchers 4-day split	**Workloads:** Position players Beginners: do all reps in the first set Advanced players: do a pyramid Core–5 × 8 Core–1 × 8; 1 × 5; 4 × 4 × 85% Assist–3 × 8 Assist–3 × 8 × 80% See table 3.3 for specific exercises **Workloads:** Pitchers Beginners: do all reps in the first set Advanced players: do a pyramid Core–5 × 8 Core–1 × 8; 1 × 5; 4 × 4 × 85% Assist–3 × 8 Assist–3 × 8 × 80% See table 3.3 for specific exercises
	Shoulders	Cuff and scapula (1 × 10)
	Trunk	Daily core 3 × 50 series, 3 × 100 series, leg drops (2 × 20) MD drills (1 × 10): off-center (3 positions), rocky twist feet up, rocky twist feet down, seated toss-over
	Wrist and hand	Wrist (3 × 20): superset 3 exercises Hand (3 × 20): rice drill #2, plate squeeze
	Plyometrics	Box crossover (3 × 10), 12-inch box jump (4 × 5), 18-inch box jump (4 × 5), 24-inch box jump (4 × 5), 36-inch box jump (4 × 5)
	COOL-DOWN AND FLEXIBILITY	Jog and walk 5 min Daily dozen (do 3 sets of each exercise and hold for 10-15 sec)

(continued)

Table 3.6 Preseason (Week 16) – Performance Training – "Train to Compete"

	Activity	Exercises and Drills
TUESDAY	**WARM-UP AND FLEXIBILITY**	Jog 5 min, general warm-up (1 × 10), dynamic warm-up #2 (1 × 10) Daily dozen (1 × 10)
	SPEED/QUICKNESS	
	Speed	10-sec bursts, 3 × 6 × 10 sec
	Aerobics	Position players and pitchers: jog 20 min @ 7:00-7:30-per-mile pace, jump rope 10 min
	STRENGTH/POWER	
	Position players and pitchers 4-day split	**Workloads:** Position players Beginners: do all reps in the first set Core–5 × 8 Assist–3 × 8 See table 3.3 for specific exercises Advanced players: do a pyramid Core–1 × 8; 1 × 5; 4 × 4 × 85% Assist–3 × 8 × 80% **Workloads:** Pitchers Beginners: do all reps in the first set Core–5 × 8 Assist–3 × 8 See table 3.3 for specific exercises Advanced players: do a pyramid Core–1 × 8; 1 × 5; 4 × 4 × 85% Assist–3 × 8 × 80%
	Trunk	Daily core 3 × 50 series, 3 × 100 series, leg drops (2 × 20) MD drills (1 × 10): lateral twist (3 positions), NC feet up, NC feet down, seated toss-over
	COOL-DOWN AND FLEXIBILITY	Jog and walk 5 min Daily dozen (do 3 sets of each exercise and hold for 10-15 sec)

Table 3.6 Preseason (Week 16) – Performance Training – "Train to Compete"

	Activity	Exercises and Drills
WEDNESDAY	**WARM-UP AND FLEXIBILITY**	Jog 5 min, general warm-up (1 × 10), dynamic warm-up #1 (1 × 10), Daily dozen (1 × 10)
	SPEED/QUICKNESS	
	Reaction time	Two-ball drops: forward (2 × 5), lateral (2 × 5)
	First-step quickness (do 2 sets of each)	Ladder drills: wide skip, crossover skip, Icky shuffle, crossover, alternate-foot hopscotch Pick-ups (3 × 25)
	Speed	10 × 100 yd in 10 min
	STRENGTH/POWER	
	Aerobics	Pitchers and position players: jog 20 min @ 7:00-7:30-per-mile pace, jump rope 10 min

Table 3.6 Preseason (Week 16) – Performance Training – "Train to Compete"

	Activity	Exercises and Drills
WEDNESDAY	**STRENGTH/POWER** *(continued)*	
	Shoulders	Cuff and scapula (1 × 10)
	Trunk	Daily core 3 × 50 series, 3 × 100 series, leg drops (2 × 20) MD drills (1 × 10): off-center (3 positions), rocky twist feet up, rocky twist feet down, seated toss-over
	Wrist and hand	Wrist (3 × 20): superset 3 exercises Hand (3 × 20): rice drill #2, plate squeeze
	COOL-DOWN AND FLEXIBILITY	Jog and walk 5 min Daily dozen (do 3 sets of each exercise and hold for 10-15 sec)

Table 3.6 Preseason (Week 16) – Performance Training – "Train to Compete"

	Activity	Exercises and Drills
THURSDAY	**WARM-UP AND FLEXIBILITY**	Jog 5 min, general warm-up (1 × 10), dynamic warm-up #2 (1 × 10) Daily dozen (1 × 10)
	SPEED/QUICKNESS	
	Speed	Hollow sprints, 2 × 10 × 50 yd
	Aerobics	Pitchers: jog 30 min @ 7:00-7:30-per-mile pace
	STRENGTH/POWER	
	Position players and pitchers 4-day split	**Workloads:** Position players Beginners: do all reps in the first set Advanced players: do a pyramid Core–5 × 8 Core–1 × 8; 1 × 5; 4 × 4 × 85% Assist–3 × 8 Assist–3 × 8 × 80% See table 3.3 for specific exercises **Workloads:** Pitchers Beginners: do all reps in the first set Advanced players: do a pyramid Core–5 × 8 Core–1 × 8; 1 × 5; 4 × 4 × 85% Assist–3 × 8 Assist–3 × 8 × 80% See table 3.3 for specific exercises
	Trunk	Daily core 3 × 50 series, 3 × 100 series, leg drops (2 × 20) MD drills (1 × 10): lateral twist (3 positions), NC feet up, NC feet down, seated toss-over
	Plyometrics	Jumps, hops, and sprints (5 yd): standing long jump and sprint forward (1 × 5); hop and sprint forward (1 × 5); lateral hop, open hips, and lateral sprint (1 × 5); lateral hop, crossover, and lateral sprint (1 × 5)
	COOL-DOWN AND FLEXIBILITY	Jog and walk 5 min Daily dozen (do 3 sets of each exercise and hold for 10-15 sec)

(continued)

Table 3.6 Preseason (Week 16) – Performance Training – "Train to Compete"

	Activity	Exercises and Drills
FRIDAY	**WARM-UP AND FLEXIBILITY**	Jog 5 min, general warm-up (1 × 10), dynamic warm-up #1 (1 × 10) Daily dozen (1 × 10)
	SPEED/QUICKNESS	
	Reaction time	Two-ball drops: forward (2 × 5), lateral (2 × 5)
	First-step quickness (do 2 sets of each)	Hurdle drills: high step with 4 hurdles, high step with 2 hurdles, high step crossover with 2 hurdles Cone jumps with 5-yd forward sprint: side/side (2 × 5), front/back (2 × 5) Pick-ups (3 × 25)
	Speed	Speed-endurance, 4 × 300 @ 60:180
	STRENGTH/POWER	
	Position players and pitchers 4-day split	**Workloads:** Position players Beginners: do all reps in the first set Core–5 × 8 Assist–3 × 8 See table 3.3 for specific exercises Advanced players: do a pyramid Core–1 × 8; 1 × 5; 4 × 4 × 85% Assist–3 × 8 × 80% **Workloads:** Pitchers Beginners: do all reps in the first set Core–5 × 8 Assist–3 × 8 See table 3.3 for specific exercises Advanced players: do a pyramid Core–1 × 8; 1 × 5; 4 × 4 × 85% Assist–3 × 8 × 80%
	Aerobics	Position players and pitchers: jog 20 min @ 7:00-7:30-per-mile pace, jump rope 10 min
	Shoulders	Cuff and scapula (1 × 10)
	Trunk	Daily core 3 × 50 series, 3 × 100 series, leg drops (2 × 20) MD drills (1 × 10): off-center (3 positions), rocky twist feet up, rocky twist feet down, seated toss-over
	Wrist and hand	Wrist (3 × 20): superset 3 exercises Hand (3 × 20): rice drill #2, plate squeeze
	COOL-DOWN AND FLEXIBILITY	Jog and walk 5 min Daily dozen (do 3 sets of each exercise and hold for 10-15 sec)

Table 3.7 Preseason (Week 17) – Performance Training – "Train to Compete"

	Activity	Exercises and Drills
MONDAY	**WARM-UP AND FLEXIBILITY**	Jog 5 min, general warm-up (1 × 10), dynamic warm-up #1 (1 × 10) Daily dozen (1 × 10)
	SPEED/QUICKNESS	
	Reaction time	Wall runs (3 × 10)
	First-step quickness (do 2 sets of each)	Ladder drills: wide skip, backward wide skip, backward wide skip, crossover skip, backward crossover skip, hopscotch, alternate-foot hopscotch Pick-ups (3 × 25)
	Speed	30-second bursts, 1 × 10 × 30 sec
	Aerobics	Position players and pitchers: jog 20 min @ 7:00-7:30-per-mile pace, jump rope 10 min
	Speed-Strength (forward sprint 10 yd after last rep in each set)	SAT: back/front (4 × 5), side/side (4 × 5)
	STRENGTH/POWER	
	Position players and pitchers 4-day split	**Workloads:** Position players Beginners: do all reps in the first set Advanced players: do a pyramid Core–5 × 8 Core–1 × 8; 1 × 5; 4 × 3 × 90% Assist–3 × 8 Assist–1 × 10; 1 × 8; 1 × 6 × 85% See table 3.3 for specific exercises **Workloads:** Pitchers Beginners: do all reps in the first set Advanced players: do a pyramid Core–5 × 8 Core–1 × 8; 1 × 5; 4 × 3 × 90% Assist–3 × 8 Assist–1 × 10; 1 × 8; 1 × 6 × 85% See table 3.3 for specific exercises
	Shoulders	Cuff and scapula (1 × 10)
	Trunk	Daily core 3 × 50 series, 3 × 100 series, 4 × 4, leg drops (2 × 20) MD drills (1 × 10): off-center (3 positions), rocky twist feet up, seated toss-over
	Wrist and hand	Wrist (3 × 20): superset 3 exercises Hand (3 × 20): rice drill #2, plate squeeze
	Plyometrics	Run-bound-run (5 × 30 yd) Bound-run-bound (5 × 30 yd)
	COOL-DOWN AND FLEXIBILITY	Jog and walk 5 min Daily dozen (do 3 sets of each exercise and hold for 10-15 sec)

(continued)

Table 3.7 Preseason (Week 17) – Performance Training – "Train to Compete"

	Activity	Exercises and Drills
TUESDAY	**WARM-UP AND FLEXIBILITY**	Jog 5 min, general warm-up (1 × 10), dynamic warm-up #2 (1 × 10) Daily dozen (1 × 10)
	SPEED/QUICKNESS	
	Speed	10 × 100 yd in 10 min
	Aerobics	Position players and pitchers: jog 30 min @ 7:00-7:30-per-mile pace
	STRENGTH/POWER	
	Position players and pitchers 4-day split	**Workloads:** Position players Beginners: do all reps in the first set Advanced players: do a pyramid Core–5 × 8 Core–1 × 8; 1 × 5; 4 × 3 × 90% Assist–3 × 8 Assist–1 × 10; 1 × 8; 1 × 6 × 85% See table 3.3 for specific exercises **Workloads:** Pitchers Beginners: do all reps in the first set Advanced players: do a pyramid Core–5 × 8 Core–1 × 8; 1 × 5; 4 × 3 × 90% Assist–3 × 8 Assist–1 × 10; 1 × 8; 1 × 6 × 85% See table 3.3 for specific exercises
	Trunk	Daily core 3 × 50 series, 3 × 100 series, 4 × 4, leg drops (2 × 20) MD drills (1 × 10): lateral twist (3 positions), NC feet up, seated toss-over
	COOL-DOWN AND FLEXIBILITY	Jog and walk 5 min Daily dozen (do 3 sets of each exercise and hold for 10-15 sec)

Table 3.7 Preseason (Week 17) – Performance Training – "Train to Compete"

	Activity	Exercises and Drills
WEDNESDAY	**WARM-UP AND FLEXIBILITY**	Jog 5 min, general warm-up (1 × 10), dynamic warm-up #1 (1 × 10) Daily dozen (1 × 10)
	SPEED/QUICKNESS	
	Reaction time	Dot drill (3 ×)
	First-step quickness (do 2 sets of each)	Hurdle drills: high step with 4 hurdles, high step with 2 hurdles, high step crossover with 2 hurdles Cone jumps with 5-yd lateral sprint: side/side (2 × 5), front/back (2 × 5) Pick-ups (3 × 25)
	Speed	Hollow sprints, 3 × 10 × 60 yd
	STRENGTH/POWER	
	Aerobics	Position players and pitchers: jog 20 min @ 7:00-7:30-per-mile pace, jump rope 10 min

Table 3.7 Preseason (Week 17) – Performance Training – "Train to Compete"

	Activity	Exercises and Drills
WEDNESDAY	**STRENGTH/POWER** *(continued)*	
	Shoulders	Cuff and scapula (1 × 10)
	Trunk	Daily core 3 × 50 series, 3 × 100 series, 4 × 4, leg drops (2 × 20) MD drills (1 × 10): off-center (3 positions), rocky twist feet up, seated toss-over
	Wrist and hand	Wrist (3 × 20): superset 3 exercises Hand (3 × 20): rice drill #2, plate squeeze
	COOL-DOWN AND FLEXIBILITY	Jog and walk 5 min Daily dozen (do 3 sets of each exercise and hold for 10-15 sec)

Table 3.7 Preseason (Week 17) – Performance Training – "Train to Compete"

	Activity	Exercises and Drills
THURSDAY	**WARM-UP AND FLEXIBILITY**	Jog 5 min, general warm-up (1 × 10), dynamic warm-up #1 (1 × 10) Daily dozen (1 × 10)
	SPEED/QUICKNESS	
	Speed	LSA (5-10-5) × 10
	Aerobics	Pitchers: jog 30 min @ 7:00-7:30-per-mile pace
	Speed-strength	SAT: back/front (4 × 5), side/side (4 × 5) (forward sprint 10 yd after last rep in each set)
	STRENGTH/POWER	
	Position players and pitchers 4-day split	**Workloads:** Position players Beginners: do all reps in the first set Advanced players: do a pyramid Core–5 × 8 Core–1 × 8; 1 × 5; 4 × 3 × 90% Assist–3 × 8 Assist–1 × 10; 1 × 8; 1 × 6 × 85% See table 3.3 for specific exercises Advanced players: do a pyramid Core–1 × 8; 1 × 5; 4 × 3 × 90% Assist–1 × 10; 1 × 8; 1 × 6 × 85%
	Trunk	Daily core 3 × 50 series, 3 × 100 series 4 × 4, leg drops (2 × 20) MD drills (1 × 10): lateral twist (3 positions), NC feet up, seated toss-over
	Plyometrics	Run-bound-run (5 × 30 yd) Bound-run-bound (5 × 30 yd)
	COOL-DOWN AND FLEXIBILITY	Jog and walk 5 min Daily dozen (do 3 sets of each exercise and hold for 10-15 sec)

(continued)

Table 3.7 Preseason (Week 17) – Performance Training – "Train to Compete"

	Activity	Exercises and Drills
FRIDAY	**WARM-UP AND FLEXIBILITY**	Jog 5 min, general warm-up (1 × 10), dynamic warm-up #1 (1 × 10) Daily dozen (1 × 10)
	SPEED/QUICKNESS	
	Reaction time	Quicks (3 × 10)
	First-step quickness (do 2 sets of each)	Ladder drills: wide skip, backward wide skip, crossover skip, back crossover skip, hopscotch, alternate-foot hopscotch Pick-ups (3 × 25)
	Speed	Speed-endurance, 3 × 400 @ 70:210
	STRENGTH/POWER	
	Position players and pitchers 4-day split	**Workloads: Position players** Beginners: do all reps in the first set Core–5 × 8 Advanced players: do a pyramid Assist–3 × 8 Core–1 × 8; 1 × 5; 4 × 3 × 90% See table 3.3 for specific exercises Assist–1 × 10; 1 × 8; 1 × 6 × 85% **Workloads: Pitchers** Beginners: do all reps in the first set Core–5 × 8 Advanced players: do a pyramid Assist–3 × 8 Core–1 × 8; 1 × 5; 4 × 3 × 90% See table 3.3 for specific exercises Assist–1 × 10; 1 × 8; 1 × 6 × 85%
	Aerobics	Position players and pitchers: jog 20 min @ 7:00-7:30-per-mile pace, jump rope 10 min
	Shoulders	Cuff and scapula (1 × 10)
	Trunk	Daily core 3 × 50 series, 3 × 100 series 4 × 4, leg drops (2 × 20) MD drills (1 × 10): off-center (3 positions), rocky twist feet up, seated toss-over
	Wrist and hand	Wrist (3 × 20): superset 3 exercises Hand (3 × 20): rice drill #2, plate squeeze
	COOL-DOWN AND FLEXIBILITY	Jog and walk 5 min Daily dozen (do 3 sets of each exercise and hold for 10-15 sec)

Table 3.8 Preseason (Week 18) – Performance Training – "Train to Compete"

	Activity	Exercises and Drills
MONDAY	**WARM-UP AND FLEXIBILITY**	Jog 5 min, general (1 × 10), dynamic warm-up #1 (1 × 10) Daily dozen (1 × 10)
	SPEED/QUICKNESS	
	Reaction time	Wall runs (3 × 10) X-jumps forward and backward down the line (3 ×)
	First-step quickness (do 2 sets of each)	Hurdle drills: high step with 4 hurdles, high step with 2 hurdles, high step crossover with 2 hurdles Cone hops with 5-yd lateral sprint: side/side (2 × 5) Pick-ups (3 × 25)
	Speed	Sprints, 3 × 6 × 60 yd
	Aerobics	Position players and pitchers: jog 20 min @ 7:00-7:30-per-mile pace, jump rope 10 min
	Speed-Strength	SAT: diagonal back/front (4 × 5), side/side (4 × 5)
	STRENGTH/POWER	
	Position players and pitchers 4-day split	**Workloads: Position players** Beginners: do all reps in the first set Advanced players: do a pyramid Core–5 × 6 Core–1 × 8; 1 × 5; 4 × 2 × 95% Assist–3 × 8 Assist–1 × 8; 2 × 6 × 85% See table 3.3 for specific exercises **Workloads: Pitchers** Beginners: do all reps in the first set Advanced players: do a pyramid Core–5 × 8 Core–1 × 8; 1 × 5; 4 × 2 × 95% Assist–3 × 8 Assist–1 × 8; 2 × 6 × 85% See table 3.3 for specific exercises
	Shoulders	Cuff and scapula (1 × 10)
	Trunk	Daily core 4 × 50 series, 4 × 100 series, leg drops (2 × 20) MD drills (1 × 10): off-center (3 positions), rocky twist feet up, seated toss-over
	Wrist and hand	Wrist (3 × 20): superset 3 exercises Hand (3 × 20): rice drill #2, plate squeeze
	Plyometrics	Run-bound-run (5 × 30 yd), Bound-run-bound (5 × 30 yd)
	COOL-DOWN AND FLEXIBILITY	Jog and walk 5 min Daily dozen (do 3 sets of each exercise and hold for 10-15 sec)

(continued)

Table 3.8 Preseason (Week 18) – Performance Training – "Train to Compete"

	Activity	Exercises and Drills
TUESDAY	**WARM-UP AND FLEXIBILITY**	Jog 5 min, general warm-up (1 × 10), dynamic warm-up #2 (1 × 10) Daily dozen (1 × 10)
	SPEED/QUICKNESS	
	Speed	10 × 100 yd in 10 min
	Aerobics	Position players and pitchers: jog 30 min @ 7:00-7:30-per-mile pace
	STRENGTH/POWER	
	Position players and pitchers 4-day split	**Workloads: Position players** Beginners: do all reps in the first set Core–5 × 6 Assist–3 × 8 See table 3.3 for specific exercises Advanced players: do a pyramid Core–1 × 8; 1 × 5; 4 × 2 × 95% Assist–1 × 8; 2 × 6 × 85% **Workloads: Pitchers** Beginners: do all reps in the first set Core–5 × 8 Assist–3 × 8 See table 3.3 for specific exercises Advanced players: do a pyramid Core–1 × 8; 1 × 5; 4 × 2 × 95% Assist–1 × 8; 2 × 6 × 85%
	Trunk	Daily core 4 × 50 series, 4 × 100 series, leg drops (2 × 20) MD drills (1 × 10): lateral twist (3 positions), NC feet up, seated toss-over
	COOL-DOWN AND FLEXIBILITY	Jog and walk 5 min Daily dozen (do 3 sets of each exercise and hold for 10-15 sec)

Table 3.8 Preseason (Week 18) – Performance Training – "Train to Compete"

	Activity	Exercises and Drills
WEDNESDAY	**WARM-UP AND FLEXIBILITY**	Jog 5 min, general warm-up (1 × 10), dynamic warm-up #1 (1 × 10) Daily dozen (1 × 10)
	SPEED/QUICKNESS	
	Reaction time	Dot drill (3 ×), X-jumps lateral down the line (3 ×)
	First-step quickness (do 2 sets of each)	Ladder drills: wide skip, backward wide skip, crossover skip, crossover, alternate-foot hopscotch Pick-ups (3 × 25)
	Speed	Hollow sprints, 3 × 10 × 80 yd
	STRENGTH/POWER	
	Aerobics	Position players and pitchers: jog 20 min @ 7:00-7:30-per-mile pace, jump rope 10 min

Table 3.8 Preseason (Week 18) – Performance Training – "Train to Compete"

	Activity	Exercises and Drills
WEDNESDAY	**STRENGTH/POWER** *(continued)*	
	Shoulders	Cuff and scapula (1 × 10)
	Trunk	Daily core 4 × 50 series, 4 × 100 series, leg drops (2 × 20) MD drills (1 × 10): off-center (3 positions), rocky twist feet up, seated toss-over
	Wrist and hand	Wrist (3 × 20): superset 3 exercises Hand (3 × 20): rice drill #2, plate squeeze
	COOL-DOWN AND FLEXIBILITY	Jog and walk 5 min Daily dozen (do 3 sets of each exercise and hold for 10-15 sec)

Table 3.8 Preseason (Week 18) – Performance Training – "Train to Compete"

	Activity	Exercises and Drills
THURSDAY	**WARM-UP AND FLEXIBILITY**	Jog 5 min, general warm-up (1 × 10), dynamic warm-up #2 (1 × 10) Daily dozen (1 × 10)
	SPEED/QUICKNESS	
	Speed	LSA, (5-10-5) × 10
	STRENGTH/POWER	
	Position players and pitchers 4-day split	**Workloads:** Position players Beginners: do all reps in the first set Advanced players: do a pyramid Core–5 × 6 Core–1 × 8; 1 × 5; 4 × 2 × 95% Assist–3 × 8 Assist–1 × 8; 2 × 6 × 85% See table 3.3 for specific exercises **Workloads:** Pitchers Beginners: do all reps in the first set Advanced players: do a pyramid Core–5 × 8 Core–1 × 8; 1 × 5; 4 × 2 × 95% Assist–3 × 8 Assist–1 × 8; 2 × 6 × 85% See table 3.3 for specific exercises
	Aerobics	Pitchers: jog 30 min @ 7:00-7:30-per-mile pace
	Speed-Strength (forward sprint 10 yd after last rep in each set)	SAT: diagonal back/front (4 × 5), side/side (4 × 5)
	Trunk	Daily core 4 × 50 series, 4 × 100 series, leg drops (2 × 20) MD drills (1 × 10): lateral twist (3 positions), NC feet up, seated toss-over
	Plyometrics	Run-bound-run (5 × 30 yd) Bound-run-bound (5 × 30 yd)
	COOL-DOWN AND FLEXIBILITY	Jog and walk 5 min Daily dozen (do 3 sets of each exercise and hold for 10-15 sec)

(continued)

Table 3.8 Preseason (Week 18) – Performance Training – "Train to Compete"

	Activity	Exercises and Drills
FRIDAY	**WARM-UP AND FLEXIBILITY**	Jog 5 min, general warm-up (1 × 10), dynamic warm-up #1 (1 × 10) Daily dozen (1 × 10)
	SPEED/QUICKNESS	
	Reaction time	Quicks (3 × 10), X-jumps forward and backward down the line (3 ×)
	First-step quickness (do 2 sets of each)	Hurdle drills: high step with 4 hurdles, high step with 2 hurdles, high step crossover with 2 hurdles Cone hops with 5-yd lateral sprint: side/side (2 × 5) Pick-ups (3 × 25)
	Speed	4 × 400 @ 70:210
	STRENGTH/POWER	
	Position players and pitchers 4-day split	**Workloads: Position players** Beginners: do all reps in the first set Advanced players: do a pyramid Core–5 × 6 Core–1 × 8; 1 × 5; 4 × 2 × 95% Assist–3 × 8 Assist–1 × 8; 2 × 6 × 85% See table 3.3 for specific exercises

Workloads: Pitchers Beginners: do all reps in the first set Advanced players: do a pyramid Core–5 × 8 Core–1 × 8; 1 × 5; 4 × 2 × 95% Assist–3 × 8 Assist–1 × 8; 2 × 6 × 85% See table 3.3 for specific exercises |
	Aerobics	Position players and pitchers: jog 20 min @ 7:00-7:30-per-mile pace, jump rope 10 min
	Shoulders	Cuff and scapula (1 × 10)
	Trunk	Daily core 4 × 50 series, 4 × 100 series, leg drops (2 × 20) MD drills (1 × 10): off-center (3 positions), rocky twist feet up, seated toss-over
	Wrist and hand	Wrist (3 × 20): superset 3 exercises Hand (3 × 20): rice drill #2, plate squeeze
	COOL-DOWN AND FLEXIBILITY	Jog and walk 5 min Daily dozen (do 3 sets of each exercise and hold for 10-15 sec)

Practice receiving the ball daily. Start with 5 minutes. Add a minute per day to a maximum of 15 minutes. Block 50 balls per day using soft cloth balls or tennis balls. Work on hand speed and reaction time by doing crazy ball drills or by catching Frisbees from a receiving position. Use the throwing program outlined in table 3.9. Make all short throws on a flat line and use an arc when throwing long.

DEVELOPING A QUICK CATCHER'S GLOVE

The most important skill for a catcher is catching the ball. As you climb the ladder, pitchers throw harder, throw pitches at different speeds, and have movement on their pitches. Being able to handle all types of pitches is a must. Three effective ways to improve catching skills are to (1) catch as many different pitchers as you can, (2) catch balls at different speeds from a pitching machine, and (3) catch Frisbees.

Start by learning how to handle different speeds. Get 10 large Frisbees. Assume a receiving position with a partner kneeling about 30 feet in front of you. Have him or her throw one Frisbee at a time at a relatively slow speed. Catch the Frisbee with your bare glove hand, place it on the ground behind you, and get ready to receive the next one. Catch 10 throws, rest one or two minutes, and repeat. After catching two or three sets of 10 throws, increase throwing speed. When you can handle faster speeds, use smaller Frisbees.

Next, work on reaction time and hand-eye quickness. Again, start with large Frisbees. Have your partner throw Frisbees, one after another, as quickly as possible. As soon as you catch one, the second should be on the way. When you can catch two or three sets of 10 throws, switch to smaller Frisbees. For additional improvement, repeat the drills from different positions (down and up), with your partner standing closer and farther away or using a mix of large and small Frisbees.

Hitters

Swing the bat at least 200 times a day. Start with 50 free swings and then hit 50 balls off a T and 50 in soft toss. Mix in at least 25 bunts and five minutes of pepper each day. Add 50 swings per day to a maximum of 500. Hit off a machine to toughen your hands. Develop timing by hitting off a live arm whenever possible. Always warm up before swinging and hitting.

Infielders

Think legs. You can't field, throw, or hit with weak legs. Do forward and lateral walking lunges on leg days. Do ball pick-ups three times per week and field at least 100 ground balls five or six times per week. Take 25 ground balls straight at you, go side-to-side for 50, and finish by charging 25 slow rollers. Practice making double plays. Work on getting the ball out of your glove and making quick tosses.

Play catch three times per week and throw for arm strength three times per week using the program outlined in table 3.10 on page 79. Finish with 15 to 20 crisp throws at 50 feet. Make all short throws on a flat line and use an arc when throwing long. Sprint for speed and acceleration, do shuttles for LSA, and run 10 × 100 in 10 minutes for endurance. Jump rope for agility and balance.

Table 3.9 Six-Week Throwing Program for Catchers

Week	Day	Action	Distance (ft)	Week	Day	Action	Distance (ft)
1	1, 3, 5	Warm-up toss	45	1	2, 4, 6	Warm-up toss	60
		Throw 15 ×	45			Throw 15 ×	75
		Rest 1-2 min				Rest 1-2 min	
		Warm-up toss	45			Warm-up toss	60
		Throw 20 ×	45			Throw 20 ×	60
2	1, 3, 5	Warm-up toss	75	2	2, 4, 6	Warm-up toss	90
		Throw 15 ×	85			Throw 15 ×	90
		Rest 1-2 min				Rest 1-2 min	
		Warm-up toss	75			Throw 20 ×	90
		Throw 20 ×	75			Long toss 20 ×	120
3	1, 3, 5	Warm-up toss	90	3	2	Warm-up toss	115
		Throw 20 ×	90			Throw 15 ×	115
		Rest 1-2 min				Rest 1-2 min	
		Throw 20 ×	60			Throw 20 ×	115
		Throw 20 ×	90			Long toss 20 ×	140
3	4	Warm-up toss	130	3	6	Warm-up toss	145
		Throw 20 ×	130			Throw 20 ×	145
		Rest 1-2 min				Rest 1-2 min	
		Throw 20 ×	130			Throw 20 ×	145
		Long toss 20 ×	150			Long toss 20 ×	160
4	1, 3, 5	Warm-up toss	90	4	2, 4, 6	Warm-up toss	160
		Throw 25 ×	90			Throw 25 ×	160
		Rest 1-2 min				Rest 1-2 min	
		Throw 25 ×	60			Throw 20 ×	160
		Throw 25 ×	90			Long toss 20 ×	180
5	1, 3, 5	Warm-up toss	90	5	2	Warm-up toss	150
		Throw 30 ×	90			Throw 15 ×	60
		Rest 1-2 min				Rest 1-2 min	
		Throw 30 ×	60			Throw 20 ×	60
		Throw 30 ×	90			Throw 10 ×	90
						Throw 20 ×	60
						Long toss 20 ×	120

Week	Day	Action	Distance (ft)	Week	Day	Action	Distance (ft)
5	4	Warm-up toss	150	5	6	Warm-up toss	180
		Throw 15 ×	60			Throw 25 ×	60
		Rest 1-2 min				Rest 1-2 min	
		Throw 10 ×	90			Throw 20 ×	60
		Throw 20 ×	60			Long toss 20 ×	120
		Long toss 20 ×	120				
6	1, 3, 5	Warm-up toss	100	6	2	Warm-up toss	150
		Throw 25 ×	60			Throw 15 ×	60
		Rest 1-2 min				Rest 1-2 min	
		Throw 25 ×	60			Throw 20 ×	60
		Throw 25 ×	60			Throw 10 ×	90
						Throw 20 ×	60
						Long toss 20 ×	120
6	4	Warm-up toss	180	6	6	Warm-up toss	150
		Throw 25 ×	60			Throw 15 ×	60
		Rest 1-2 min				Rest 1-2 min	
		Throw 20 ×	60			Throw 20 ×	60
		Long toss 20 ×	120			Throw 10 ×	90
						Throw 20 ×	60
						Long toss 20 ×	120

If your arm is sore and does not improve after warm-up, take the day off and repeat the previous day's workout in your next training session. If the soreness disappears after warm-up, continue the program as outlined.

Outfielders

Run, field, and throw every workout. Sprint for speed, run 10×100 yards in 10 minutes for endurance, and do 15:15s for speed-endurance. Play catch three times per week and throw for arm strength three times per week using the program outlined in table 3.11 on page 82. Make all short throws on a flat line and use an arc when throwing long. Stretch your arm before and after throwing. Hang from a pull-up bar for two to three minutes each day.

IMPROVING ARM STRENGTH

Most players ask, "How can I make my arm stronger?" The key to throwing starts with your legs! You can lift weights or pull on tubing until you turn blue in the face, but until you learn how to use your legs, you'll never achieve maximum arm strength. When an outfielder throws a runner out at the plate, the announcers rave about how strong his arm is, but the truth is that the force that he imparts to the ball is initiated in the legs and then transferred through the trunk to his arm and hand where it is eventually applied to the ball. Velocity and distance are determined by the *sum* of forces generated by the legs, trunk, arm, and hand.

You can do four things to improve your throwing:

1. Start all throws with your legs. For maximum force, pivot on your back foot until it's parallel to the target. Think "throw like a pitcher, not like a dart thrower." Dart throwers point their toes at the target. With toes forward, you can't bend you knees, so you don't get any leg force. Also, with toes forward, the hips are open and can't rotate and contribute to the throw. A pitcher pivots until his foot is parallel to the plate. Pivoting lets him bend his back leg to get more force and then transfer this force through the hips to the arm and hand.

2. Reach forward with your glove and point it directly at the target. Reaching forward will make you take a longer step. The longer the step, the more leg force you can generate. For every action there is an equal and opposite reaction. Wherever your glove hand goes, your throwing hand follows. If you point your glove at the target, you'll get maximum force from your hips and legs. If you pull your glove across the chest, your hips will open too soon and you'll lose most of your leg force, getting nothing on the ball.

3. Throw directly overhand with your hand squarely behind the ball. Overhand throws let you get maximum force from the legs, hips, and arm behind the ball. Distance and accuracy are sacrificed with other release points.

4. Strengthen your core. The forces used in throwing come from the legs, hips, trunk, arm, and hand, not just the arm and hand.

Pitchers

Do sprints and hollow sprints for power and LSA for agility. Jog and run 10×100 in 10 minutes for endurance. Run intervals for speed-endurance. Your goal is to get ready for spring training, not opening day. Throw three times per week but don't try to be game ready in February. Get your arm in shape so that spring drills will be easier. Stretch before and after throwing to minimize soreness and the chances of injury. Play catch on flat ground and do long-toss drills for two weeks before throwing off a mound. Follow the throwing program outlined in table 3.12 on page 84. Make quality throws. Throw the ball straight, without an arc or lob. Use your total body, especially your hips and legs, to minimize stress on your arm. If you don't have access to a mound, do all your throwing off flat ground.

You don't need a mound to get your arm in shape. Nolan Ryan would start just behind pitchers mound with 50 balls. He would place a ball on the ground, bend down, pick it up like an outfielder, and using a crow hop throw it into a backstop about 125 feet away. After 50 throws, he would pick the balls up, move to just behind second base and repeat the drill. Nolan finished the long-toss drill by throwing 50 balls from center field and 50 from deep center. After 150 to 200 long tosses, Nolan would finish with 5 to 10 minutes of flat-ground work to a partner about 55 feet away. Starting each long toss with the ball on the ground and throwing off flat ground shifted most of the stress from his arm to his hips and legs.

Table 3.10 Six-Week Throwing Program for Infielders

Week	Day	Action	Distance (ft)	Week	Day	Action	Distance (ft)
1	1, 3, 5	Warm-up toss	45	1	2, 4, 6	Warm-up toss	60
		Throw 15 ×	45			Throw 15 ×	75
		Rest 1-2 min				Rest 1-2 min	
		Warm-up toss	45			Warm-up toss	60
		Throw 20 ×	45			Throw 20 ×	60
2	1, 3, 5	Warm-up toss	75	2	2, 4, 6	Warm-up toss	90
		Throw 15 ×	85			Throw 15 ×	90
		Rest 1-2 min				Rest 1-2 min	
		Warm-up toss	75			Throw 20 ×	90
		Throw 20 ×	75			Long toss 20 ×	120
						Throw 20 ×	50
3	1, 3, 5	Warm-up toss	90	3	2	Warm-up toss	100
		Throw 20 ×	90			Throw 15 ×	100
		Rest 1-2 min				Rest 1-2 min	
		Throw 20 ×	60			Throw 20 ×	100
		Throw 20 ×	90			Long toss 20 ×	120
						Throw 20 ×	50
3	4	Warm-up toss	120	3	6	Warm-up toss	130
		Throw 20 ×	120			Throw 20 ×	130
		Rest 1-2 min				Rest 1-2 min	
		Throw 20 ×	120			Throw 20 ×	130
		Long toss 20 ×	140			Long toss 20 ×	150
		Throw 20 ×	50			Throw 20 ×	50
4	1, 3, 5	Warm-up toss	90	4	2, 4, 6	Warm-up toss	150
		Throw 25 ×	90			Throw 25 ×	150
		Rest 1-2 min				Rest 1-2 min	
		Throw 25 ×	60			Throw 20 ×	150
		Throw 25 ×	90			Long toss 20 ×	170
						Throw 20 ×	50
5	1, 3, 5	Warm-up toss	90	5	2	Warm-up toss	170
		Throw 30 ×	90			Throw 15 ×	60
		Rest 1-2 min				Rest 1-2 min	
		Throw 30 ×	60			Throw 20 ×	60
		Throw 30 ×	90			Long toss 20 ×	120

(continued)

Table 3.10 *(continued)*

Week	Day	Action	Distance (ft)	Week	Day	Action	Distance (ft)
5	4	Warm-up toss	150	5	6	Warm-up toss	180
		Throw 15 ×	60			Throw 25 ×	60
		Rest 1-2 min				Rest 1-2 min	
		Throw 20 ×	60			Throw 20 ×	60
		Throw 10 ×	90			Long toss 20 ×	120
		Throw 20 ×	60			Throw 20 ×	50
		Long toss 20 ×	120				
		Throw 20 ×	50				
6	1, 3, 5	Warm-up toss	100	6	2	Warm-up toss	150
		Throw 25 ×	60			Throw 15 ×	60
		Rest 1-2 min				Rest 1-2 min	
		Throw 25 ×	60			Throw 20 ×	60
		Throw 25 ×	90			Throw 10 ×	90
						Throw 20 ×	60
						Long toss 20 ×	120
						Throw 20 ×	50
6	4	Warm-up toss	180	6	6	Warm-up toss	150
		Throw 25 ×	60			Throw 15 ×	60
		Rest 1-2 min				Rest 1-2 min	
		Throw 20 ×	60			Throw 20 ×	60
		Long toss 20 ×	120			Throw 10 ×	90
						Throw 20 ×	60
						Long toss 20 ×	120
						Throw 20 ×	50

If your arm is sore and does not improve after warm-up, take the day off and repeat the previous day's workout in your next training session. If the soreness disappears after warm-up, continue the program as outlined.

AVOIDING ARM PROBLEMS

The main cause of arm injury is repetitive throwing with bad mechanics. Preventing arm pain involves three related steps. First, learn proper mechanics. Second, develop flexibility and strength in the muscles of the arm and shoulder. Third, limit the number of throws made in games and practice sessions. The typical major-league pitcher throws about 15 pitches per inning, or 125 to 135 in a nine-inning game. The typical young amateur pitcher, however, throws 25 to 30 pitches per inning, with some throwing up to 40 per inning. He also throws in practice and before and after games. It is not uncommon for young pitchers to make as many pitches to friends, parents, and coaches as they do in competition. The cause of many arm problems is found not on the baseball diamond but on the practice field.

A major cause of arm problems is throwing too much. Excessive throwing, especially in those with a developing arm, bad mechanics, and low strength puts a lot of stress on the muscles and support structures of the elbow and shoulder. Repetitive stress can cause the muscles, tendons, and ligaments to become inflamed. The player experiences pain and stiffness in the elbow or shoulder and changes his mechanics to avoid pain.

You can't throw through this problem. The more you throw, the more pain you get. And with pain comes a loss of control and velocity. The only cure for arm pain is a lot of rest.

Prevention is the best way to avoid arm injury. Pay attention to mechanics and the number of pitches thrown per week. A pitch count in the range of 150 to 200 total pitches per week should be reasonable for those without arm problems. Coaches should observe these guidelines and use common sense to protect young arms. If a pitcher is wild and throws 100 to 120 pitches Saturday afternoon, don't ask him to go home and throw more to work on mechanics. If he couldn't throw a strike in the game, when the arm was strong, he won't be able to throw a strike later in the day when his arm is tired.

Fueling the Body: Supplements

Supplements are the trendiest area in sports nutrition today. Most manufacturers claim that their products contain some secret ingredient that will increase speed, improve endurance, relieve muscle soreness, increase muscle mass, or reduce body fat beyond that achieved under normal dietary conditions. Claims are usually based on testimonials by well-known athletes or on case histories. Few claims can be validated by scientific research, but athletes continue to buy them in record numbers. Why? Because they are looking for a magic bullet to give them an edge over the competition.

Unfortunately, many supplements offer no benefits, and some are harmful. Avoid products with bogus claims like fat burner, fat metabolizer, energy enhancer, performance booster, strength booster, ergogenic aid, natural steroid, anabolic optimizer, and genetic optimizer. Eating a diet high in carbohydrate and training hard are the best ergogenic aids available. They are safe, cheap, and effective.

Muscle Builders–Testosterone Boosters

*"Will taking asteroids make me a better pitcher?"—**Ramon Garcia***

Testosterone, the four-carbon ring from which every anabolic steroid is derived, is the most coveted muscle-building hormone in existence. It is the hormone that separates men from boys. Testosterone and its chemical cousins, anabolic steroids, are illegal and hard to get. If used improperly, they can have serious side effects.

Anabolic Steroids

Steroids increase muscle size and strength but not without serious side effects that could be life threatening. Steroid use is associated with an increased risk of

Table 3.11 Six-Week Throwing Program for Outfielders

Week	Day	Action	Distance (ft)	Week	Day	Action	Distance (ft)
1	1, 3, 5	Warm-up toss	90	1	2, 4, 6	Warm-up toss	90
		Throw 15 ×	90			Throw 15 ×	90
		Rest 1-2 min				Rest 1-2 min	
		Warm-up toss	60			Throw 20 ×	90
		Throw 20 ×	90			Long toss 20 ×	120
2	1, 3, 5	Warm-up toss	120	2	2	Warm-up toss	145
		Throw 20 ×	120			Throw 15 ×	145
		Rest 1-2 min				Rest 1-2 min	
		Warm-up toss	90			Throw 20 ×	145
		Throw 20 ×	120			Long toss 20 ×	160
2	4	Warm-up toss	130	2	6	Warm-up toss	145
		Throw 20 ×	130			Throw 20 ×	145
		Rest 1-2 min				Rest 1-2 min	
		Throw 20 ×	130			Throw 20 ×	145
		Long toss 20 ×	150			Long toss 20 ×	160
3	1, 3, 5	Warm-up toss	140	3	2, 4, 6	Warm-up toss	160
		Throw 25 ×	140			Throw 25 ×	160
		Rest 1-2 min				Rest 1-2 min	
		Throw 25 ×	90			Throw 20 ×	160
		Throw 25 ×	140			Long toss 20 ×	175
4	1, 3, 5	Warm-up toss	150	4	2	Warm-up toss	175
		Throw 30 ×	150			Throw 15 ×	175
		Rest 1-2 min				Rest 1-2 min	
		Throw 30 ×	90			Throw 10 ×	120
		Throw 30 ×	150			Throw 10 ×	140
						Long toss 20 ×	190
4	4	Warm-up toss	190	4	6	Warm-up toss	200
		Throw 15 ×	190			Throw 15 ×	200
		Rest 1-2 min				Rest 1-2 min	
		Throw 10 ×	130			Throw 10 ×	140
		Throw 10 ×	160			Throw 10 ×	170
		Long toss 20 ×	200			Long toss 20 ×	215

Week	Day	Action	Distance (ft)	Week	Day	Action	Distance (ft)
5	1, 3, 5	Warm-up toss	160	5	2	Warm-up toss	215
		Throw 25 ×	160			Throw 15 ×	215
		Rest 1-2 min				Rest 1-2 min	
		Throw 25 ×	90			Throw 10 ×	150
		Throw 25 ×	160			Throw 10 ×	180
						Throw 10 ×	200
						Long toss 20 ×	225
5	4	Warm-up toss	150	5	6	Warm-up toss	220
		Throw 15 ×	150			Throw 25 ×	220
		Rest 1-2 min				Rest 1-2 min	
		Throw 20 ×	150			Throw 20 ×	180
		Throw 10 ×	120			Throw 20 ×	180
		Throw 20 ×	90			Throw 20 ×	200
		Long toss 20 ×	120			Throw 20 ×	220
		Throw 20 ×	160			Throw 20 ×	225
6	1, 3, 5	Warm-up toss	170	6	2	Warm-up toss	225
		Throw 25 ×	170			Throw 15 ×	225
		Rest 1-2 min				Rest 1-2 min	
		Throw 25 ×	90			Throw 10 ×	150
		Throw 25 ×	170			Throw 10 ×	180
						Throw 10 ×	210
						Long toss 20 ×	230
6	4	Warm-up toss	230	6	6	Warm-up toss	240
		Throw 15 ×	230			Throw 15 ×	240
		Rest 1-2 min				Rest 1-2 min	
		Throw 10 ×	150			Throw 10 ×	150
		Throw 10 ×	190			Throw 10 ×	200
		Throw 10 ×	220			Throw 10 ×	225
		Long toss 20 ×	240			Long toss 20 ×	250

If your arm is sore and does not improve after warm-up, take the day off and repeat the previous day's workout in your next training session. If the soreness disappears after warm-up, continue the program as outlined.

Table 3.12 Six-Week Throwing Program for Pitchers

Week	Day	Action, time (min), and distance (ft)	Week	Day	Action, time (min), and distance (ft)
1	MWF	Warm-up toss: 1 min at 40 ft 1 min at 50 ft 1 min at 60 ft 2 min at 70 ft Long toss: 1 min at 100 ft 1 min at 110 ft 1 min at 120 ft	2	MWF	Warm-up toss: 1 min at 40 ft 1 min at 50 ft 1 min at 60 ft 2 min at 70 ft Long toss: 1 min at 100 ft 1 min at 110 ft 1 min at 120 ft Flat ground—all pitches: 5 min at 60 ft
3	MWF	Warm-up toss: 1 min at 40 ft 1 min at 50 ft 1 min at 60 ft 2 min at 70 ft Long toss: 1 min at 80 ft 1 min at 90 ft 1 min at 100 ft 1 min at 110 ft 1 min at 120 ft Flat ground—all pitches: 5 min at 60 ft Mound—all pitches at 60%: 5-7 min	4	MWF	Warm-up toss: 1 min at 40 ft 1 min at 50 ft 1 min at 60 ft 2 min at 70 ft Long toss: 1 min at 80 ft 1 min at 90 ft 1 min at 100 ft 1 min at 110 ft 1 min at 120 ft 1 min at 130 ft Flat ground—all pitches: 5 min at 60 ft Mound—all pitches at 70%: 8-10 min
5	MWF	Warm-up toss: 1 min at 40 ft 1 min at 50 ft 1 min at 60 ft 2 min at 70 ft Long toss: 1 min at 90 ft 1 min at 100 ft 1 min at 110 ft	6	MWF	Warm-up toss: 1 min at 40 ft 1 min at 50 ft 1 min at 60 ft 2 min at 70 ft Long toss: 1 min at 100 ft 1 min at 110 ft 1 min at 120 ft

(continued)

Week	Day	Action, time (min), and distance (ft)	Week	Day	Action, time (min), and distance (ft)
5	MWF	1 min at 120 ft	6	MWF	1 min at 130 ft
(continued)		1 min at 130 ft	(continued)		1 min at 140 ft
		1 min at 140 ft			1 min at 150 ft
		Flat ground—all pitches:			Flat ground—all pitches:
		5 min at 60 ft			5 min at 60 ft
		Mound—all pitches at 80%:			Mound—all pitches at 90%:
		11-13 min			14-16 min

If your arm is sore and does not improve after warm-up, take the day off and repeat the previous day's workout in your next training session. If the soreness disappears after warm-up, continue the program as outlined.

liver damage, heart disease, stroke, and cancer. Other side effects include acne, baldness, fluid retention, oily skin, deepening of the voice, unnatural hair growth on the face and body, breast enlargement, impotence, and sterility.

The body has its own wisdom. Too much androgen (steroid) shuts off the body's production of testosterone. This can impair normal testicular function. Steroid users also experience severe personality changes ranging from mild aggressiveness to extreme hostility ("roid rage") and an increased risk of injury. Injuries occur when the structural strength of the tendons, ligaments, and bones cannot withstand the increased force of contraction of the muscles treated with steroids. Finally, the Drug Enforcement Agency (DEA) has made steroids a Class III drug, which means a user can receive up to a year in prison and a $1,000 fine. Sellers can receive 5 years in prison and a $250,000 fine, and a second offense can bring as much as 10 years and a $500,000 fine.

Androstenedione ("Andro")

This "natural" hormone is produced in the body and converted in just one step to testosterone. Andro, while not classified as a steroid, functions like one to boost testosterone levels so you train harder and recover more quickly. Is it safe? We don't know. It appears to be OK in its natural state in meats and plants. But the pills you buy are more concentrated and may produce unwanted consequences. We do know that the potential side effects of excess testosterone production include acne, mood swings, male pattern baldness, abnormal prostate growth, increased sex drive, and enlarged breasts. Doctors suspect that it could also cause liver problems (especially if you drink), create heart problems, and stunt adolescent growth. The NFL, NCAA, and USOC ban it. The Association of Professional Team Doctors recommends that it be banned from all sports.

DHEA (Dehydroepiandrosterone)

Watch out with this product! It's not an herb; it's a powerful steroid hormone produced by the adrenal gland. It's two steps up the hormonal metabolic pathway from testosterone production. It's so powerful that the FDA says it should not be sold without a prescription. While DHEA is sold as the "steroid of youth" to build muscle, burn fat, and slow the aging process, research has not shown that it can do any of these things. It will, however, shrink your testicles, make your skin oily, cause acne, grow body hair, enlarge your liver, and make you more aggressive. Astros' team physician Dr. William Bryan, calls it the "fountain of prostate cancer." And don't believe the claim that you can form your own DHEA by eating Mexican yams (dioscoria). You can't.

Muscle Builders–Energy Enhancers

These substances are chemical agents, not steroids, designed to increase the delivery of energy and nutrients into the muscle to allow you to train harder. Creatine appears to be the real deal for putting on size and strength. It is a muscle fuel (amino acid) found primarily in meat and fish but also available in tablet and powder forms. Research (see "For More Information" at the back of this book) indicates that creatine helps you work harder, train longer, and build muscle faster by raising the energy level within muscles.

There is an upper limit to the creatine levels that can be achieved, so taking larger dosages does not help more; once the muscle becomes saturated, excess creatine is simply excreted by the kidneys. Vegetarians and occasional meat eaters achieve the most pronounced effect from supplementation, while beefy meat eaters accumulate a negligible amount of additional creatine.

Creatine increases the *capacity to train,* and the increase in training eventually increases strength, size, and performance. Although no long-term medical risks appear to be associated with creatine use, some athletes taking creatine are more susceptible to muscle cramps, spasms, and pulls. Creatine can cause a 10 to 15 pound increase in body weight due to water retention in the muscles. This extra weight can negatively impact performance, reducing first-step quickness, acceleration, and speed.

Most college and pro teams recommend that players avoid creatine supplements, especially immediately before and during the season. The risks of injury outweigh the benefits. Creatine helps you train harder, but at a price. What good is it to be big if you lose a step? It will not make you a better baseball player. If you insist on taking creatine, use it very carefully and only early in the off-season when you're building a fitness base. Injuries are highest when you combine creatine, training, and heat. Take it at least 30 minutes before exercise and take it with plenty of water to avoid dehydration. Get off it before Christmas and stay off until the season is over!

HMB

HMB, or beta-hydroxy-beta-methylbutyrate, is marketed as being the breakthrough supplement to decrease muscle breakdown after exercise, speed muscle repair, and increase muscle mass and strength during resistance training. Only two studies support the manufacturer's claims, but both of these were conducted by the men who hold the patent on HMB (see Nissen and Abumrad and Nissen et al.).

You are probably already getting enough HMB through protein in your diet to achieve your training objectives. The HMB supplements cost about $35 for a 10-day supply, and the physiological effects of extended use are unknown. Don't buy hype.

Protein Supplements

You don't need lots of protein, and excess protein is usually stored as fat. A typical 200-pounder needs about seven ounces of protein per day from all sources (meat, beans, milk, whole-grain breads, and eggs). Most of us don't need amino acid supplements. How much protein your body uses is determined by how much you need, not by the amount in the diet.

The best supplements are branch-chain amino acids (BCAAs), but there's a lot more energy in carbohydrate-rich foods and it's a lot cheaper. Most BCAAs cost $2 to $3 per day or about $100 per pound of muscle.

Baseball Readiness Test

If you are uncertain of your fitness status, warm up and take the readiness test outlined below. It will tell you how close you are to being game ready. The test measures both general fitness and sport-specific fitness factors like strength, speed, agility, and power. Norms come from the scores obtained just before or during the first week of spring drills on players from A ball to MLB.

General Fitness—All Players

One-and-a-Half-Mile Run. Run one and a half miles as fast as you can and record your time to determine aerobic fitness. A high level of aerobic fitness lets you recover between pitches, innings, bases, and games. It's very hard to pitch more than two or three innings with a low aerobic capacity. Likewise, it's almost impossible for a position player to develop speed and go through routine fielding drills without first developing a sound aerobic base. Pitchers, whether high school, college, or pro, should be able to finish in 10:00 to 11:00; position players in 10:30 to 11:30. If you can't come close to these values, run 10×100 yards in 10 minutes on MWF and intervals on TTh (run repeat 220s and 440s with 3:1 rest-to-work ratios).

Sit and Reach. This test measures flexibility in the low back and hamstrings and is a predictor of potential hamstring and low-back problems. Sit with your legs extended straight in front of you and feet together. Place the soles of your feet against the end of a 12-inch high box. Lay a yardstick across the top of the box so that the 15-inch mark is even with the soles of your feet. Keep your knees straight, bend forward, and, with hands overlapped, reach as far as you can. Hold for a second and have a partner read where the tips of your fingers reach on the ruler. Pitchers should be able to touch 20 to 22 inches, that is, reach 5 to 7 inches beyond their toes. Position players should touch 18 to 20 inches, about 3 to 5 inches beyond their toes. If you fail to make these standards, spend more time on static hamstring and hip stretches. Start with three to five sets. Hold each stretch for 6 to 10 seconds. Progress to 3×10 seconds and work to 1×30 seconds.

Waist Circumference—Percent Body Fat. The number found where the columns containing your waist size and body weight in table 3.13 to get a rough estimate of percent body fat. This approach is not as accurate as skinfolds, but it's better than height-weight tables. Pitchers should be less than 13 or 14 percent fat; position players less than 11 or 12 percent fat. If you exceed these values, reduce your dietary fat to no more than 20 percent of your total calories

Table 3.13 Weight/Circumference Chart

Weight (lb)	Waist Circumference (in.)				
	32	33	34	35	36
180	10.8	13.1	15.4	17.7	20.0
185	10.2	11.3	14.6	16.7	19.1
190	9.8	12.0	14.1	16.3	18.5
195	9.2	11.4	13.5	15.6	17.7
200	8.9	11.0	13.0	15.1	17.2
205	8.4	10.4	12.4	14.4	16.4
210	8.1	10.1	12.0	14.0	16.0
215	7.6	9.5	11.5	13.4	15.3
220	7.3	9.2	11.0	13.0	14.9
225	6.9	8.8	10.6	12.4	14.3
230	6.7	8.5	10.3	12.1	13.9
235	6.3	8.0	9.8	11.6	13.3
240	6.0	7.8	9.5	11.2	13.0
245	5.7	7.4	9.1	10.8	12.4
250	5.5	7.1	8.8	10.4	12.1

and do more distance work. Each mile you run burns 175 to 200 calories, and you need to burn 3,500 calories to lose a pound of fat (about 15 miles per pound). Measure yourself around your abdomen at the level of your navel. Then find your abdominal circumference and your weight in the following table. Go down the column that lists circumference until it intersects the row that lists your weight. The number at the intersection is your percent body fat.

Sport-Specific Fitness—All Players

Agility (5-10-5).   This test measures your ability to start, stop, change directions, and run again. Place three cones five yards apart. Stand behind the middle cone. Use a crossover step and sprint as fast as you can to your right to the third cone and touch the cone with your hand. Quickly change directions and sprint to your left to the first cone and touch the cone with your hand. Change directions and sprint back to the middle. Record your time from start to finish. Rest and repeat in the opposite direction, that is, go left for 5 yards, right for 10 yards, and left for 5 yards. Your two times should not differ by more than one second. Pitchers should finish the test in 8.3 to 9.2 seconds; position players in 8.2 to 9.1 seconds. If you are below standards do the 5-10-5 drill.

30-Second Cone Jumps—Repetitive Power. This test measures your ability to exert power in a repetitive manner. It's a good index of your ability to run fast and throw hard in the late innings. Stand to the left of a 12-inch cone. Jump side to side over the cone on both feet as many times as you can in 30 seconds. Pitchers should make 58 to 65 jumps; position players 60 to 71. Failure to meet standards indicates a need to do more all-out explosive work. Increase power by doing box jumps, long jumps, and hops.

Sport-Specific Fitness—Pitchers

Vertical Jump—Power. This test measures leg power. Stand with your throwing arm next to a wall. Reach up with your throwing arm and touch as high on the wall as you can with the tips of your fingers. Have a partner mark this spot with chalk or a pencil. This is your standing height. Now bend you hips and legs and jump as high as you can and touch the wall. Put chalk or water on your finger tips so you can leave a mark on the wall. This is your jumping height. Use a yardstick and measure the distance between your standing and jumping height. This value is your vertical jump. Make three jumps and calculate the average. Pitchers should jump 26 to 38 inches; position players 27 to 39 inches. Power pitchers and power hitters usually jump more than 27 inches. If you fail to reach these standards, do lower-body strength and plyometric work.

300-Yard Shuttle—Willpower. This test will tell you whether you have done enough high-intensity anaerobic work during the off-season. It's also a good index of who will quit when the going gets tough. Mark off a 25-yard straight away. Stand behind the starting line and then sprint to the end and back six times as fast as you can. Record your total time in seconds. Rest five minutes and repeat. Pitchers should complete the first trial in 55 to 60 seconds. All players should run the second trial no more than 2 seconds slower than the first. If you score low on this test, run more 15:15s, 30:30s, 30- and 90-second bursts, pole sprints, and 220- to 440-yard shuttles.

Sport-Specific Fitness—Position Players

30-Yard Sprint—Acceleration-Speed. About 90 percent of top speed is reached within 30 yards. This test measures your ability to accelerate and run fast. Run 30 yards as fast as you can from a standing position using a crossover step. Run three times and calculate the average of the three. Your goal is 3.3 to 3.5 seconds. A slow time indicates the need to run all-out short sprints. Work on starting ability and do more leg work and lower-body plyometric exercises. Do 10- to 60-yard sprints, bounds, skips, walking lunges, and steps-ups. Pitchers don't need to take this test.

Standing Long Jump—Starting Ability. This test measures explosive power and starting ability. Stand behind a tape measure stretched out on grass or a soft mat. Bend at the hips, knees, and ankle. Swing both arms forward and explode as far forward as possible. Measure the distance from the tip of your toes in the starting position to the back of your rear heel in the landing position. Make three jumps and compute the average of the three. MLB average is 102 to 120 inches for pitchers and 105 to 129 inches for position players. If your score is low, do squats, lunges, and step-ups for strength and plyometrics (hops, long jumps, and box jumps) for power. Run sprints for speed and do starts, quicks, wall runs, and ladder drills for first-step quickness.

300-Yard Shuttle. See instructions in the section for pitchers. Position players should complete the first trial in 51 to 56 seconds.

Preseason II— Training to Play

GOAL *Get ready to start the season, converting sport-specific strength and fitness into baseball-specific strength, speed, and power*

To get a good start to the spring season, you'll concentrate on converting the sport-specific training and conditioning that you've been doing into specific baseball skills. Follow the program outlined in tables 4.1 through 4.8. High school, college, and minor-league players do the first four weeks of the program. Major leaguers train for six weeks.

Working the Body

You can use a four-day split and reduce the number of exercises to three or four per day to conserve energy for skill work. Work explosively when doing core lifts to turn on fast-twitch fibers. Train the smaller muscles at a slower rate.

Warm-Up and Flexibility

For early work, do each exercise in warm-up routine #1 each day to prepare for first-step drills. Do two or three quickness drills. Then do prepractice warm-ups and flexibility exercises as a team. Start with the general warm-up exercises and then do dynamic warm-up routine #2 to get ready for game-related running. Stretch (daily dozen) before and cool down after workouts.

Practice

Do drills, fielding, hitting, throwing, and so on as a team.

Running and Speed

Position players should run six times a week. For the first two weeks, work on stamina (10 × 100 yards in 10 minutes) on Monday, speed (build-ups and hollow sprints) on Tuesday and Friday, jog on Wednesday, do speed-endurance (15:15 runs) on Thursday, and do speed-endurance and run the bases on Saturday. Take Sunday off or jog.

Pitchers run six times a week. For the first two weeks, work on stamina (10 × 100 yards in 10 minutes) on Monday and Saturday, endurance and speed (poles and 60s) on Tuesday and Thursday, speed and endurance (100s) and jogging on Wednesday, and speed-endurance (30:30) on Friday. Take Sunday off or jog. Run the bases once or twice per week, starting in week 3. Add pole sprints in week 3.

Simulated Inning Training

Once games begin, pitchers can vary the running program to simulate the metabolic effect of pitching additional innings. To make your training more sport specific, workouts should match the time and energy requirements of game situations. Most major-league pitchers take about 5 to 10 seconds to get the sign, check the runner or runners, and deliver the ball to the plate. They rest 15 to 20 seconds between pitches and throw about 15 pitches per inning. The average inning lasts approximately five minutes. Using these guidelines, you can develop workouts to simulate the energy requirements of pitching in game situations.

Start with three innings and 15 reps each inning. Start at one foul line and sprint away from the foul line for 5 seconds (about 15 yards). Without stopping, turn and jog or walk back to the starting point (foul line) in about 15 seconds. Use a work-to-rest ratio of 1:4 (beginner) or 1:3 (advanced) and get back to the starting point in 15 to 20 seconds. To make these target times, you will probably have to jog about 10 yards and walk the last 5 yards. Repeat the process 15 times and then rest for five minutes. Do 100 sit-ups while resting. Repeat the process three to six times (innings). Vary the work-to-rest interval each inning to make the drill more game specific. For example, sprint for 5 seconds and rest for 15 seconds in the first inning. Then sprint for 3 to 9 seconds in the second inning. Follow each short sprint (3-second effort) with a long sprint (9-second effort). Follow each long sprint with a medium sprint (5- or 6-second effort). Sprint for 3 to 12 seconds in inning three and 3 to 15 seconds in inning four.

The drill is adaptable to any form of aerobic training machine or device. Successful programs have been developed using StairMaster-like stepping devices, rowing machines, and slideboards. For more variety, cross-train by varying the method of work. Cycle in inning one, StairMaster in inning two, use a slideboard in inning three, run in inning four, and so on.

Strength

Work the trunk every day. Do the daily core plus 200 to 300 sit-ups, MD ball twists, wood choppers, and seated back toss-overs each day. (see table 4.1)

Advanced players continue with a split program and reduce the number of exercises to three to four per day to conserve energy for skill work. Do large, multijoint exercises quickly and explosively for strength-power. Work smaller muscle groups at a slower rate for strength-endurance. Use the program outlined in table 4.2. Reduce intensity in week 6 to prepare for Opening Day. Train the rotator cuff, scapula, wrist, and hands three times per week.

Use a four-day split for strength training. Beginners use a load that will allow them to do all reps in the first set; advanced players use a pyramid program.

Fueling the Body to Play

*"It was the only English I knew—three-piece chicken, Coca-Cola. So when I got real hungry, I'd say, 'Three-piece chicken, Coca-Cola, three-piece chicken, Coca-Cola,' and I'd get two boxes of chicken and two cokes."—**Rafael Ramirez** on why he ate the same meal three times a day for 30 days*

You will expend more energy and need more nutrients during spring training than during almost any other time in the year. Don't go to the park or to class on an empty stomach. If you're living at home or in the dorm, start the day with one of the seven power breakfasts outlined in chapter 2 and take something with you to eat during the day. If you eat out, watch what you order at McDonald's or Denny's-type restaurants—most of their meals are high in calories and fat. The Grand Slam Breakfast, for example, with two eggs, two pancakes, two strips of

Table 4.1 Spring Training Strength-Training Workouts—Beginners

Week	Exercise	Set × Rep	Exercise	Set × Rep
19	Core	4 × 8	Assist	3 × 10
20		4 × 8		3 × 10
21		4 × 6		3 × 10
22		4 × 6		3 × 8
23		4 × 4		3 × 8
24		4 × 6		3 × 10

Do all reps in the first set.

Table 4.2 Spring Training Strength-Training Workouts—Advanced Players

Week	Exercise	Set × Rep × Load	Exercise	Set × Rep × Load
19	Core	1 × 8; 4 × 6 × 75%	Assist	3 × 10 × 65%
20		1 × 8; 4 × 6 × 80%		2 × 10; 1 × 8 × 70%
21		1 × 8; 4 × 6 × 85%		1 × 10; 2 × 8 × 75%
22		1 × 8; 4 × 4 × 88%		3 × 8 × 80%
23		1 × 8; 4 × 3 × 90%		2 × 8; 1 × 6 × 85%
24		1 × 8; 4 × 6 × 85%		1 × 10; 2 × 8 × 75%

Table 4.3 Spring Training (Week 19) – Performance Training – "Train to Play"

	Activity	Exercises and Drills
MONDAY	**SPEED/QUICKNESS**	
	Early work	Warm-up: routine #1 Quickness: X-jump (3 × 10)
	Warm-up for practice	Warm-up: jog 1/2 mile or about 5 min, general warm-up and dynamic warm-up routine #2 Flexibility: daily dozen Trunk: daily core Running: 100 yd pick-ups (6 ×), backward run (4 × 30 yd), breaks from 1B with shuffle (6 × 30 yd)
	Running	Position players: 10 × 100 yd in 10 min Pitchers: 10 × 100 yd in 10 min
	Core	Sit-ups: 3 × 50 series, 1 × 100 series, 2 × 10 leg drops MD balls: off-center (3 positions), back toss-over
	Cool-down	Daily dozen
	STRENGTH/POWER	
	Strength	**Workloads:** Beginners: do all reps in the first set Advanced players: do a pyramid Core–4 × 8 Core–1 × 8; 4 × 6 × 75% Assist–3 × 10 Assist–3 × 10 × 65% **Exercises:** Position players: DB lunge (core), calf raise, leg press (core), leg curl, multihip, back extension Pitchers: DB lunge (core), calf raise, leg press (core), leg curl, multihip, back extension
	Shoulder	Cuff and scapula
	Wrist and hand	Superset (3 × 20)

Table 4.3 Spring Training (Week 19) – Performance Training – "Train to Play"

	Activity	Exercises and Drills
TUESDAY	**SPEED/QUICKNESS**	
	Early work	Warm-up: routine #1 Quickness: X-hop (3 × 10)
	Warm-up for practice	Warm-up: jog 1/2 mile or about 5 min, general warm-up and dynamic warm-up routine #2 Flexibility: daily dozen Trunk: daily core Running: 100 yd pick-ups (6 ×), backward run (4 × 30 yd), breaks from 1B with shuffle (6 × 30 yd)

Table 4.3 Spring Training (Week 19) – Performance Training – "Train to Play"

	Activity	Exercises and Drills
TUESDAY	**SPEED/QUICKNESS**	
	Running	Position players: build-up 10 × 50 yd Pitchers: poles 5 ×, 10 × 60 yd
	Core	Sit-ups: 3 × 50 series 1 × 100 series 2 × 10 leg drops MD balls: off-center (3 positions) Back toss-over
	Cool-down	Daily dozen
	STRENGTH/POWER	
	Strength	**Workloads:** Beginners: do all reps in the first set · Advanced players: do a pyramid Core–4 × 8 · Core–1 × 8; 4 × 6 × 75% Assist–3 × 10 · Assist–3 × 10 × 65% **Exercises:** Position players: DB bench (core), lat pull (w), DB incline fly, seated row, triceps press, DB curl Pitchers: DB bench +, lat pull (w), DB shrug, triceps press, DB curl + substitute push-up or push-up plus

Table 4.3 Spring Training (Week 19) – Performance Training – "Train to Play"

	Activity	Exercises and Drills
WEDNESDAY	**SPEED/QUICKNESS**	
	Early work	Warm-up: routine #1 Quickness: wall run (3 × 10)
	Warm-up for practice	Warm-up: jog 1/2 mile or about 5 min, general warm-up and dynamic warm-up routine #2 Flexibility: daily dozen Trunk: daily core Running: 100 yd pick-ups (6 ×), backward run (4 × 30 yd), breaks from 1B with shuffle (6 × 30 yd)
	Running	Position players: jog 12 min Pitchers: 14 × 100 yd, jog 10 min
	Core	Sit-ups: 3 × 50 series, 1 × 100 series, 2 × 10 leg drops MD balls: lat twist (3 positions), wood chopper

(continued)

Table 4.3 Spring Training *(Week 19, continued)*

	Activity	Exercises and Drills
WEDNESDAY	**Cool-down**	Daily dozen
	STRENGTH/POWER	
	Strength	**Workloads:** Beginners: do all reps in the first set Advanced players: do a pyramid Core–4 × 8 Core–1 × 8; 4 × 6 × 75% Assist–3 × 10 Assist–3 × 10 × 65%
	Shoulder	Cuff and scapula
	Wrist and hand	Superset (3 × 20)

Table 4.3 Spring Training (Week 19) – Performance Training – "Train to Play"

	Activity	Exercises and Drills
THURSDAY	**SPEED/QUICKNESS**	
	Early work	Warm-up: routine #1 Quickness: dot drill (3 ×)
	Warm-up for practice	Warm-up: jog 1/2 mile or about 5 min, general warm-up and dynamic warm-up routine #2 Flexibility: daily dozen Trunk: daily core Running: 100 yd pick-ups (6 ×), backward run (4 × 30 yd), breaks from 1B with shuffle (6 × 30 yd)
	Running	Position players: 8 × (15:15) Pitchers: poles × 12, 10 × 60 yards
	Core	Sit-ups: 3 × 50 series, 1 × 100 series, 2 × 10 leg drops MD balls: lat twist (3 positions), wood chopper
	Cool-down	Daily dozen
	STRENGTH/POWER	
	Strength	**Workloads:** Beginners: do all reps in the first set Advanced players: do a pyramid Core–4 × 8 Core–1 × 8; 4 × 6 × 75% Assist–3 × 10 Assist–3 × 10 × 65% **Exercises:** Position players: DB squat (core), calf raise, step-up (core), leg curl, split-squat, back extension Pitchers: DB squat (core), calf raise, step-up (core), leg curl, split-squat, back extension

Table 4.3 Spring Training (Week 19) – Performance Training – "Train to Play"

	Activity	Exercises and Drills
FRIDAY	**SPEED/QUICKNESS**	
	Early work	Warm-up: routine #1 Quickness: hip twist (3 × 10)
	Warm-up for practice	Warm-up: jog 1/2 mile or about 5 min, general warm-up and dynamic warm-up routine #2 Flexibility: daily dozen Trunk: daily core Running: 100 yd pick-ups (6 ×), backward run (4 × 30 yd), breaks from 1B with shuffle (6 × 30 yd)
	Running	Position players: hollow sprint 10 × 50 yd Pitchers: 10 × (30:30), jog 10 min
	Core	Sit-ups: 3 × 50 series, 1 × 100 series, 2 × 10 leg drops MD balls: off-center (3 positions), back toss-over
	Cool-down	Daily dozen
	STRENGTH/POWER	
	Strength	**Workloads:** Beginners: do all reps in the first set	Advanced players: do a pyramid Core–4 × 8	Core–1 × 8; 4 × 6 × 75% Assist–3 × 10	Assist–3 × 10 × 65% **Exercises:** Position players:	DB inc (core), lat pull (u), DB fly, DB row, rope tri, arm curl* Pitchers:	DB inc +, lat pull (u), DB fly, DB row, rope tri, arm curl* +substitute push-up or push-up plus *substitute machine or hammer curl
	Shoulder	Cuff and scapula
	Wrist and hand	Superset (3 × 20)

Table 4.3 Spring Training (Week 19) – Performance Training – "Train to Play"

	Activity	Exercises and Drills
SATURDAY	**SPEED/QUICKNESS**	
	Early work	Warm-up: routine #1 Quickness: quicks (3 × 10)
	Warm-up for practice	Warm-up: jog 1/2 mile or about 5 min, general warm-up and dynamic warm-up routine #2

(continued)

Table 4.3 Spring Training *(Week 19, continued)*

	Activity	Exercises and Drills
SATURDAY	**SPEED/QUICKNESS** *(continued)*	
	Warm-up for practice *(continued)*	Flexibility: daily dozen Trunk: daily core Running: 100 yd pick-ups (6 ×), backward run (4 × 30 yd), breaks from 1B with shuffle (6 × 30 yd)
	Running	Position players: bases (5 ×): H to 1B, 1B to 3B, H to 2B, 2B to H, H to 3B, H to H (1×) Pitchers: 10 × 100 yd in 10 min
	Core	Sit-ups: 3 × 50 series, 2 × 100 series, 2 × 20 leg drops MD balls: off-center (3 positions), back toss-over
	Cool-down	Daily dozen

Table 4.3 Spring Training (Week 19) – Performance Training – "Train to Play"

	Activity	Exercises and Drills
SUNDAY	**SPEED/QUICKNESS**	
	Early work	Warm-up: routine #1
	Warm-up for practice	Warm-up: jog 1/2 mile or about 5 min, general warm-up and dynamic warm-up routine #2 Flexibility: daily dozen Trunk: daily core Running: 100 yd pick-ups (6 ×), backward run (4 × 30 yd), breaks from 1B with shuffle (6 × 30 yd)
	Running	Position players: optional Pitchers: optional
	Core	Sit-ups: 3 × 50 series, 1 × 100 series, 2 × 10 leg drops MD balls: off-center (3 positions), back toss-over
	Cool-down	Daily dozen

Table 4.4 Spring Training (Week 20) – Performance Training – "Train to Play"

	Activity	Exercises and Drills
MONDAY	**SPEED/QUICKNESS**	
	Early work	Warm-up: routine #1 Quickness: ladder (2 ×): crossover, back crossover, hopscotch, alt hopscotch
	Warm-up for practice	Warm-up: jog 1/2 mile or about 5 min, general warm-up and dynamic warm-up routine #2 Flexibility: daily dozen

Table 4.4 Spring Training (Week 20) – Performance Training – "Train to Play"

	Activity	Exercises and Drills
MONDAY	**SPEED/QUICKNESS (continued)**	
	Warm-up for practice (continued)	Trunk: daily core Running: 100 yd pick-ups (6 ×), backward run (4 × 30 yd), breaks from 1B with shuffle (6 × 30 yd)
	Running	Position players: 10 × 100 yd in 10 min Pitchers: 10 × 100 yd in 10 min
	Core	Sit-ups: 3 × 50 series, 2 × 100 series, 2 × 20 leg drops MD balls: off-center (3 positions), back toss-over
	Cool-down	Daily dozen
	STRENGTH/POWER	
	Strength	**Workloads:** Position players Beginners: do all reps in the first set Advanced players: do a pyramid Core–4 × 8 Core–1 × 8; 4 × 6 × 80% Assist–3 × 10 Assist–2 × 10; 1 × 8 × 70% See table 4.3 for specific exercises
	Shoulder	Cuff and scapula
	Wrist and hand	Superset (3 × 20)

Table 4.4 Spring Training (Week 20) – Performance Training – "Train to Play"

	Activity	Exercises and Drills
TUESDAY	**SPEED/QUICKNESS**	
	Early work	Warm-up: routine #1 Quickness: hurdle (2 ×): high with 4, high with 3, high with 2, crossover with 2
	Warm-up for practice	Warm-up: jog 1/2 mile or about 5 min, general warm-up and dynamic warm-up routine #2 Flexibility: daily dozen Trunk: daily core Running: 100 yd pick-ups (6 ×); backward run (4 × 30 yd) breaks from 1B with shuffle (6 × 30 yd)
	Running	Position players: build-up 10 × 50 yd Pitchers: poles × 14, 10 × 60 yd
	Core	Sit-ups: 3 × 50 series, 2 × 100 series, 2 × 20 leg drops MD balls: off-center (3 positions), back toss-over
	Cool-down	Daily dozen

(continued)

Table 4.4 Spring Training *(Week 20, continued)*

	Activity	Exercises and Drills
TUESDAY	**STRENGTH/POWER**	
	Strength	**Workloads:** Position players Beginners: do all reps in the first set Core–4 × 8 Assist–3 × 10 Advanced players: do a pyramid Core–1 × 8; 4 × 6 × 80% Assist–2 × 10; 1 × 8 × 70% See table 4.3 for specific exercises

Table 4.4 Spring Training (Week 20) – Performance Training – "Train to Play"

	Activity	Exercises and Drills
WEDNESDAY	**SPEED/QUICKNESS**	
	Early work	Warm-up: routine #1 Quickness: hip twist 5-10-5 (2 ×): forward, backward, shuffle, F/B/shuffle

	Warm-up for practice	Warm-up: jog 1/2 mile or about 5 min, general warm-up and dynamic
		  warm-up routine #2
		Flexibility: daily dozen
		Trunk: daily core
		Running: 100 yd pick-ups (6 ×), backward run (4 × 30 yd), breaks from 1B
		  with shuffle (6 × 30 yd)

	Running	Position players: jog 12 min Pitchers: 14 × 100 yd, jog 10 min
	Core	Sit-ups: 3 × 50 series, 2 × 100 series, 2 × 20 leg drops MD balls: lat twist (3 positions), wood chopper
	Cool-down	Daily dozen
	STRENGTH/POWER	
	Shoulder	Cuff and scapula
	Wrist and hand	Superset (3 × 20)

Table 4.4 Spring Training (Week 20) – Performance Training – "Train to Play"

	Activity	Exercises and Drills
THURSDAY	**SPEED/QUICKNESS**	
	Early work	Warm-up: routine #1 Quickness: get up (2 ×): head-first, feet-first, dive back
	Warm-up for practice	Warm-up: jog 1/2 mile or about 5 min, general warm-up and dynamic warm-up routine #2

Table 4.4 Spring Training (Week 20) – Performance Training – "Train to Play"

	Activity	Exercises and Drills
THURSDAY	**SPEED/QUICKNESS** *(continued)*	
	Warm-up for practice *(continued)*	Flexibility: daily dozen Trunk: daily core Running: 100 yd pick-ups (6 ×), backward run (4 × 30 yd), breaks from 1B with shuffle (6 × 30 yd)
	Running	Position players: 8 × (15:15) Pitchers: poles × 12, 10 × 60
	Core	Sit-ups: 3 × 50 series, 2 × 100 series, 2 × 20 leg drops MD balls: lat twist (3 positions), wood chopper
	Cool-down	Daily dozen
	STRENGTH/POWER	
	Strength	**Workloads:** Position players Beginners: do all reps in the first set Advanced players: do a pyramid Core–4 × 8 Core–1 × 8; 4 × 6 × 80% Assist–3 × 10 Assist–2 × 10; 1 × 8 × 70% See table 4.3 for specific exercises

Table 4.4 Spring Training (Week 20) – Performance Training – "Train to Play"

	Activity	Exercises and Drills
FRIDAY	**SPEED/QUICKNESS**	
	Early work	Warm-up: routine #1 Quickness: ladder (2 ×): crossover, back crossover, hopscotch, alt hopscotch
	Warm-up for practice	Warm-up: jog 1/2 mile or about 5 min, general warm-up and dynamic warm-up routine #2 Flexibility: daily dozen Trunk: daily core Running: 100 yd pick-ups (6 ×), backward run (4 × 30 yd), breaks from 1B with shuffle (6 × 30 yd)
	Running	Position players: hollow sprint 10 × 50 yd Pitchers: 10 × (30:30), jog 10 min
	Core	Sit-ups: 3 × 50 series, 2 × 100 series, 2 × 20 leg drops MD balls: off center (3 positions), back toss-over
	Cool-down	Daily dozen
	STRENGTH/POWER	
	Strength	**Workloads:** Position players Beginners: do all reps in the first set Advanced players: do a pyramid Core–4 × 8 Core–1 × 8; 4 × 6 × 80% Assist–3 × 10 Assist–2 × 10; 1 × 8 × 70% See table 4.3 for specific exercises

(continued)

Table 4.4 Spring Training *(Week 20, continued)*

	Activity	Exercises and Drills
FRIDAY	**STRENGTH/POWER** *(continued)*	
	Shoulder	Cuff and scapula
	Wrist and hand	Superset (3 × 20)

Table 4.4 Spring Training (Week 20) – Performance Training – "Train to Play"

	Activity	Exercises and Drills
SATURDAY	**SPEED/QUICKNESS**	
	Early work	Warm-up: routine #1 Quickness: hurdle (2 ×): high with 4, high with 3, high with 2, crossover with 2
	Warm-up for practice	Warm-up: jog 1/2 mile or about 5 min, general warm-up and dynamic warm-up routine #2 Flexibility: daily dozen Trunk: daily core Running: 100 yd pick-ups (6 ×), backward run (4 × 30 yd), breaks from 1B with shuffle (6 × 30 yd)
	Running	Position players: bases (5 ×): H to 1B, 1B to 3B, H to 2B, 2B to H, H to 3B, H to H (1 ×) Pitchers: 10 × 100 yd in 10 min
	Core	Sit-ups: 3 × 50 series, 2 × 100 series, 2 × 20 leg drops MD balls: off-center (3 positions), back toss-over
	Cool-down	Daily dozen

Table 4.4 Spring Training (Week 20) – Performance Training – "Train to Play"

	Activity	Exercises and Drills
SUNDAY	**SPEED/QUICKNESS**	
	Early work	Warm-up: routine #1 Quickness: get-up (2 ×): head-first, feet-first, dive back
	Warm-up for practice	Warm-up: jog 1/2 mile or about 5 min, general warm-up and dynamic warm-up routine #2 Flexibility: daily dozen Trunk: daily core Running: 100 yd pick-ups (6 ×), backward run (4 × 30 yd), breaks from 1B with shuffle (6 × 30 yd)
	Running	Position players: optional Pitchers: optional
	Core	Sit-ups: repeat Wed/Thurs workout
	Cool-down	Daily dozen

Table 4.5 Spring Training (Week 21) – Performance Training – "Train to Play"

	Activity	Exercises and Drills
MONDAY	**SPEED/QUICKNESS**	
	Early work	Warm-up: routine #1 Quickness: ladder (2 ×): crossover, back crossover, hopscotch, alt hopscotch
	Warm-up for practice	Warm-up: jog 1/2 mile or about 5 min, general warm-up and dynamic warm-up routine #2 Flexibility: daily dozen Trunk: daily core Running: 100 yd pick-ups (6 ×), backward run (4 × 30 yd), breaks from 1B with shuffle (6 × 30 yd)
	Running	Position players: bases (5 ×): H to 1B, 1B to 3B, H to 2B, 2B to H, H to 3B, H to H (1 ×) Game pitcher: choose one of the following options after coming out of the game: 1. 10 pole sprints @ 45 sec 2. 10 × (15:15) 3. 10 poles and 10 × 100 yd 4. Simulate 4 innings Non-game pitcher: run 10 × 100 yd in 10 min
	Core	Sit-ups: 4 × 50 series, 2 × 100 series, 2 × 20 leg drops MD balls: off-center (3 positions), back toss-over
	Cool-down	Daily dozen
	STRENGTH/POWER	
	Strength	**Workloads:** Position players Beginners: do all reps in the first set Core–4 × 6 Assist–3 × 10 See table 4.3 for specific exercises Advanced players: do a pyramid. Core–1 × 8; 4 × 6 × 85% Assist–1 × 10; 2 × 8 × 75%
	Shoulder	Cuff and scapula
	Wrist and hand	Superset (3 × 20)

Table 4.5 Spring Training (Week 21) – Performance Training – "Train to Play"

	Activity	Exercises and Drills
TUESDAY	**SPEED/QUICKNESS**	
	Early work	Warm-up: routine #1 Quickness: hurdle (2 ×): high with 4, high with 3, high with 2, crossover with 2
	Warm-up for practice	Warm-up: jog 1/2 mile or about 5 min, general warm-up and dynamic warm-up routine #2 Flexibility: daily dozen Trunk: daily core Running: 100 yd pick-ups (6 ×), backward run (4 × 30 yd), breaks from 1B with shuffle (6 × 30 yd)

(continued)

Table 4.5 Spring Training *(Week 21, continued)*

	Activity	Exercises and Drills
TUESDAY	**SPEED/QUICKNESS** *(continued)*	
	Running	Position players: 10 × 100 yd Game pitcher: choose one of the following options after coming out of the game: 1. 10 pole sprints @ 45 sec 2. 10 × (15:15) 3. 10 poles and 10 ×100 yd 4. Simulate 4 innings Non-game pitcher: bases (5 ×): H to 1B, 1B to 3B, H to 2B, 2B to H, H to 3B, H to H (1 ×)
	Core	Sit-ups: 4 × 50 series, 2 × 100 series, 2 × 20 leg drops MD balls: off-center (3 positions), back toss-over
	Cool-down	Daily dozen
	STRENGTH/POWER	
	Strength	**Workloads:** Position players Beginners: do all reps in the first set Advanced players: do a pyramid Core–4 × 6 Core–1 × 8; 4 × 6 × 85% Assist–3 × 10 Assist–1 × 10; 2 × 8 × 75% See table 4.3 for specific exercises
	Shoulder	Cuff and scapula

Table 4.5 Spring Training (Week 21) – Performance Training – "Train to Play"

	Activity	Exercises and Drills
WEDNESDAY	**SPEED/QUICKNESS**	
	Early work	Warm-up: routine #1 Quickness: hip twist 5-10-5 (2 ×): forward, backward, shuffle, F/B/shuffle
	Warm-up for practice	Warm-up: jog 1/2 mile or about 5 min, general warm-up and dynamic warm-up routine #2 Flexibility: daily dozen Trunk: daily core Running: 100 yd pick-ups (6 ×), backward run (4 × 30 yd), breaks from 1B with shuffle (6 × 30 yd)
	Running	Position players: breaks 10 × 60 yd Game pitcher: choose one of the following options after coming out of the game: 1. 10 pole sprints @ 45 sec 2. 10 × (15:15) 3. 10 poles and 10 × 100 yd 4. Simulate 4 innings Non-game pitcher: pole sprint 10 ×, 10 × 60 yd

Table 4.5 Spring Training (Week 21) – Performance Training – "Train to Play"

	Activity	Exercises and Drills
WEDNESDAY	**SPEED/QUICKNESS** *(continued)*	
	Core	Sit-ups: 4 × 50 series, 2 × 100 series, 2 × 20 leg drops MD balls: lat twist (3 positions), wood chopper
	Cool-down	Daily dozen
	STRENGTH/POWER	
	Shoulder	Cuff and scapula
	Wrist and hand	Superset (3 × 20)

Table 4.5 Spring Training (Week 21) – Performance Training – "Train to Play"

	Activity	Exercises and Drills
THURSDAY	**SPEED/QUICKNESS**	
	Early work	Warm-up: routine #1 Quickness: get up (2 ×): head first, feet-first, dive back

	Warm-up for practice	Warm-up: jog 1/2 mile or about 5 min, general warm-up and dynamic
		  warm-up routine #2
		Flexibility: daily dozen
		Trunk: daily core
		Running: 100 yd pick-ups (6 ×), backward run (4 × 30 yd), breaks from 1B
		  with shuffle (6 × 30 yd)

	Running	Position players: 10 × (15:15) Game pitcher: choose one of the following options after coming out of the game: 1. 10 pole sprints @ 45 sec 2. 10 × (15:15) 3. 10 poles and 10 ×100 yd 4. Simulate 4 innings Non-game pitcher: poles × 16, 10 × 60 yd
	Core	Sit-ups: 4 × 50 series, 2 × 100 series, 2 × 20 leg drops MD balls: lat twist (3 positions), wood chopper
	Cool-down	Daily dozen
	STRENGTH/POWER	
	Strength	**Workloads:** Position players Beginners: do all reps in the first set / Advanced players: do a pyramid Core–4 × 6 / Core–1 × 8; 4 × 6 × 85% Assist–3 × 10 / Assist–1 × 10; 2 × 8 × 75% See table 4.3 for specific exercises

(continued)

Table 4.5 Spring Training (Week 21) – Performance Training – "Train to Play"

	Activity	Exercises and Drills
FRIDAY	**SPEED/QUICKNESS**	
	Early work	Warm-up: routine #1 Quickness: ladder (2 ×): crossover, back crossover, hopscotch, alt hopscotch
	Warm-up for practice	Warm-up: jog 1/2 mile or about 5 min, general warm-up and dynamic warm-up routine #2 Flexibility: daily dozen Trunk: daily core Running: 100 yd pick-ups (6 ×), backward run (4 × 30 yd), breaks from 1B with shuffle (6 × 30 yd)
	Running	Position players: breaks 10 × 60 yd Game pitcher: choose one of the following options after coming out of the game: 1. 10 pole sprints @ 45 sec 2. 10 × (15:15) 3. 10 poles and 10 × 100 yd 4. Simulate 4 innings Non-game pitcher: 10 × (30:30), jog in 10 min
	Core	Sit-ups: 4 × 50 series, 2 × 100 series, 2 × 20 leg drops MD balls: off center (3 positions), back toss-over
	Cool-down	Daily dozen
	STRENGTH/POWER	
	Strength	**Workloads:** Position players Beginners: do all reps in the first set Advanced players: do a pyramid Core–4 × 6 Core–1 × 8; 4 × 6 × 85% Assist–3 × 10 Assist–1 × 10; 2 × 8 × 75% See table 4.3 for specific exercises
	Shoulder	Cuff and scapula
	Wrist and hand	Superset (3 × 20)

Table 4.5 Spring Training (Week 21) – Performance Training – "Train to Play"

	Activity	Exercises and Drills
SATURDAY	**SPEED/QUICKNESS**	
	Early Work	Warm-up: routine #1 Quickness: hurdle (2 ×): high with 4, high with 3, high with 2, crossover with 2
	Warm-up for practice	Warm-up: jog 1/2 mile or about 5 min, general warm-up and dynamic warm-up routine #2 Flexibility: daily dozen

Table 4.5 Spring Training (Week 21) – Performance Training – "Train to Play"

	Activity	Exercises and Drills
	SPEED/QUICKNESS *(continued)*	
SATURDAY	**Warm-up for practice** *(continued)*	Trunk: daily core Running: 100 yd pick-ups (6 ×), backward run (4 × 30 yd), breaks from 1B with shuffle (6 × 30 yd)
	Running	Postion players: 10 × 100 yd in 10 min Game pitcher: choose one of the following options after coming out of the game: 1. 10 pole sprints @ 45 sec 2. 10 × (15:15) 3. 10 poles and 10 ×100 yd 4. Simulate 4 innings Non-game pitcher: poles × 16 10 × 60 yd
	Core	Sit-ups: 4 × 50 series, 2 × 100 series, 2 × 20 leg drops MD balls: lat twist (3 positions), wood chopper
	Cool-down	Daily dozen

Table 4.5 Spring Training (Week 21) – Performance Training – "Train to Play"

	Activity	Exercises and Drills
	SPEED/QUICKNESS	
SUNDAY	**Early work**	Warm-up: routine #1 Quickness: get up (2 ×): head-first, feet-first, dive back
	Warm-up for practice	Warm-up: jog 1/2 mile or about 5 min, general warm-up and dynamic warm-up routine #2 Flexibility: daily dozen Trunk: daily core Running: 100 yd pick-ups (6 ×), backward run (4 × 30 yd), breaks from 1B with shuffle (6 × 30 yd)
	Running	Position players: optional Game pitcher: choose one of the following options after coming out of the game: 1. 10 pole sprints @ 45 sec 2. 10 × (15:15) 3. 10 poles and 10 × 100 yd 4. Simulate 4 innings Non-game pitcher: pole sprint 10 ×, 10 × 60 yd
	Core	Sit-ups: 4 × 50 series, 2 × 100 series, 2 × 20 leg drops MD balls: lat twist (3 positions), wood chopper
	Cool-down	Daily dozen

(continued)

Table 4.6 Spring Training (Week 22) – Performance Training – "Train to Play"

	Activity	Exercises and Drills
MONDAY	**SPEED/QUICKNESS**	
	Early work	Warm-up: routine #1 Quickness: dot drill (3 ×)
	Warm-up for practice	Warm-up: jog 1/2 mile or about 5 min, general warm-up and dynamic warm-up routine #2 Flexibility: daily dozen Trunk: daily core Running: 100 yd pick-ups (6 ×), backward run (4 × 30 yd), breaks from 1B with shuffle (6 × 30 yd)
	Running	Position players: bases (5 ×) Game pitcher: choose one of the following options after coming out of the game: 1. 10 pole sprints @ 45 sec 2. 10 × (15:15) 3. 10 poles and 10 × 100 yd 4. Simulate 4 innings Non-game pitcher: 10 × 100 yd in 10 min
	Core	Sit-ups: 4 × 50 series, 2 × 100 series, 2 × 20 leg drops MD balls: off-center (3 positions), back toss-over
	Cool-down	Daily dozen
	STRENGTH/POWER	
	Strength	**Workloads:** Position players Beginners: do all reps in the first set Advanced players: do a pyramid Core–4× 6 Core–1 × 8; 4 × 4 × 88% Assist–3 × 8 Assist–3 × 8 × 80% See table 4.3 for specific exercises
	Shoulder	Cuff and scapula
	Wrist and hand	Superset (3 × 20)

Table 4.6 Spring Training (Week 22) – Performance Training – "Train to Play"

	Activity	Exercises and Drills
TUESDAY	**SPEED/QUICKNESS**	
	Early work	Warm-up: routine #1 Quickness: hip twist (3 × 10)
	Warm-up for practice	Warm-up: jog 1/2 mile or about 5 min, general warm-up and dynamic warm-up routine #2 Flexibility: daily dozen Trunk: daily core Running: 100 yd pick-ups (6 ×), backward run (4 × 30 yd), breaks from 1B with shuffle (6 × 30 yd)

Table 4.6 Spring Training (Week 22) – Performance Training – "Train to Play"

	Activity	Exercises and Drills
TUESDAY	**SPEED/QUICKNESS** *(continued)*	
	Running	Position players: 10 × 100 yd Game pitcher: choose one of the following options after coming out of the game: 1. 10 pole sprints @ 45 sec 2. 10 × (15:15) 3. 10 poles and 10 × 100 yd 4. Simulate 4 innings Non-game pitcher: pole sprints 10 ×, 10 × 60 yd
	Core	Sit-ups: 4 × 50 series, 2 × 100 series, 2 × 20 leg drops MD balls: off-center (3 positions), back toss-over
	Cool-down	Daily dozen
	STRENGTH/POWER	
	Strength	**Workloads:** Position players Beginners: do all reps in the first set Advanced players: do a pyramid Core–4 × 6 Core–1 × 8; 4 × 4 × 88% Assist–3 × 8 Assist–3 × 8 × 80% See table 4.3 for specific exercises

Table 4.6 Spring Training (Week 22) – Performance Training – "Train to Play"

	Activity	Exercises and Drills
WEDNESDAY	**SPEED/QUICKNESS**	
	Early Work	Warm-up: routine #1 Quickness: quicks (3 × 10)
	Warm-up for practice	Warm-up: jog 1/2 mile or about 5 min, general warm-up and dynamic warm-up routine #2 Flexibility: daily dozen Trunk: daily core Running: 100 yd pick-ups (6 ×), backward run (4 × 30 yd), breaks from 1B with shuffle (6 × 30 yd)
	Running	Position players: breaks 10 × 60 yd Game pitcher: choose one of the following options after coming out of the game: 1. 10 pole sprints @ 45 sec 2. 10 × (15:15) 3. 10 poles and 10 × 100 yd 4. Simulate 4 innings Non-game pitcher: 10 × 100 yd in 10 min
	Core	Sit-ups: 4 × 50 series, 2 × 100 series, 2 × 20 leg drops MD balls: lat twist (3 positions), wood chopper

(continued)

Table 4.6 Spring Training *(Week 22, continued)*

	Activity	Exercises and Drills
WEDNESDAY	**Cool-down**	Daily dozen
	STRENGTH/POWER	
	Shoulder	Cuff and scapula
	Wrist and hand	Superset (3 × 20)

Table 4.6 Spring Training (Week 22) – Performance Training – "Train to Play"

	Activity	Exercises and Drills
THURSDAY	**SPEED/QUICKNESS**	
	Early work	Warm-up: routine #1 Quickness: get up (2 ×): head-first, feet-first, dive back
	Warm-up for practice	Warm-up: jog 1/2 mile or about 5 min, general warm-up and dynamic warm-up routine #2 Flexibility: daily dozen Trunk: daily core Running: 100 yd pick-ups (6 ×), backward run (4 × 30 yd), breaks from 1B with shuffle (6 × 30 yd)
	Running	Position players: 10 × (15:15) Game pitcher: choose one of the following options after coming out of the game: 1. 10 pole sprints @ 45 sec 2. 10 × (15:15) 3. 10 poles and 10 × 100 yd 4. Simulate 4 innings 1. 10 pole sprints @ 45 sec 2. 10 × (15:15) Non-game pitcher: poles × 16, 10 × 60 yd
	Core	Game pitcher: choose one of the following options after coming out of the game: Sit-ups: 4 × 50 series, 2 × 100 series, 2 × 20 leg drops MD balls: lat twist (3 positions), wood chopper
	Cool-down	Daily dozen
	STRENGTH/POWER	
	Strength	**Workloads:** Position players Beginners: do all reps in the first set — Advanced players: do a pyramid Core–4 × 6 — Core–1 × 8; 4 × 4 × 88% Assist–3 × 8 — Assist–3 × 8 × 80% See table 4.3 for specific exercises

Table 4.6 Spring Training (Week 22) – Performance Training – "Train to Play"

	Activity	Exercises and Drills
FRIDAY	**SPEED/QUICKNESS**	
	Early work	Warm-up: routine #1 Quickness: ladder (2 ×): crossover, back crossover, hopscotch, alt hopscotch
	Warm-up and practice	Warm-up: jog 1/2 mile or about 5 min, general warm-up and dynamic warm-up routine #2 Flexibility: daily dozen Trunk: daily core Running: 100 yd pick-ups (6 ×), backward run (4 × 30 yd), breaks from 1B with shuffle (6 × 30 yd)
	Running	Position players: breaks 10 × 60 yd Game pitcher: choose one of the following options after coming out of the game: 1. 10 pole sprints @ 45 sec 2. 10 × (15:15) 3. 10 poles and 10 × 100 yd 4. Simulate 4 innings Non-game pitcher: 10 × (30:30) jog in 10 min
	Core	Sit-ups: 4 × 50 series, 2 × 100 series, 2 × 20 leg drops MD balls: off center (3 positions), back toss-over
	Cool-down	Daily dozen
	STRENGTH/POWER	
	Strength	**Workloads:** Position players Beginners: do all reps in the first set Core–4 × 6 Assist–3 × 8 See table 4.3 for specific exercises Advanced players: do a pyramid Core–1 × 8; 4 × 4 × 88% Assist–3 × 8 × 80%
	Shoulder	Cuff and scapula
	Wrist and hand	Superset (3 × 20)

Table 4.6 Spring Training (Week 22) – Performance Training – "Train to Play"

	Activity	Exercises and Drills
SATURDAY	**SPEED/QUICKNESS**	
	Early work	Warm-up: routine #1 Quickness: hurdle (2 ×): high with 4, high with 3, high with 2, crossover with 2
	Warm-up for practice	Warm-up: jog 1/2 mile or about 5 min, general warm-up and dynamic warm-up routine #2 Flexibility: daily dozen Trunk: daily core

(continued)

Table 4.6 Spring Training *(Week 22, continued)*

	Activity	Exercises and Drills
SATURDAY	**SPEED/QUICKNESS** *(continued)*	
	Warm-up for practice *(continued)*	Running: 100 yd pick-ups (6 ×), backward run (4 × 30 yd), breaks from 1B with shuffle (6 × 30 yd)
	Running	Position players: 10 × 100 yd in 10 min Game pitcher: choose one of the following options after coming out of the game: 1. 10 pole sprints @ 45 sec 2. 10 × (15:15) 3. 10 poles and 10 ×100 yd 4. Simulate 4 innings Non-game pitcher: 10 × 100 yd in 10 min
	Core	Sit-ups: 4 × 50 series, 2 × 100 series, 2 × 20 leg drops MD balls: lat twist (3 positions), wood chopper
	Cool-down	Daily dozen
	STRENGTH/POWER	
	Strength	**Workloads:** Position players Beginners: do all reps in the first set Advanced players: do a pyramid Core–4 × 6 Core–1 × 8; 4 × 4 × 88% Assist–3 × 8 Assist–3 × 8 × 80% See table 4.3 for specific exercises

Table 4.6 Spring Training (Week 22) – Performance Training – "Train to Play"

	Activity	Exercises and Drills
SUNDAY	**SPEED/QUICKNESS**	
	Early work	Warm-up: routine #1 Quickness: hip twist (3 × 10)
	Warm-up for practice	Warm-up: jog 1/2 mile or about 5 min, general warm-up and dynamic warm-up routine #2 Flexibility: daily dozen Trunk: daily core Running: 100 yd pick-ups (6 ×), backward run (4 × 30 yd), breaks from 1B with shuffle (6 × 30 yd)
	Running	Position players: optional Game pitcher: choose one of the following options after coming out of the game: 1. 10 pole sprints @ 45 sec 2. 10 × (15:15) 3. 10 poles and 10 × 100 yd 4. Simulate 4 innings Non-game pitcher: optional
	Core	Sit-ups: repeat Wed/Thurs workout
	Cool-down	Daily dozen

Table 4.7 Spring Training (Week 23) – Performance Training – "Train to Play"

	Activity	Exercises and Drills
MONDAY	**SPEED/QUICKNESS**	
	Early work	Warm-up: routine #1 Quickness: dot drill (3 ×)
	Warm-up for practice	Warm-up: jog 1/2 mile or about 5 min, general warm-up and dynamic warm-up routine #2 Flexibility: daily dozen Trunk: daily core Running: 100 yd pick-ups (6 ×), backward run (4 × 30 yd), breaks from 1B with shuffle (6 × 30 yd)
	Running	Position players: breaks 10 × 60 yd Game pitcher: choose one of the following options after coming out of the game: 1. 10 pole sprints @ 45 sec 2. 10 × (15:15) 3. 10 poles and 10 × 100 yd 4. Simulate 4 innings Non-game pitcher: 10 × 100 yd in 10 min
	Core	Sit-ups: 4 × 50 series, 2 × 100 series, 2 × 20 leg drops MD balls: off-center (3 positions), back toss-over
	Cool-down	Daily dozen
	STRENGTH/POWER	
	Strength	**Workloads:** Position players Beginners: do all reps in the first set Advanced players: do a pyramid Core–4 × 4 Core–1 × 8; 4 × 3 × 90% Assist–3 × 8 Assist–2 × 8; 1 × 6 × 85% See table 4.3 for specific exercises
	Shoulder	Cuff and scapula
	Wrist and hand	Superset (3 × 20)

Table 4.7 Spring Training (Week 23) – Performance Training – "Train to Play"

	Activity	Exercises and Drills
TUESDAY	**SPEED/QUICKNESS**	
	Early work	Warm-up: routine #1 Quickness: hip twist (3 × 10)
	Warm-up for practice	Warm-up: jog 1/2 mile or about 5 min, general warm-up and dynamic warm-up routine #2 Flexibility: daily dozen Trunk: daily core

Table 4.7 Spring Training *(Week 23, continued)*

<table>
<tr><th colspan="2">Activity</th><th>Exercises and Drills</th></tr>
<tr><td rowspan="11" style="writing-mode:vertical">TUESDAY</td><td colspan="2">SPEED/QUICKNESS (continued)</td></tr>
<tr><td>Warm-up for practice (continued)</td><td>Running: 100 yd pick-ups (6 ×), backward run (4 × 30 yd), breaks from 1B with shuffle (6 × 30 yd)</td></tr>
<tr><td>Running</td><td>Position players: 10 × 100 yd
Game pitcher: choose one of the following options after coming out of the game:
1. 10 pole sprints @ 45 sec
2. 10 × (15:15)
3. 10 poles and 10 × 100 yd
4. Simulate 4 innings
Non-game pitcher: pole sprints 10 × 10 × 60 yd</td></tr>
<tr><td>Core</td><td>Sit-ups: 4 × 50 series, 2 × 100 series, 2 × 20 leg drops
MD balls: off-center (3 positions), back toss-over</td></tr>
<tr><td>Cool-down</td><td>Daily dozen</td></tr>
<tr><td colspan="2">STRENGTH/POWER</td></tr>
<tr><td>Strength</td><td>Workloads: Position players
Beginners: do all reps in the first set   Advanced players: do a pyramid
Core–4 × 4   Core–1 × 8; 4 × 3 × 90%
Assist–3 × 8   Assist–2 × 8; 1 × 6 × 85%
See table 4.3 for specific exercises</td></tr>
</table>

Table 4.7 Spring Training (Week 23) – Performance Training – "Train to Play"

<table>
<tr><th colspan="2">Activity</th><th>Exercises and Drills</th></tr>
<tr><td rowspan="5" style="writing-mode:vertical">WEDNESDAY</td><td colspan="2">SPEED/QUICKNESS</td></tr>
<tr><td>Early work</td><td>Warm-up: routine #1
Quickness: quicks (3 × 10)</td></tr>
<tr><td>Warm-up for practice</td><td>Warm-up: jog 1/2 mile or about 5 min, general warm-up and dynamic warm-up routine #2
Flexibility: daily dozen
Trunk: daily core
Running: 100 yd pick-ups (6 ×), backward run (4 × 30 yd), breaks from 1B with shuffle (6 × 30 yd)</td></tr>
<tr><td>Running</td><td>Position players: breaks 10 × 60 yd
Game pitcher: choose one of the following options after coming out of the game:
1. 10 pole sprints @ 45 sec
2. 10 × (15:15)
3. 10 poles and 10 × 100 yd
4. Simulate 4 innings
Non-game pitcher: 10 × 100 yd in 10 min</td></tr>
</table>

Table 4.7 Spring Training (Week 23) – Performance Training – "Train to Play"

	Activity	Exercises and Drills
WEDNESDAY	**SPEED/QUICKNESS** *(continued)*	
	Core	Sit-ups: 4 3 50 series, 2 3 100 series, 2 3 20 leg drops MD balls: lat twist (3 positions), wood chopper
	Cool-down	Daily dozen
	STRENGTH/POWER	
	Strength	**Workloads:** Position players Beginners: do all reps in the first set Advanced players: do a pyramid Core–4 × 4 Core–1 × 8; 4 × 3 × 90% Assist–3 × 8 Assist–2 × 8; 1 × 6 × 85% See table 4.3 for specific exercises
	Shoulder	Cuff and scapula

Table 4.7 Spring Training (Week 23) – Performance Training – "Train to Play"

	Activity	Exercises and Drills
THURSDAY	**SPEED/QUICKNESS**	
	Early work	Warm-up: routine #1 Quickness: get up (2 ×): head-first, feet-first, dive back

	Warm-up for practice	Warm-up: jog 1/2 mile or about 5 min, general warm-up and dynamic
		  warm-up routine #2
		Flexibility: daily dozen
		Trunk: daily core
		Running: 100 yd pick-ups (6 ×), backward run (4 × 30 yd), breaks from 1B
		  with shuffle (6 × 30 yd)

	Running	Position players: 10 × (15:15) Game pitcher: choose one of the following options after coming out of the game: 1. 10 pole sprints @ 45 sec 2. 10 × (15:15) 3. 10 poles and 10 ×100 yd 4. Simulate 4 innings Non-game pitcher: poles × 18, 10 × 60 yd
	Core	Sit-ups: 4 × 50 series, 2 × 100 series, 2 × 20 leg drops MD balls: lat twist (3 positions), wood chopper
	Cool-down	Daily dozen
	STRENGTH/POWER	
	Strength	**Workloads:** Position players Beginners: do all reps in the first set Advanced players: do a pyramid Core–4 × 4 Core–1 × 8; 4 × 3 × 90% Assist–3 × 8 Assist–2 × 8; 1 × 6 × 85% See table 4.3 for specific exercises

(continued)

Table 4.7 Spring Training (Week 23) – Performance Training – "Train to Play"

	Activity	Exercises and Drills
FRIDAY	**SPEED/QUICKNESS**	
	Early Work	Warm-up: routine #1 Quickness: ladder (2 ×): crossover, back crossover, hopscotch, alt hopscotch
	Warm-up for practice	Warm-up: jog 1/2 mile or about 5 min, general warm-up and dynamic warm-up routine #2 Flexibility: daily dozen Trunk: daily core
	Running	Position players: breaks 10 × 60 yd Game pitcher: choose one of the following options after coming out of the game: 1. 10 pole sprints @ 45 sec 2. 10 × (15:15) 3. 10 poles and 10 × 100 yd 4. Simulate 4 innings Non-game pitcher: 10 × (30:30), jog 10 min
	Core	Sit-ups: 4 × 50 series, 2 × 100 series, 2 × 20 leg drops MD balls: off-center (3 positions), back toss-over
	Cool-down	Daily dozen
	STRENGTH/POWER	
	Strength	**Workloads:** Position players Beginners: do all reps in the first set / Advanced players: do a pyramid Core–4 × 4 / Core–1 × 8; 4 × 3 × 90% Assist–3 × 8 / Assist–2 × 8; 1 × 6 × 85% See table 4.3 for specific exercises
	Shoulder	Cuff and scapula
	Wrist and hand	Superset (3 × 20)

Table 4.7 Spring Training (Week 23) – Performance Training – "Train to Play"

	Activity	Exercises and Drills
SATURDAY	**SPEED/QUICKNESS**	
	Early work	Warm-up: routine #1 Quickness: hurdle (2 ×): high with 4, high with 3, high with 2, crossover with 2
	Warm-up for practice	Warm-up: jog 1/2 mile or about 5 min, general warm-up and dynamic warm-up routine #2 Flexibility: daily dozen Trunk: daily core Running: 100 yd pick-ups (6 ×), backward run (4 × 30 yd), breaks from 1B with shuffle (6 × 30 yd)

Table 4.7 Spring Training (Week 23) – Performance Training – "Train to Play"

	Activity	Exercises and Drills
SATURDAY	SPEED/QUICKNESS *(continued)*	
	Running	Position players: 10 × 100 yd in 10 min Game pitcher: choose one of the following options after coming out of the game: 1. 10 pole sprints @ 45 sec 2. 10 × (15:15) 3. 10 poles and 10 × 100 yd 4. Simulate 4 innings Non-game pitcher: 10 × 100 yd in 10 min
	Core	Sit-ups: 4 × 50 series, 2 × 100 series, 2 × 20 leg drops MD balls: off-center (3 positions), back toss-over
	Cool-down	Daily dozen
	STRENGTH/POWER	
	Strength	**Workloads:** Position players Beginners: do all reps in the first set · Advanced players: do a pyramid Core–4 × 4 · Core–1 × 8; 4 × 3 × 90% Assist–3 × 8 · Assist–2 × 8; 1 × 6 × 85% See table 4.3 for specific exercises

Table 4.7 Spring Training (Week 23) – Performance Training – "Train to Play"

	Activity	Exercises and Drills
SUNDAY	SPEED/QUICKNESS	
	Early work	Warm-up: routine #1 Quickness: hip twist (3 × 10)
	Warm-up for practice	Warm-up: jog 1/2 mile or about 5 min, general warm-up and dynamic warm-up routine #2 Flexibility: daily dozen Trunk: daily core Running: 100 yd pick-ups (6 ×), backward run (4 × 30 yd), breaks from 1B with shuffle (6 × 30 yd)
	Running	Position players: optional Game pitcher: choose one of the following options after coming out of the game: 1. 10 pole sprints @ 45 sec 2. 10 × (15:15) 3. 10 poles and 10 × 100 yd 4. Simulate 4 innings Non-game pitcher: optional
	Core	Sit-ups: repeat Wed/Thurs workout

(continued)

Table 4.7 Spring Training *(Week 23, continued)*

	Activity	Exercises and Drills
SUNDAY	**SPEED/QUICKNESS** *(continued)*	
	Cool-down	Daily dozen
	STRENGTH/POWER	
	Strength	**Workloads:** Position players Beginners: do all reps in the first set Core–4 × 4 Assist–3 × 8 See table 4.3 for specific exercises Advanced players: do a pyramid Core–1 × 8; 4 × 3 × 90% Assist–2 × 8; 1 × 6 × 85%

Table 4.8 Spring Training (Week 24) – Performance Training – "Train to Play"

	Activity	Exercises and Drills
MONDAY	**SPEED/QUICKNESS**	
	Early work	Warm-up: routine #1 Quickness: dot drill (3 ×)
	Warm-up for practice	Warm-up: jog 1/2 mile or about 5 min, general warm-up and dynamic warm-up routine #2 Flexibility: daily dozen Trunk: daily core Running: 100 yd pick-ups (6 ×), backward run (4 × 30 yd), breaks from 1B with shuffle (6 × 30 yd)
	Running	Position players: breaks 5 × 30 yd, 5 × 60 yd Game pitcher: choose one of the following options after coming out of the game: 1. 10 pole sprints @ 45 sec 2. 10 × (15:15) 3. 10 poles and 10 × 100 yd 4. Simulate 4 innings Non-game pitcher: 10 × 100 yd in 10 min
	Core	Sit-ups: 4 × 50 series, 2 × 100 series, 2 × 20 leg drops MD balls: off-center (3 positions), back toss-over
	Cool-down	Daily dozen
	STRENGTH/POWER	
	Strength	**Workloads:** Position players Beginners: do all reps in the first set Core–4 × 6 Assist–3 × 10 See table 4.3 for specific exercises Advanced players: do a pyramid Core–1 × 8; 4 × 6 × 85% Assist–1 × 10; 2 × 8 × 75%
	Shoulder	Cuff and scapula
	Wrist and hand	Superset (3 × 20)

Table 4.8 Spring Training (Week 24) – Performance Training – "Train to Play"

	Activity	Exercises and Drills
TUESDAY	**SPEED/QUICKNESS**	
	Early work	Warm-up: routine #1 Quickness: hip twist (3 × 10)
	Warm-up for practice	Warm-up: jog 1/2 mile or about 5 min, general warm-up and dynamic warm-up routine #2 Flexibility: daily dozen Trunk: daily core Running: 100 yd pick-ups (6 ×), backward run (4 × 30 yd), breaks from 1B with shuffle (6 × 30 yd)
	Running	Position players: 10 × 100 yd Game pitcher: choose one of the following options after coming out of the game: 1. 10 pole sprints @ 45 sec 2. 10 × (15:15) 3. 10 poles and 10 × 100 yd 4. Simulate 4 innings Non-game pitcher: pole sprints 10 × 10 × 60 yd
	Core	Sit-ups: 4 × 50 series, 2 × 100 series, 2 × 20 leg drops MD balls: off-center (3 positions), back toss-over
	Cool-down	Daily dozen
	STRENGTH/POWER	
	Strength	**Workloads:** Position players Beginners: do all reps in the first set Advanced players: do a pyramid Core–4 × 6 Core–1 × 8; 4 × 6 × 85% Assist–3 × 10 Assist–1 × 10; 2 × 8 × 75% See table 4.3 for specific exercises

Table 4.8 Spring Training (Week 24) – Performance Training – "Train to Play"

	Activity	Exercises and Drills
WEDNESDAY	**SPEED/QUICKNESS**	
	Early work	Warm-up: routine #1 Quickness: quicks (3 × 10)
	Warm-up for practice	Warm-up: jog 1/2 mile or about 5 min, general warm-up and dynamic warm-up routine #2 Flexibility: daily dozen Trunk: daily core Running: 100 yd pick-ups (6 ×), backward run (4 × 30 yd), breaks from 1B with shuffle (6 × 30 yd)
	Running	Position players: for breaks 5 × 30 yd 10 × 60 yd

(continued)

Table 4.8 Spring Training *(Week 24, continued)*

	Activity	Exercises and Drills
WEDNESDAY	**SPEED/QUICKNESS** *(continued)*	
	Running *(continued)*	Game pitcher: choose one of the following options after coming out of the game: 1. 10 pole sprints @ 45 sec 2. 10 × (15:15) 3. 10 poles and 10 × 100 yd 4. Simulate 4 innings Non-game pitcher: 10 × 100 yd, jog 10 min
	Core	Sit-ups: 4 × 50 series, 2 × 100 series, 2 × 20 leg drops MD balls: lat twist (3 positions), wood chopper
	Cool-down	Daily dozen
	STRENGTH/POWER	
	Shoulder	Cuff and scapula
	Wrist and hand	Superset (3 × 20)

Table 4.8 Spring Training (Week 24) – Performance Training – "Train to Play"

	Activity	Exercises and Drills
THURSDAY	**SPEED/QUICKNESS**	
	Early work	Warm-up: routine #1 Quickness: get up (2 ×): head-first, feet-first, dive back
	Warm-up for practice	Warm-up: jog 1/2 mile or about 5 min, general warm-up and dynamic warm-up routine #2 Flexibility: daily dozen Trunk: daily core Running: 100 yd pick-ups (6 ×), backward run (4 × 30 yd), breaks from 1B with shuffle (6 × 30 yd)
	Running	Position players: breaks 5 × 30 yd, 10 × 60 yd Game pitcher: choose one of the following options after coming out of the game: 1. 10 pole sprints @ 45 sec 2. 10 × (15:15) 3. 10 poles and 10 × 100 yd 4. Simulate 4 innings Non-game pitcher: poles × 18, 10 × 60 yd
	Core	Sit-ups: 4 × 50 series, 2 × 100 series, 2 × 20 leg drops MD balls: lat twist (3 positions), wood chopper
	Cool-down	Daily dozen
	STRENGTH/POWER	
	Strength	**Workloads:** Position players Beginners: do all reps in the first set Advanced players: do a pyramid Core–4 × 6 Core–1 × 8; 4 × 6 × 85% Assist–3 × 10 Assist–1 × 10; 2 × 8 × 75% See table 4.3 for specific exercises

Table 4.8   Spring Training (Week 24) – Performance Training – "Train to Play"

	Activity	Exercises and Drills
FRIDAY	**SPEED/QUICKNESS**	
	Early work	Warm-up: routine #1 Quickness: ladder (2 ×): crossover, back crossover, hopscotch, alt hopscotch
	Warm-up for practice	Warm-up: jog 1/2 mile or about 5 min, general warm-up and dynamic warm-up routine #2 Flexibility: daily dozen Trunk: daily core Running: 100 yd pick-ups (6 ×), backward run (4 × 30 yd), breaks from 1B with shuffle (6 × 30 yd)
	Running	Position players: breaks 5 × 30 yd, 10 × 60 yd Game pitcher: choose one of the following options after coming out of the game: 1. 10 pole sprints @ 45 sec 2. 10 × (15:15) 3. 10 poles and 10 × 100 yd 4. Simulate 4 innings Non-game pitcher: 10 × (30:30), jog 10 min
	Core	Sit-ups: 4 × 50 series, 2 × 100 series, 2 × 20 leg drops MD balls: off-center (3 positions), back toss-over
	Cool-down	Daily dozen
	STRENGTH/POWER	
	Strength	**Workloads:** Position players Beginners: do all reps in the first set Advanced players: do a pyramid Core–4 × 6 Core–1 × 8; 4 × 6 × 85% Assist–3 × 10 Assist–1 × 10; 2 × 8 × 75% See table 4.3 for specific exercises
	Shoulder	Cuff and scapula
	Wrist and hand	Superset (3 × 20)

Table 4.8   Spring Training (Week 24) – Performance Training – "Train to Play"

	Activity	Exercises and Drills
SATURDAY	**SPEED/QUICKNESS**	
	Early work	Warm-up: routine #1 Quickness: dot drill (3 ×)
	Warm-up for practice	Warm-up: jog 1/2 mile or about 5 min, general warm-up and dynamic warm-up routine #2 Flexibility: daily dozen Trunk: daily core Running: 100 yd pick-ups (6 ×), backward run (4 × 30 yd), breaks from 1B with shuffle (6 × 30 yd)

(continued)

Table 4.8 Spring Training *(Week 24, continued)*

	Activity	Exercises and Drills
SATURDAY	**SPEED/QUICKNESS** *(continued)*	
	Running	Position players: 5 × 30 yd, 10 × 60 yd Game pitcher: choose one of the following options after coming out of the game: 1. 10 pole sprints @ 45 sec 2. 10 × (15:15) 3. 10 poles and 10 × 100 yd 4. Simulate 4 innings Non-game pitcher: 10 × 100 yd in 10 min
	Core	Sit-ups: 4 × 50 series, 2 × 100 series, 2 × 20 leg drops MD balls: off-center (3 positions), back toss-over
	Cool-down	Daily dozen

Table 4.8 Spring Training (Week 24) – Performance Training – "Train to Play"

	Activity	Exercises and Drills
SUNDAY	**SPEED/QUICKNESS**	
	Early work	Warm-up: routine #1 Quickness: hip twist (3 × 10)
	Warm-up for practice	Warm-up: jog 1/2 mile or about 5 min, general warm-up and dynamic warm-up routine #2 Flexibility: daily dozen Trunk: daily core Running: 100 yd pick-ups (6 ×), backward run (4 × 30 yd), breaks from 1B with shuffle (6 × 30 yd)
	Running	Position players: optional Game pitcher: choose one of the following options after coming out of the game: 1. 10 pole sprints @ 45 sec 2. 10 × (15:15) 3. 10 poles and 10 × 100 yd 4. Simulate 4 innings Non-game pitcher: optional
	Core	Sit-ups: repeat Wed/Thurs workout
	Cool-down	Daily dozen

bacon and two sausage links, is like eating two Big Macs (1,100 calories and 49 grams of fat). You can make it better by requesting egg substitutes or an egg white omelet. Denny's Slim Slam with only 610 calories and 13 grams of fat is a better choice. The scrambled eggs are made with Egg Beaters, the fatty sausage and bacon are replaced by lean grilled ham, and pieces of real fruit appear with the pancakes instead of butter or margarine. If you order pancakes, hold the margarine and order fresh fruit instead of sausage or bacon. Avoid the Southern Slam. Even without biscuits and gravy, it has as much fat and saturated fat as a half pound of Spam. With biscuits and gravy, it has as much as nine chocolate frosted donuts. Skip the Belgian waffle. One waffle with whipped topping has as much saturated fat as two Quarter Pounders and as many calories as three hot fudge sundaes. Ham and cheese omelets are no better. The fat in the eggs, ham, cheese, hash browns, and margarine is equal to three corned beef sandwiches. Limit side dishes to ham and toast with jelly. Skip the hash browns and bacon. Don't even think about ordering sausage. It's the worst side dish you can get. Four links have 32 grams or about a half day's worth of fat. Don't get off to a bad start by eating a lot of fat (see table 4.9).

College and high school players start to work out two to three hours after lunch. All players should have a high-carbohydrate snack within 30 to 60 minutes after workouts and spring games to replenish muscle and liver glycogen stores for the next day's workout and game. Drink plenty of fluids throughout the day. Consume 6 to 8 ounces of water or electrolyte drink every 15 or 20 minutes and drink another 12 to 20 ounces immediately after workouts and games. Eat a good dinner and drink a lot of fluids throughout the evening. Minimize your intake of soft drinks and alcohol. Have a meal replacement drink or some fruit (fresh or dried) or low-fat cheese, yogurt, or pudding about two hours after dinner to top off your glycogen stores.

Table 4.9 Better Breakfast Choices

Day	CHO	Protein	Fruit or juice
1	cold whole-wheat cereal whole-wheat toast	low-fat milk lean ham	OJ or strawberries
2	pancakes w/o margarine	low-fat milk low-fat yogurt	OJ or melon
3	Cream of Wheat bagel	low-fat milk cottage cheese	Grapefruit juice or banana
4	egg white omelets or egg substitute whole-wheat toast	low-fat milk lean ham	OJ or pineapple
5	oatmeal with brown sugar English muffin	low-fat milk low-fat yogurt	OJ or fruit medley

TEN FAST-FOOD TIPS

1. The best hamburger is a small hamburger. Most hamburgers contain about 20 grams of fat per patty; with cheese and special sauce they are almost 60 percent fat. Get the smallest hamburger they make and add a piece of fruit and a glass of low-fat milk.

2. The worst hamburger is a "monster fatburger." Eighteen- to 24-year-old males go to fast-food restaurants more often than anyone else, and they have two things in mind: get the most food (calories) for the dollar and get filled up. Jack in the Box has the Colossus, or "Suicide Burger," and more recently the Ultimate Cheeseburger. Hardee's has a Monster Burger and In-N-Out Burger of California has the 4 by 4.

3. The best chicken sandwich is the McGrilled Classic. Nine of them have less fat than just one Burger King Broiler Chicken sandwich (29 grams). Why the difference? BK fries its chicken and slathers it with mayo. Leave off the mayo and lose 80 percent of the fat.

4. Pizza pizza is two too many. Each year, we eat enough pizzas to cover nearly 13,000 baseball fields. Two slices of a medium pepperoni pizza from Pizza Hut, for example, contain 20 to 23 grams of fat. Stop at two if you can.

5. Skim milk can fool most drinkers. OK, you know that skim milk is better for you than whole milk, but you can't stand the watery taste. In a recent taste test by the Center for Science in the Public Interest, only 5 percent of the tasters could accurately identify whole, 2 percent, 1 percent, and skim milk, and at least 25 percent couldn't even distinguish whole milk from skim. Try again. You'll learn to like it, and it's a lot better for you.

6. Hold the chicken skin and lose the fat. Removing the skin from chicken can cut the fat content by 75 percent and the calories by nearly 50 percent.

7. If you like coleslaw, make it yourself. Most coleslaw contains mayo, and a single cup gets nearly 70 percent of its 200 calories from fat. If you make your own, substitute nonfat yogurt for mayo to eliminate most of the fat, while keeping all the fiber, vitamin C, and other nutrients. If you're eating out, ask for extra beans rather than slaw.

8. Try a Subway sandwich. If you're in the habit of stopping by fast-food chains on your way to the park, you might want to skip the burger joints: a Big Mac or Whopper with all the trimmings, an order of fries, and a shake gets you 1,000 to 1,500 calories. Try a Subway sandwich, ordering turkey or roast beef on whole-wheat bread with mustard (hold the oil, olives, salt, cheese, and mayo).

9. No, you don't want fries with that. If you must have a hamburger, hold the fries. A large order at McDonald's has 22 grams of fat and 450 calories. Fries are not a side dish. They're a main dish of fat and calories.

10. Snackwells may be fat-free, but they're not calorie-free. They're zero fat, so they must be good for you, right? True, if you're concerned about heart disease and cancer. But if you're eating them to lose weight, you're in for a surprise. Snackwells and Chips Ahoy both contain about 50 calories per cookie.

Energy Supplements

Sports Drinks.   Most sports drinks contain water for rehydration, carbs for energy, minerals for electrolyte balance, and no fats or proteins. Select a brand that tastes good and contains a mix of glucose, sucrose, fructose, high-fructose corn syrup, and maltodextrins (complex chains of glucose). Drink 8 to 16 ounces one hour or more before workouts to superhydrate the body. Drink another 4 to 8 ounces at 15- to 20-minute intervals during workouts and another 8 to 16 ounces after workouts to get carbs and fluids back into the body. During the season, drink at least a cup every half inning to maintain fluid balance and drink 8 to 16 ounces as soon as possible after games to get carbs and fluids back into the body. Avoid using high-sugar fluids like soft drinks, fruit drinks, and fruit juices for fluid replacement. They don't work.

Energy Bars and Gels.   Energy bars are a good source of fuel for performance. They're compact, convenient, and expensive—about $1.75 for a two-ounce bar. But their number-one ingredient is sugar. True, it's fructose (fruit sugar), but it's still sugar. The bottom line, according to a report in *Scan's Pulse,* is that "bars and gels do not provide any nutritional advantage over other food, although consumers often believe otherwise." These products may contain vitamins and minerals, but they don't make up for a poor diet. They lack fiber, phytochemicals, and significant amounts of high-quality protein. Energy is just another word for calories, and food is still your best bet for energy.

Meal Replacement Powders.   Powdered nutritional products like Ultramet, MET-Rx, Myoplex, and Lean Body claim to be the perfect food for athletes needing to lose fat. Their primary ingredient is protein. The average hard-working 200-pound athlete needs no more than 180 grams, or about six ounces, per day. You can get the same extra protein for a lot less money by drinking low-fat milk or eating low-fat dairy products. Most meal replacement products go for about $60 for a box of 20 packets, so you could spend about $85 per week for these products. Try this instead: every time you drink milk or put milk on your cereal, add one-third cup of nonfat powdered milk to a glass of nonfat milk. A one-third cup of powdered milk gives you an additional 8 grams of protein. Do this three times per day and you get an extra 24 grams of protein. Add this to the real skim milk you use and you get all your calcium needs for pennies a day.

Chapter

In-Season— Training to Win

GOAL *Be prepared to play at a level that will help your team win*

During the season you want to improve performance, reduce the risk of injury, and maintain at least 90 percent of the sport-specific strength, speed, and power you developed previously.

Working the Body

Because you will begin to lose strength and fitness about six days after the cessation of training, you must continue to train throughout the season. Follow the program outlined in table 5.1 to maintain fitness, reduce the risk of injury, and enhance performance. Run five or six times per week. Position players run sprints each day. Starting pitchers run distance the day after pitching and then do intervals and sprints for three days leading up to the next start. Relievers run intervals or short sprints each day and jog 12 to 15 minutes once per week. All players lift at least twice per week using alternate days of heavy and moderate loads. Limit the number of lifts to those specific to your position and train two to three times per week for 15 to 20 minutes per workout. Beginners use the required reps method with a load that will allow you to do all reps in the first set. Advanced athletes set training loads on a percentage of maximum.

Vary workouts at 6- to 8-week intervals to avoid overtraining, staleness, and boredom. Divide the season into three 8-week training blocks. Increase training intensity every sixth week and increase work rate every seventh week. Follow this with a week of explosive training using lighter loads and then repeat the first six weeks with 3 to 5 percent heavier loads. Warm up, stretch, cool down, and do sit-ups every day. Do MD ball and cuff exercises three times per week.

Warm-Up, Early Work, and Flexibility

Warm up at 4 P.M. to get ready for pregame practice at 4:30 P.M. Get physically and mentally prepared to take quality batting practice (BP), throw, and field. Warm-up raises body temperature, increases blood flow, reduces stiffness, and makes your muscles contract and relax faster. It improves range of motion and protects your body against sudden, unexpected movements. Warm-up helps you practice better, and better practice yields more success. It keeps you from having to waste 10 to 12 swings in BP to get in a groove or play catch for 5 to 10 minutes to get loose. It increases your number of quality swings and throws and keeps you from wasting two very valuable resources—time and batting practice arms. Failure to warm up increases your risk of injury and wastes practice time.

If you have extra work scheduled, get to the park early and do dynamic warm-up routine #1 to prepare for the work to come. Don't throw on the side, take extra BP, or field balls without warming up unless you want to pull your rib muscles.

Running

"J.R. Richard is the luckiest pitcher in the world. He always pitches on days when the other team doesn't score many runs."—Kenny Forsch

Most players lose a step between opening day and the end of the season. Why? Because they don't run hard enough or often enough during the season. Speed, like hitting and fielding, improves with practice and decreases with inactivity. The running that most players do before the game will not maintain speed. You can't run from foul line to second base at half- to three-quarters speed five or six times before the game and expect to maintain speed. Likewise, running hard from home to first three or four times per week will not maintain speed. You have to run at 90 percent or faster to maintain speed.

Position Players. The average starting player in MLB runs to first base about 300 times per season. More than 50 percent of these runs are below the threshold for speed development. Most players run at threshold speed less than once per game. You have to run hard and run often to maintain speed for an entire season. Run 8 to 10 sprints per day and run most of these at 90 percent or better. Do five 30-yard sprints at near maximum speed. Walk back and run again. Finish with five 60-yard sprints at near maximum speed. Adjust your running schedule to match your performance. If you ran out two or three ground balls, scored from second on a close play, stole a base, and had two or three hit-and-run attempts fouled off the night before, run a little less. If, however, you took an "0-fer" with a couple of pop-ups and a K, run hard. Don't go two days in a row without working on speed.

Extra Men. If you don't play every day, run more and run hard. Run for speed four times per week and run for endurance twice per week. Do sprints at near maximum speed. Run intervals (6 × 15:15) for endurance. You stride 50 yards, turn, and sprint back. Your goal is to go down and back in 15 seconds. You then rest 15 seconds and repeat the run. Alternatively, do 10 × 100 yards in 10 minutes once or twice per week.

Starting Pitchers. Do distance for endurance and sprints for strength-power each day (table 5.2 on page 135). The day after you pitch, run for 25 to 30 minutes

Table 5.1 In-Season (Weeks 25-52) – Performance Training – "Train to Win"—
(Repeat cycle every 8 weeks)

	Activity	Exercises and Drills
MONDAY	**SPEED/QUICKNESS**	
	Early work	Warm-up: routine #1

	Warm-up for pre-game drills	Warm-up: jog 2 min, general warm-up, and dynamic warm-up routine #2
		Flexibility: daily dozen
		Trunk: daily core
		Running: build-ups (jog-stride-sprint-walk 6 × 30 yd), breaks from 1B with shuffle (6 × 30 yd)
		  Starters: breaks 10 × 60 yd
		  Extra men: breaks 10 × 60 yd, 10 × 100 yd in 10 min
		  Starting pitchers: jog 30 min, 10 × 100 yd
		  Relievers: jog 10 min, 10 × 60 yd

	Core	Sit-ups: 2 × 50 series, 2 × 100 series, 2 × 20 leg drops MD balls: off-center (3 positions), back toss-over
	Cool-down	Daily dozen
	STRENGTH/POWER	
	Strength	**Workloads:** Beginners: do all reps in first set Advanced: Week 1–6 Core—3-4 × 6-10 × 85% Assist—2-3 × 10-12 × 75% Week 7 Core—3-5 × 3-4 × 90% Assist—2-4 × 6-8 × 80% Week 8 Core—2-4 × 6-10 × 70% Assist—2-4 × 6-10 × 70% **Exercises:** Position players: DB bench^, DB inc fly, EZ tri, tri press Starting pitchers: DB lunge^, calf raise, DB squat, leg press^, leg curl, step-up, back ext Relievers: DB lunge^, calf raise, leg press^, leg curl, step-up
	Shoulder	Cuff and scapula
	Wrist and hand	Superset (3 × 20)

^Core lift

(continued)

Table 5.1 In-Season *(Weeks 25-52, continued)*

	Activity	Exercises and Drills
TUESDAY	**SPEED/QUICKNESS**	
	Early work	Warm-up: routine #1
	Warm-up for pre-game drills	Warm-up: jog 2 min, general warm-up, and dynamic warm-up routine #2 Flexibility: daily dozen Trunk: daily core Running: build-ups (jog-stride-sprint-walk 6 × 30 yd), breaks from 1B with shuffle (6 × 30 yd) Starters: 10 × 100 yd Extra men: 10 × 100 yd Starting pitchers: 10 × (30:30), 10 × 80 yd Relievers: jog 10 min, 10 × 60 yd
	Core	Sit-ups: 2 × 50 series, 2 × 100 series, 2 × 20 leg drops MD balls: off-center (3 positions) back toss-over
	Cool-down	Daily dozen
	STRENGTH/POWER	
		Workloads: Beginners: do all reps in first set Advanced: Week 1–6 Core—3-4 × 6-10 × 85% Assist—2-3 × 10-12 × 75% Week 7 Core—3-5 × 3-4 × 90% Assist—2-4 × 6-8 × 80% Week 8 Core—2-4 × 6-10 × 70% Assist—2-4 × 6-10 × 70% **Exercises:** Position players: DB lunge^, calf raise, leg curl, step-up Starting pitchers: DB bench+, lat pull (wide), DB shrug, DB row, tri kick, DB row, DB curl Relievers: DB bench+, lat pull (wide), DB row, tri kick, DB curl

^Core lift

Substitute: + Push-up; + Push-up plus; + Protraction/retraction

Table 5.1   In-Season (Weeks 25-52) – Performance Training – "Train to Win"—
(Repeat cycle every 8 weeks)

	Activity	Exercises and Drills
WEDNESDAY	**SPEED/QUICKNESS**	
	Early work	Warm-up: routine #1
	Warm-up for pre-game drills	Warm-up: jog 2 min, general warm-up, and dynamic warm-up routine #2 Flexibility: daily dozen Trunk: daily core Running: build-ups (jog-stride-sprint-walk 6 × 30 yd), breaks from 1B with shuffle (6 × 30 yd) Starters: breaks 10 × 60 yd Extra men: breaks 10 × 60 yd Starting pitchers: jog 20 min, 10 × 60 yd Relievers: jog 10 min, 10 × 60 yd
	Core	Sit-ups: 2 × 50 series, 2 × 100 series, 2 × 20 leg drops MD balls: lat twist (3 positions), wood chopper
	Cool-down	Daily dozen
	STRENGTH/POWER	
	Shoulder	Cuff and scapula
	Wrist and hand	Superset (3 × 20)
		Workloads: Beginners: do all reps in first set Advanced: Week 1–6 Core—3-4 × 6-10 × 85% Assist—2-3 × 10-12 × 75% Week 7 Core—3-5 × 3-4 × 90% Assist—2-4 × 6-8 × 80% Week 8 Core—2-4 × 6-10 × 70% Assist—2-4 × 6-10 × 70% **Exercises:** Position players: Lat pull (wide), seated row, DB shrug, DB curl

Table 5.1   In-Season (Weeks 25-52) – Performance Training – "Train to Win"—
(Repeat cycle every 8 weeks)

	Activity	Exercises and Drills
THURSDAY	**SPEED/QUICKNESS**	
	Early work	Warm-up: routine #1
	Warm-up for pre-game drills	Warm-up: jog 2 min., general warm-up, and dynamic warm-up routine #2 Flexibility: daily dozen Trunk: daily core build-ups (jog-stride-sprint-walk 6 × 30 yd) Running: breaks from 1B with shuffle (6 × 30 yd) Starters: 10 × 100 yd Extra men: 6 × (15:15) Starting pitchers: jog 15 min, 10 x 60 yd Relievers: jog 10 min, 10 × 60 yd

(continued)

Table 5.1   In-Season *(Weeks 25-52, continued)*

<table>
<tr><th></th><th>Activity</th><th>Exercises and Drills</th></tr>
<tr><td rowspan="6">THURSDAY</td><td>Core</td><td>Sit-ups: 2 × 50 series, 2 × 100 series, 2 × 20 leg drops
MD balls: Lat twist (3 positions), wood chopper</td></tr>
<tr><td>Cool-down</td><td>Daily dozen</td></tr>
<tr><td colspan="2">STRENGTH/POWER</td></tr>
<tr><td></td><td>

Workloads:
Beginners: all reps in first set
Advanced:

Week 1–6 Core—3-4 × 6-10 × 85%	Assist—2-3 × 10-12 × 75%
Week 7 Core—3-5 × 3-4 × 90%	Assist—2-4 × 6-8 × 80%
Week 8 Core—2-4 × 6-10 × 70%	Assist—2-4 × 6-10 × 70%

Exercises:
Position players: off
</td></tr>
</table>

Table 5.1   In-Season (Weeks 25-52) – Performance Training – "Train to Win"—
(Repeat cycle every 8 weeks)

<table>
<tr><th></th><th>Activity</th><th>Exercises and Drills</th></tr>
<tr><td rowspan="8">FRIDAY</td><td colspan="2">SPEED/QUICKNESS</td></tr>
<tr><td>Early work</td><td>Warm-up: routine #1</td></tr>
<tr><td>Warm-up for pre-game drills</td><td>Warm-up: jog 2 min, general warm-up, and dynamic warm-up routine #2
Flexibility: daily dozen
Trunk: daily core
Running: build-ups (jog-stride-sprint-walk 6 × 30 yd), breaks from 1B with
   shuffle (6 × 30 yd)
   Starters: breaks 10 × 60 yd
   Extra men: breaks 10 × 60 yd
   Starting pitchers: pitch
   Relievers: jog 10 min, 10 × 60 yd</td></tr>
<tr><td>Core</td><td>Sit-ups: 2 × 50 series, 2 × 100 series, 2 × 20 leg drops
MD balls: off-center (3 positions), back toss-over</td></tr>
<tr><td>Cool-down</td><td>Daily dozen</td></tr>
<tr><td colspan="2">STRENGTH/POWER</td></tr>
<tr><td>Shoulder</td><td>Cuff and scapula</td></tr>
<tr><td>Wrist and hand</td><td>Superset (3 × 20)</td></tr>
</table>

Table 5.1 In-Season (Weeks 25-52) – Performance Training – "Train to Win"—
(Repeat cycle every 8 weeks)

	Activity	Exercises and Drills
FRIDAY		**Workloads:** Beginners: do all reps in first set Advanced: Week 1–6 Core—3-4 × 6-10 × 85% Assist—2-3 × 10-12 × 75% Week 7 Core—3-5 × 3-4 × 90% Assist—2-4 × 6-8 × 80% Week 8 Core—2-4 × 6-10 × 70% Assist—2-4 × 6-10 × 70% **Exercises:** Position players: DB inc^, DB fly, rope tri, tri dip

^Core lift

Table 5.1 In-Season (Weeks 25-52) – Performance Training – "Train to Win"—
(Repeat cycle every 8 weeks)

	Activity	Exercises and Drills
SATURDAY	**SPEED/QUICKNESS**	
	Early work	Warm-up: routine #1
	Warm-up for pre-game drills	Warm-up: jog 2 min, general warm-up, and dynamic warm-up routine #2 Flexibility: daily dozen Trunk: daily core Running: build-ups (jog-stride-sprint-walk 6 × 30 yd), breaks from 1B with shuffle (6 × 30 yd) Starters: 10 × 100 yd in 10 min Starting pitcher: jog 30 min and 10 × 100 yd Extra men: 10 × 100 yd in 10 min Relievers: jog 10 min, 10 × 60 yd
	Core	Sit-ups: 2 × 50 series, 2 × 100 series, 2 × 20 leg drops MD balls: off-center (3 positions), back toss-over
	Cool-down	Daily dozen
	STRENGTH/POWER	
		Workloads: Beginners: do all reps in first set Advanced: Week 1–6 Core—3-4 × 6-10 × 85% Assist—2-3 × 10-12 × 75% Week 7 Core—3-5 × 3-4 × 90% Assist—2-4 × 6-8 × 80% Week 8 Core—2-4 × 6-10 × 70% Assist—2-4 × 6-10 × 70% **Exercises:** Position players: Leg press, calf raise, leg curl, split-squat Relievers: DB squat^, calf raise, step-up^, leg curl, split-squat

^Core lift

(continued)

Table 5.1 In-Season *(Weeks 25-52, continued)*

	Activity	Exercises and Drills
SUNDAY	**SPEED/QUICKNESS**	
	Early work	Warm-up: routine #1
	Warm-up for pre-game drills	Warm-up: jog 2 min, general warm-up, and dynamic warm-up routine #2 Flexibility: daily dozen Trunk: daily core Running: build-ups (jog-stride-sprint-walk 6 × 30 yd), breaks from 1B with shuffle (6 × 30 yd) Starters: optional Extra men: optional Starting pitcher: 10 × (30:30) and 10 × 80 yd Relievers: optional
	Core	Repeat Wed/Thur workout
	Cool-down	Daily dozen
	STRENGTH/POWER	
		Workloads: Beginners: do all reps in first set Advanced:

	Workloads (Advanced)	
Week 1-6 Core—3-4 × 6-10 × 85%	Assist—2-3 × 10-12 × 75%
Week 7 Core—3-5 × 3-4 × 90%	Assist—2-4 × 6-8 × 80%
Week 8 Core—2-4 × 6-10 × 70%	Assist—2-4 × 6-10 × 70%

Exercises:

Position players: Lat pull (w), seated row, DB shrug, DB curl

Relievers: DB inc+, lat pull (u), DB row, rope tri, DB curl*

Substitute: + Push-up; + Push-up plus; + Protraction/retraction; *Machine or hammer curl

at a 8:00- or 9:00-per-mile pace to loosen up and help remove residual soreness. Then run 10 × 100 yards at 80 to 85 percent of maximum speed for strength-power. Day 2 is a quality day. Run poles for 10 minutes at 8:00- or 9:00-per-mile pace to warm up. Then do 10 × 30:30 for speed-endurance. Finish with 10 × 80 yards at 85 to 90 percent for speed-power. Reduce distance on days 3 and 4. On day 3, run poles for 15 minutes at 8:00- or 9:00-per-mile pace and then do 10 × 60 yards at 85 to 90 percent pace. On day 4, jog for 10 minutes and do 10 × 60 yards at 85 to 90 percent. On game day, run six poles to warm up and then do 10 × 60 yards at moderate pace before going to the pen to throw. After you come out of the game, ice and cycle or use the StairMaster for 5 to 10 minutes to help redistribute blood flow from your arm to the rest of your body.

Table 5.2 In-Season Running Program for Starting Pitchers

Day	Endurance	Speed-power
1	Jog 25-30 min	10 × 100 yd
2	10 poles	10 × (30:30) and 10 × 80 yd
3	Jog 15 min	10 × 60 yd
4	Jog 10 min	10 × 60 yd
5	Warm-up (6 poles and 10 × 60 yd)	
	Pitch	
	Cool-down (cycle 5-10 min)	

Relief Pitchers.   It's hard for a reliever to know exactly how much to run. You need to run intervals for endurance and sprints for power, but not so much that you're too tired to pitch. Middle relievers run six times per week for 8 to 10 minutes per day at 8:00- to 9:00-per-mile pace for endurance and then do 10 × 60 yards at 85 to 90 percent for speed-power. Adjust your running to your workload. If you go three innings or more one night, you probably won't work the next. Run longer (10 to 12 minutes) the next day and skip the sprints. Sprints are more important than distance for closers. Run 10 × 60 yards at 85 to 90 percent, five or six times per week. Do distance (one to two miles at 8:00- to 9:00-per-mile pace) on days that you know you won't be used. If you don't like to run before the game, do five or six sprints during BP to warm up and then do the following cycle program for speed-power after the game. Warm up for two minutes at 90 rpm. Increase speed to 150 rpm and sprint all out for 5 seconds. Reduce speed to 90 rpm and ride comfortably for 15 seconds. Repeat the process five times. Sprinting all out for 5 seconds is the metabolic equivalent of running a 40- or 50-yard sprint. Give maximum or near maximum effort on each trial.

RUNNING DOES NOT BUILD LEG STRENGTH

Running three to five times per week in the off-season and almost every day during the season will not increase leg strength. The key to strength is intensity, not volume. Intensity is an index of how hard you work; volume is a measure of how much total work you do. Playing baseball requires high-intensity work. Long-distance running is high-volume work. You have to run short, all-out sprints, sprint uphill, run against resistance, and lift relatively heavy weights to develop leg strength. Distance running helps control body weight and increase aerobic fitness but does little or nothing for strength. The leg strength of champion marathon runners, for example, is only slightly higher than that of the spectators lining the streets. Strength is the result of high-intensity, low-rep work. You achieve gains by working with loads that you can lift 3 to 10 times. The loads in distance running are so light that you can repeat them thousands of times. For maximum strength lift weights with multiple sets of 3 to 10 RM loads. The upshot is this: lift for strength and run for endurance.

Strength

During the season, continue to work on strength. How you approach it depends on the position you play.

Trunk. Do two or three different MD ball drills before leaving the clubhouse and 100 sit-ups (daily dozen) in pregame warm-up. Pitchers and extra men do 300 to 400 more sit-ups after running.

Shoulder. Do exercises for the rotator cuff and scapula three times per week.

Wrist and Hands. Work the wrist and hand three to four times per week, always after practice.

Strength for Position Players. Lift two to three times per week if doing a total-body workout. Use heavy and moderate loads on alternate days. Lift six times per week if doing a split. Do chest and triceps on one day; legs on the next; and shoulders, back, and biceps on the third. Take a day off and repeat the sequence. Limit the number of lifts to those most specific to your position and train for 15 to 20 minutes per workout. Advanced athletes determine training loads on a percentage of maximum. Beginners use the required rep method with a load that allows them to do all reps in the first set, and use the loads in table 5.3. Lift after games when at home and before or after when on the road. Advanced players should use the loads in table 5.4.

Vary your workouts at eight-week intervals to avoid overtraining, staleness, and boredom. Increase training intensity every seventh week and increase work rate every eighth. Do three to five sets of 3 to 4 reps of core exercises and three to four sets of 6 to 8 reps for assist exercises in week 7. Follow this with a week of explosive training using lighter loads (two to four sets of 6 to 10 reps) and then repeat the first eight weeks with 3 to 5 percent heavier training loads.

Strength for Starting Pitchers. Lift twice between starts. Do legs the day after and upper body the next day. Take two days off and pitch. Some pitchers prefer to lift more often. Limit the number of lifts to those most specific to your position and train for 15 to 20 minutes per workout. Advanced athletes base training loads on a percentage of maximum. Beginners use the required rep method with a load that allows them to do all reps in all sets. Lift before games at home and on the road. Use the same load all season.

Strength for Relief Pitchers. Relievers tend to do well on a four-day split. Do legs one day and upper body the next. Take one or two days off and repeat the sequence. Limit the number of lifts to those most specific to your position and train for 15 to 20 minutes per workout. Advanced athletes determine training loads on a percentage of maximum. Beginners use the required rep method with a load that allows them to do all reps in all sets. Lift after games when at home. Lift before 4:00 P.M. when on the road. Use the same load all season.

Staleness

Abe Lemmons to Johnny Bench during his induction to the Oklahoma Sports Hall of Fame: "Had you accepted a basketball scholarship to OCU instead of signing with the Reds, you'd be principal of Binger High School today."

Table 5.3 In-Season—Maintenance Program for Position Players (Beginners)

Week	Exercise	Set × rep	Exercise	Set × rep
1	Core	3 × 10	Assist	3 × 10
2		3 × 10		3 × 10
3		3 × 8		3 × 10
4		3 × 8		3 × 10
5		3 × 6		3 × 10
6		3 × 6		3 × 10
7		3 × 4		3 × 10
8		3 × 10		

Do all reps in first set.

Table 5.4 In-Season—Maintenance Program for Position Players (Advanced)

Week	Exercise	Set × rep × % max	Exercise	Set × rep × % max
1	Core	3-4 × 6-10 × 85%	Assist	2-3 × 10-12 × 75%
2		3-4 × 6-10 × 85%		2-3 × 10-12 × 75%
3		3-4 × 6-10 × 85%		2-3 × 10-12 × 75%
4		3-4 × 6-10 × 85%		2-3 × 10-12 × 75%
5		3-4 × 6-10 × 85%		2-3 × 10-12 × 75%
6		3-4 × 6-10 × 85%		2-3 × 10-12 × 75%
7		3-5 × 3-4 × 90%*		2-4 × 6-8 × 80%
8		2-4 × 6-10 × 70%^		2-4 × 6-10 × 70%

* Increase intensity to 90-93%
^ Reduce intensity to 70% and increase speed or rate of work

With less than a month to play, you're fighting for a playoff slot. You've worked hard, and it's time to reap the rewards. You should be excited, but you're tired. You have a general feeling of heaviness, and no matter how hard you try, you just can't do your best during workouts and games. Your body aches, and you're anxious and restless. You don't sleep well, and you may be getting a cold or an allergy. You've got the blahs. Your competitive flame is dim, and your performance is not what it should be.

If this sounds familiar, you may be experiencing staleness. It's caused by overtraining, and it's a "too" problem that usually occurs in highly motivated athletes who tend to do "too much," "too often," with "too little rest." Why do we work ourselves to the point of near exhaustion? There's a fine line between being in peak shape and being overtrained. Most athletes incorrectly assume that if a little bit is good, a whole lot is better. Both work and rest, however, are important—neither is beneficial without the other.

Unfortunately, there are no preliminary symptoms or tests to warn you when you're on the edge of becoming overtrained. You might try testing yourself by measuring your heart rate when you get up in the morning and after a standard bout of exercise. If it's five or six beats higher than normal for the same amount of work, you may be at risk. The best predictor, however, is performance deterioration. Unfortunately, by the time you realize that you've pushed yourself too hard, it's too late. The damage done by repeated days of excessive training can be repaired only by days or, in some cases, weeks of reduced training or complete rest.

Stress is cumulative, and the underlying cause of overtraining is often a combination of both emotional and physical factors. Staleness occurs as often from a sudden increase in anxiety as from an increase in physical stress. The emotional demands of competition, desire to win, fear of failure, attempts to compensate for injured or slumping teammates, unrealistic goals, and expectations of coaches, teammates, and family can be sources of severe emotional stress. Combine these with exercise, heat, humidity, and a poor diet and you set the stage for overtraining. Unfortunately, the condition usually persists for at least two weeks before you notice any appreciable decrease in performance.

The key to preventing staleness is to avoid overtraining, and the best way to prevent it is to follow a training program that uses alternate days and weeks of easy, moderate, and hard training *(periodization model)*. As a rule of thumb, follow each day of hard training with at least one or two days of easy training. Allow at least a week of easy training after each week of hard training.

Watch your diet. Get more rest. Try to get at least eight hours of uninterrupted sleep each night and take naps before you go to the yard. Cut back. Don't run as far or as fast in pregame workouts. Lift less weight, do fewer sets and reps, and do fewer workouts each week. Few athletes are undertrained, but many are overtrained, usually because they think that more training produces better results. Don't run out of gas and enthusiasm until the final out of the World Series.

Performance Training During Playoffs

Don't make big changes. As Darrell Royal, former football coach at the University of Texas, says, "You've got to dance with who brung you." Maintain your regular routine if you can. This might be easier for pitchers than position players. Travel requirements will probably force you to make moderate adjustments, but don't skip your work to satisfy the needs of the media. They will be there when you finish your work; without you, there is no story. Cut back if you need to, but don't stop working out. Don't change an effective routine. It got you this far. Don't give up the known for the unknown.

Fueling the Body In-Season to Win

"Yeah, OK . . . but no potatoes. I'm on a diet."—**Yogi Berra** *to a waitress when asked if he wanted French fries with his burger.*

Ideally, the in-season and off-season diet should be about the same. Realistically, however, this is not always possible. You might be able to eat six good, small meals when playing at home if you work at it and have a caring clubhouse manager or coach. But you'll find doing this impossible on the road.

Breakfast.   Eat cereal (cold or hot), fruit or fruit juice, low-fat milk, low-fat yogurt, and whole-wheat toast. Another good choice is pancakes or waffles (without butter), lean ham, low-fat milk, and juice. If you eat eggs, eat only the whites.

Midday Snack.   Have a snack about two hours after breakfast, something like a high carbo drink, fruit or fruit juice, and a NutriGrain bar or energy bar. Blend a supplement drink or eat a bagel, cup of vegetable soup, or lean-meat (turkey, chicken, or tuna) sandwich.

Lunch.   Make lunch the best meal of the day. What you eat for lunch will get you through pregame drills and most of the game. Go to a good restaurant around 1:30 or 2:00 P.M. and eat a quality meal. Start with a salad or fruit plate. Order a lean entree (baked or broiled beef, fish, or chicken), starch (potato, rice, or pasta), and at least one vegetable. Eat whole-wheat bread or rolls. Drink low-fat milk or unsweetened tea and have fresh fruit or a low-fat dessert.

EATING IN POPULAR RESTAURANTS

Be careful at upscale chains like Chili's, Bennigan's, T.G.I. Friday's, Hard Rock Cafe, and Planet Hollywood (see table 5.5 for items to order or to avoid). Some of the items on their menus are so high in calories and fat that they make fast food look good.

Pregame Snack.   Have a small meal one to two hours before game time to keep from running out of energy in the late innings. If you had an early lunch, eat soup and crackers or a small sandwich of lean meat, mustard or light mayo, lettuce, and tomato. Peanut butter is another option. It's cheap, requires no refrigeration, and most people love it. But watch how much you use. A PBJ sandwich with just two tablespoons of peanut butter—it's easy to use more, especially if you lick the spoon—will run you 20 grams of fat. Wash it down with low-fat milk or fruit juice. If you can't eat before games, try an energy bar or a carbohydrate drink like Cytomax or PowerAid. Skip the cookies, even Snackwells. They're high in sugar and can cause you to run out of fuel faster.

Postgame Meal for Muscle Reloading.   By the time the game is over, you're exhausted and starving. Some clubhouses have good food choices; some don't. Don't eat a lot of fried fat and wish you hadn't later. Eat foods that will help you recover and play better the next day. Go for pasta when you can. It's a high-carbohydrate meal that will help replenish your muscle glycogen stores much faster than will fat and protein. Spaghetti is good, and tomato sauce is better than meat sauce or sausage. Other good carbohydrate foods are potatoes, rice, beans, vegetables, fruit, bread, rolls, and milk. Chicken and fish are good low-fat sources of protein that become high in fat when fried. To rehydrate, eat watery foods and drink lots of water, sports drinks, decaffeinated tea and coffee, or low fat-milk. Fruits and vegetables are 70 to 90 percent water. For maximum rehydration, mix in some bananas, cantaloupe, cucumbers, lettuce, oranges, peaches, pears, grapefruit, tomatoes and watermelon. Top off your meal with a small dessert. Just don't over do it.

Table 5.5 Foods to Order and Foods to Avoid When Eating Out

Food to order	Foods to skip
Dinner salad, dressing on the side	Appetizers (buffalo wings, fried foods)
Grilled chicken	Fried chicken
Sirloin steak	Philly cheese steak
Baked potato	Potato skins, loaded
Chicken fajitas, very little sour cream	Chef salad with dressing
Pot roast	Chicken fingers
Vegetables	Hamburgers and fries
Stuffed turkey	Baby back ribs
Fruit	Fudge brownie sundae
Frozen yogurt, fat-free	Banana split
Sherbet, cup of ice cream	Apple pie a la mode
At steak houses	
Barbecue chicken breast	Fried onions
Sirloin steak	Cheese fries
Filet mignon	Prime rib
Pork tenderloin	Pork chops
At Italian restaurants	
Tossed salad, dressing on the side	Antipasto, fried calamari
Minestrone soup, Italian bread dry	Garlic bread with butter
Pasta (marinara, marsala, or red or white clam sauce)	Pasta alfredo or pesto sauce
	Lasagna
Chicken, veal, and fish grilled	Fried fish
Chicken marsala, side of spaghetti	Veal or eggplant parmigiana
Mexican	
Mexican rice	Go easy on the chips.
Gazpacho soup	Quesadillas
Pinto, red, or black beans	Beef and cheese nachos
Chicken or seafood fajitas	Refried beans
Chicken or seafood burritos	Fried burrito
	Enchilada dinners
	Beef chimichanga dinners
	Taco salads
	Chile rellenos

Food to order	Foods to skip
Fish	
Most fish and shellfish broiled, baked,	
blackened, or steamed	Fried fish
Steamed shrimp or clams	Tartar and other cream sauces
Clam chowder	Coleslaw
Baked potato, bit of sour cream	French fries
Oriental	
Steamed rice, vegetables	Moo shu pork
Stir-fried vegetables	Kung pao chicken
Szechuan shrimp	Sweet and sour pork
Chicken chow mein	Beef with broccoli
House lo mein	Orange crispy beef

Energy Boosters—Performance Enhancers

These substances work on the central nervous system to make you feel more alert and ready for action. Players often take them before games to get themselves up for the game. Caffeine works. It stimulates the CNS to increase alertness, enhance visual perception, and reduce fatigue during muscular work. A cup or two before workouts or games will help pick you up and get you ready to go. Although a little is good, a lot is *not* better. If caffeine makes you queasy or lightheaded during exercise, don't use it. Once ingested, caffeine enters the bloodstream within minutes and can peak in the blood within as little as 30 minutes. The half-life of caffeine is 2 to 10 hours, so you'll feel its effects long after you consume it. At rest, it tends to increase urine formation, often causing a need to urinate within an hour after consumption. The secretion of extra adrenaline during exercise appears to block urine formation during work. Because of its diuretic effect during rest, caffeine is not a good fluid replacement drink after exercise.

Tobacco

"I've come to realize that if I continue to smoke, I'll never be a good runner, so I've decided that I'm going to give up running."—*Joe Niekro*

Baseball players have used the nicotine in cigarettes and spit-tobacco as a stimulant since the days of Abner Doubleday. Some claim that it improves performance by making them more alert and better able to concentrate. Others say it helps calm jittery nerves.

Smoking is hazardous to personal health and impairs performance. Smoking robs the muscles of their maximal potential for using oxygen, reduces maximum performance during all-out work, and contributes to early fatigue in submaximum work. If you smoke, you will not achieve your true aerobic potential regardless of how hard you train.

Spit-tobacco users are trading the possibility of lung cancer for that of oral cancer. There is a direct relationship between smokeless tobacco and oral, pharyngeal, and laryngeal cancer. Some 90 percent of the nicotine in chewing tobacco is absorbed through the inner membrane of the mouth. Holding tobacco in the mouth for extended periods of time will eventually lead to oral leukoplakia (leathery white patches inside the mouth), cancer, bad breath, discolored teeth, loss of sense of taste and smell, and dental problems such as receding gums, wear and tear on tooth enamel, and tooth decay. Smokeless tobacco is not a safe alternative to smoking. Taking a dip or chew tends to give you a slight high. Unfortunately, there is also a downside. The same substances that increase arousal also decreases the rate at which the muscles can remove the substance that causes fatigue (lactic acid). Using smokeless tobacco can cause your heart to work harder and less efficiently, produce premature fatigue, and inhibit maximum performance. Minor-league baseball recently banned players from smoking, dipping, and chewing tobacco at the ballpark.

Alcohol

Some athletes drink a lot, believing that as long as they exercise alcohol isn't harmful. Others avoid alcohol entirely, believing that any amount is detrimental to health and performance. The best position is probably somewhere between these two extremes. Moderation is the key. Drinking too much the night before you work out or play can affect performance. Even if you don't experience traditional hangover symptoms like headache and nausea, you will probably be dehydrated the next day. Alcohol, like caffeine and altitude, is a diuretic that causes increased urination and water loss.

Because the body requires 8 ounces of water to metabolize a single ounce of pure alcohol, you can partially counteract the dehydrating effects of alcohol by consuming a lot of water when you drink alcohol. To minimize dehydration, you need to drink at least 8 ounces of water for every two drinks. A drink is 12 ounces of beer, 4 ounces of wine, or 1-1/2 ounces of 80 proof. Each of these provides about 1/2 ounce of pure alcohol.

Alcohol is a depressant. Drinking it before workouts or games will impair brain function, reaction time, hand-eye coordination, balance, visual perception, and performance. It will also reduce stamina. And you will have to run at least one mile to burn the calories in one alcoholic drink. Drink a six-pack and you're looking at five miles on the track. If you're fighting a weight problem, you go easy on the alcohol.

For most adult athletes, having one to three drinks the night before or after a game isn't likely to harm performance or health.

PART

II

Exercises and Drills

Training to play for optimal, injury-free baseball has few absolutes and many variables. Absolutes are ideas that stand the test of time and meet the needs of both the player and the sport. They are basic principles developed by experts in sports medicine and exercise science. Variables are factors that you can't control. *52-Week Baseball Training* is based on 16 basic principles. The more of these principles you follow, the fewer variables you'll have to control for.

Principles

Principle 1: Develop the complete athlete. In game situations, the body functions as one unit. Successful, injury-free performance requires skill, strength, speed, power, agility, balance, coordination, and flexibility. You need the total package, total fitness. What good is it to squat 300 pounds if you run to first in 4.8? What good is being flexible if you're too weak to hit a sacrifice fly or throw out a runner at the plate?

Principle 2: Condition the entire body, not just the arm. Hitting and throwing start with your legs and trunk, not with your arms. The legs and trunk are your power zone, providing over 50 percent of the force generated in hitting and throwing. Your three-link chain is the legs, trunk, and arms. Forces are initiated in the legs, transferred to the upper body through the trunk, and finally applied to the bat and ball by the hands and fingers. Like all chains, your body is only as strong as its weakest link. A weak midsection can't transfer 100 percent of the forces generated by the legs and hips to the arms and hands for application to the bat and ball. So you lose arm speed, bat speed, and power and often incur injury when you add stress on the arm and shoulder muscles to compensate for a loss of speed and power.

Principle 3: Condition the body to hit, run, and throw. Get in shape to play; don't play to get in shape. Don't hit, run, and throw for conditioning. If you're in shape you can give better effort, make quicker progress, and avoid injury. Injuries occur when you're not in shape to do the skills and drills correctly, and you can't learn if you're too tired to do the skills correctly.

Principle 4: Train movements, not muscles. Nothing happens while you're standing still. Most movements in baseball are dynamic, ballistic, and fast. They're highly reactive; you have to react to a ball, opponent, or situation. Movements are sequential; one follows another. Movements are explosive (ballistic); they require you to apply a high level of force (strength) quickly. For optimal, injury-free performance, do the sport-specific movement patterns (run, hit, throw, jump, dive, slide, change directions, and so on) required of your position. Once you can execute these movement patterns efficiently, repeat them with resistance to develop sport-specific strength, speed, and power.

Work the total body in movement patterns similar to those used in game situations. Don't train isolated muscles to move slowly. Bodybuilding programs have absolutely no place in baseball. They might make you look better in the lobby, but they won't help you where it counts—between the lines. Strength that's not functional is hollow.

Principle 5: Train strength before power or endurance. Develop basic strength before doing skill, speed, power, or endurance exercises. Strength is the foundation on which you build all other athletic performance components. Without a strong foundation, your body can't withstand the high-intensity training required to build speed and power. And without strength, you can't do the repetitions required to improve skill and endurance.

Principle 6: Train for muscle balance. Joint stability relies on the contraction of muscles on both sides of the joint. Programs that emphasize only certain muscle groups can leave the joint open to injury. Also, be sure to train both sides of the body—train both arms and both legs. Your lead leg and nonthrowing arm help rotate the trunk to enhance arm and bat speed.

Principle 7: Train for performance, not capacity. Emphasize quality of effort, not quantity. Don't max out in any exercise and don't work to exhaustion. You don't need to feel the burn to get a good workout. Avoid forced reps in which you work to exhaustion and then do a few more reps with the help of a partner. Forced reps produce less than optimal gains and increase the risk of injury. When a muscle fatigues, some of its fibers shut down. With fewer fibers contracting, it's impossible to generate enough force to complete the last rep without help. Because some of the muscle has shut down, it can't contract with maximum intensity, which is the key to growth.

Avoid partial reps, a form of cheating based on the erroneous assumption that you can force a muscle to work harder by switching to half reps or quarter reps once you reach the point where you can't do a full rep. For maximum results, do full reps through the complete range of motion (ROM). Partial reps train only the muscle part that is actually working and develop strength only in the last 25 to 50 percent of the ROM. Partial reps limit your force potential and increase your risk of muscle imbalance and injury.

Principle 8: Gradually increase skill work. Training must be specific. You have to lift weights to get stronger, run to get faster, and hit, field, and throw to become a better player. Strength and fitness training will not substitute for skill work, any more than swinging a 34-ounce bat or throwing a 5-ounce ball will increase strength, speed, or power. Practice hitting, throwing, and fielding but train smart. Work on skills when you're fresh. Play light catch and swing the bat three or four times per week in the off-season when the volume of work and resulting fatigue is high. Gradually increase the amount and quality of skill work as the season approaches.

Principle 9: Start slowly and be progressive. You can't start a high-intensity training program in the first week of the off-season. Don't be in such a hurry to get to the next level that you don't take time to establish a sound training base from which to work. You can't take 500 swings or field 500 ground balls on the first day of spring. You start with 25 to 30 and build slowly. The same is true for conditioning. Train to train. Trying to be game ready without building a base increases your risk of injury and prevents you from achieving your performance goals. The key is to match your exercise routine to your fitness level.

Remember these two rules:

1. Body weight before external resistance
2. Fundamental movement skills before sport-specific skills

Be patient. If you have problems in the field or on the bases, develop fundamental movements like starting, stopping, changing directions, and moving right and left, up and down, and forward and backward before working on skills.

Principle 10: Heed individual differences. Every athlete has a different response to, and capacity for, training. Each has individual needs, maturity, motivation, background, and limits. Players occupy different positions and have different movement requirements: some rely on speed and finesse, others on strength and power. For maximum results, you should personalize your program.

Principle 11: Understand specificity. You get what you train for. Know what you need and train to get it. Baseball is a game of speed, reaction, and power, not aerobic endurance. Although it's important to develop an aerobic base early in the off-season, switch to interval sprints to improve speed, power, and aerobic capacity in the same workout as the season approaches.

Do sport-specific exercises. Don't do an exercise just because it trains an appropriate muscle group. Manipulate reps, sets, and rest to match the energy demands of the sport. As strength and power demands increase, for example, decrease reps and increase rest. Baseball requires repeated maximum effort, separated by frequent, brief rest periods. Movement consists of a series of short sprints, lateral movements, and frequent changes of direction.

Understand the three absolutes of strength training:

1. Volume (many reps with light loads) builds endurance and size.
2. Intensity (few reps with relatively heavy loads) builds strength without size.
3. Programs are not interchangeable (volume will not build strength and vice versa).

Principle 12: Do closed kinetic-chain (CKC) exercises. Performance is the result of integrated muscular actions, not the sum of isolated joint movements. Your body is composed of a series of kinetic (moving) links, or chains, that operate in sequence. Throwing does not involve just the arm; hitting does not involve just the hands; and running does not involve just the legs. All three involve the whole body. For best results, do complex movements that cross multiple joints. Closed kinetic-chain exercises (squats, lunges, step-ups, step-downs, split-squats, squat touches, push-ups, and so on) require that at least one hand or foot be in contact with the ground. With open-chain exercises, the hands (arm curl and triceps kickback) or feet (leg curl and leg extension) are not in contact with the ground. CKC exercises not only work the prime movers in patterns similar to those used in sports but also develop the support and stabilizer muscles at each joint in the chain. Because CKC exercises require more balance and coordination than open-chain activities, they are more sport specific and time efficient.

Principle 13: Have a plan. The program presented in this text is based on a periodization training model that divides the year into five training phases. Each phase has a specific purpose and incorporates different activities, different volumes, and different work intensity. Each phase is more difficult and more sport specific than the previous one. Periodization training helps you make consistent gains, prevent injuries, avoid burnout, and give your best effort when you need it—during the season. Don't jump into a training program without giving thought to what you need, how much you need, when you need it, and how to get it. The only thing you can control in this game is how you prepare for it.

Principle 14: Rest and recover. No matter how hard you work, you don't make gains during workouts. Gains are achieved during periods of recovery. Recovery is one of the most important and most ignored principles of training. Training without adequate recovery yields poor results and injury. If you follow the adage "no pain, no gain," you walk a thin line between maximum gains and overtraining. Avoid doing two hard running workouts on consecutive days and allow at least 48 to 72 hours of recovery between hard workouts of the same muscle group.

Principle 15: "It's not the arrow, it's the Indian."—**Jose Cruz.** We tend to become caught up in wanting to use the latest and most expensive training equipment and apparel. Equipment is secondary. The most important factors are the program and the athletes. The training program must be scientific and specific to your needs, and you must be willing to put forth the consistent effort required to produce the desired results. You don't need fancy equipment to get in top shape.

Principle 16: Practice makes permanent. If you do something often enough, even if you do it wrong, it becomes fixed in your brain and nervous system. If you do it right, you will always do it right. If you do it wrong, you will always do it wrong. Do exercises in a sequence that will maximize gains. Run when you're fresh. Stretch after warm-up to maximize flexibility. Do plyometrics before strength training so you can give maximum effort. Do multijoint lifts before single-joint lifts. Do aerobic work last. Achieving peak performance takes planning. You don't get there by accident.

Warm-Up/Cool-Down and Flexibility

A workout includes three distinct parts. Warm-up is not stretching; it's an active process done before you stretch to prepare your muscles, joints, and mind for the more intense activities to follow. You use gross muscle movements such as jogging, squats, and lunges to raise body temperature and increase blood flow.

Warming Up

Start with the general warm-up (see table 6.1) to raise body temperature and increase respiration, blood flow, and joint range of motion. Jog or cycle for at least five minutes and then do dynamic warm-up exercises after you break a sweat to work the muscles used in running, jumping, throwing, and swinging in movement patterns identical to those required in practice and game situations. Do squats, lunges, trunk twists, and so on to work both the large prime-mover muscles of the hip, back, and shoulders and the smaller stabilizer muscles of the groin, leg, and ankle. Do high knees, butt kicks, skips, and so on to warm up and stretch the muscles used in games and emphasize the movement skills used in practice and games. Shuffle, carioca, skip, and run backward to develop body balance, strength, dynamic flexibility, and range of motion in game-related movement patterns. Do leg swings, over-the-bar, and under-the-bar drills to work the hip muscles and improve functional strength and balance.

Table 6.1 Warm-Up, Stretching, and Cool-Down Exercises

Function	Exercise	Set × rep
General warm-up	Squat	1 × 10-15
	Lunge	1 × 10-15
	Circle toe touch	1 × 10-15
	Good morning	1 × 10-15
	Wood chopper	1 × 10-15
	Trunk twist	1 × 10-15
	Arm circle	1 × 10-15
Dynamic warm-up routine #1	Leg swing	1 × 10-15
	Crossover leg swing	1 × 10-15
	Crossover leg swing and hold	1 × 3-5
	Hip flexion/extension	1 × 10-15
	Hip flexion	1 × 10-15
	Lateral under the bar	2 × 10-15
	Forward under the bar	2 × 10-15
	Over the bar	2 × 10-15
	Crawl under the bar	1 × 10-15
Dynamic warm-up routine #2	High knees	2 × 20-30 yd
	Butt kick	2 × 20-30 yd
	Knee-to-chest skip	2 × 20-30 yd
	Straight-leg shuffle	2 × 20-30 yd
	Shuffle	2 × 20-30 yd
	Carioca	2 × 20-30 yd
	Backward skip	2 × 20-30 yd
	Backward run	2 × 20-30 yd
Static flexibility stretches (daily dozen)	Butterfly groin	2 × 10-15 sec
	Seated back twist	2 × 10-15 sec
	Buttocks stretch	2 × 10-15 sec
	Standing quadriceps stretch	2 × 10-15 sec
	Seated hamstring stretch	2 × 10-15 sec
	Lying hamstring stretch	2 × 10-15 sec
	Lower back stretch	2 × 10-15 sec
	Hip flexor stretch	2 × 10-15 sec
	Standing calf stretch	2 × 10-15 sec
	Inclined calf stretch	2 × 10-15 sec
	Arm stretch	2 × 10-15 sec
	Forearm stretch	2 × 10-15 sec
Cool-down	Walk or jog	5 min
	Daily dozen	2 × 10 sec

General Warm-Up Routine

Do one set of 10 to 15 reps of the general warm-up exercises described below. For more strength and range of motion, do them while holding a four- to six-pound MD ball or five-pound dumbbell in both hands.

Squat

Stand with your hands on your hips, behind your head, or across your chest. Squat to parallel and return.

Lunge

Step forward with one leg until the thigh is parallel to the ground. Pause, push back with the lead leg, and return. Repeat with the other leg.

Circle Toe Touch

Stand with your feet shoulder-width apart and arms extended over your head, palms forward. Bend forward at the waist, touch outside one foot with both hands, drag your hands across the ground to the opposite foot, circle the hips, and stand erect with both hands over your head. Do 5 to 10 reps in each direction.

Wood Chopper

From the Good Morning starting position, bend forward and bring your hands between your knees as if chopping wood, pause, and return. Repeat by chopping outside each foot.

Good Morning

Stand with your feet shoulder-width apart, knees slightly bent, and your hands behind your head. Bend at the waist until your chest is parallel to the ground. Pause and return.

Trunk Twist

Stand with your feet shoulder-width apart and arms bent and palms forward. Slowly twist side-to-side.

Arm Circle

Stand with your feet shoulder-width apart and arms out straight. Make large arm circles forward and backward.

Dynamic Warm-Up Routine #1— Wall Drills and Hurdles

Use routine #1 or #2 (see table 6.1) to develop strength, rhythm, flexibility, and balance. Do one set of 10 to 15 reps of each of the following drills to increase flexibility of the hip and back and strengthen the muscles of the hip, groin, and lower back.

Crossover Leg Swing

Stand facing the wall with arms out straight and both hands on the wall for support. Swing the right leg away from the body as far as possible and back across the body in a rhythmic manner. Repeat with the other leg.

Crossover Leg Swing and Hold

Stand facing the wall, as in the photo of the crossover leg swing, with arms out straight and both hands on the wall for support. Start by swinging the right leg out away from the body as far as possible. Then swing it back across the body and out again. Hold in the out position for six seconds. Next, swing the leg inward across the body, back out, and in again. Hold in the in position for six seconds. Do three reps in, three reps out, and then repeat with the other leg.

Leg Swing

Stand on your left leg with your right hand on the wall for balance. Swing the right leg forward and backward as far as possible in a rhythmic manner. Repeat with the other leg.

Hip Flexion

Stand with your back to a wall. Lean back against the wall and use your shoulders and hands for support. Keeping toe up and leg straight, raise the right leg forward as high as possible. Return and repeat. Repeat with other leg.

Hip Flexion/Extension

Stand facing the wall with arms out straight and both hands on the wall for support. With your toe up, swing the right knee up to the chest as high as possible and then extend the right hip and leg back as far as possible in a rhythmic manner. Repeat with the other leg.

Crawl Under the Bar

Place a broomstick or a weight bar across a pair of 24-inch-high boxes. Get down on your hands and toes in front of the bar. Crawl under the bar using only your hands and toes. Do not let any other part of your body touch the ground. Extend your arms and back as your hips pass under the bar, push with your feet, and stand up on the opposite side. Come back under the bar from the opposite direction. Repeat the drill 10 to 15 times. Lower the bar as your flexibility increases.

Lateral Under the Bar

Lower a track hurdle until the top is even with your navel. Use a broomstick as a barrier if you don't have access to a hurdle. Stand with your left side next to the hurdle. Step sideways under the hurdle with your left foot. Bend at the hips, knees, and ankles and keep your lower back tight and your upper back, neck, and head straight. Push with your right foot to move your body sideways under the hurdle. Stand up on the other side. Step under the hurdle with your right foot and come back under the hurdle. Go 10 to 15 times in each direction. Lower the hurdle as your flexibility increases.

Forward Under the Bar

Stand facing the hurdle (see previous exercise). Step forward under the hurdle with your right foot. Bend at the hips, knees, and ankles and place your head and back under the hurdle. Push with the left leg and drive your body under the hurdle. Square up your shoulders and stand up on the other side. Turn around and come back under the hurdle with the left foot forward. Go 10 to 15 times in each direction. Lower the hurdle as your flexibility increases.

Over the Bar

Lower the hurdle to crotch height and stand facing it. Pivot on your left foot and step over the hurdle with your right foot until your body is straddling the hurdle (right foot on one side and left foot on the other). Pivot on your right foot and bring your left foot, heel first, over the hurdle. Stand on the other side facing the hurdle. Step back across the hurdle with your left foot. Go 10 to 15 times in each direction. Raise the hurdle as your flexibility increases.

STIFF MUSCLES AND INJURY

What happens when your muscles are stiff and tight? If the tightness is in your leg muscles, your stride length will shorten and your ability to accelerate and run at top speed will be limited. If it occurs in your trunk, trunk rotation and throwing and hitting force will be restricted. If it's in your arm or shoulder, range of motion, speed, and accuracy will be reduced.

Can tight muscles increase the risk of injury? Yes. Short muscles produce less force and fatigue more quickly than long muscles. Fatigue increases the risk of injury, especially when muscles have to contract with a lot of force to produce quick movements and bursts of speed. Tight muscles are also associated with an increased risk of stress fracture and knee injury. Muscles are the primary shock absorbers in the body. Every time your foot hits the ground, your leg and foot muscles absorb an impact of three to five times body weight. Because tight muscles can't absorb much force, the force is transmitted to your bones.

Dynamic Warm-Up Routine #2—Running Drills

Do two sets of each exercise over a distance of 20 to 30 yards (see table 6.1).

Straight-Leg Shuffle

Run forward with your leg straight like a drum major leading a band. Keep the lead leg straight as you pull back and step forward with the opposite leg.

High Knees

Run forward. Bring your knees up close to your chest and pump your arms.

Butt Kick

Run forward. Bring your heels as close to your butt as possible as you pump your arms.

Knee-to-Chest Skip

Skip forward and bring one knee to your chest. Keep your head up and work your arms as in running. Repeat on the other leg. Continue the skipping cycle.

Shuffle

Run laterally using slide steps. Do not cross your feet. Go in both directions.

Carioca

Run laterally as you cross one leg over the other. Go in both directions.

Backward Skipping

Lean forward at the waist, skip backward, and bring your heel to your buttocks. Keep your head up, and work the arms as in running.

Backward Run

Lean forward at the waist, knees bent, and run backward as you pump your arms and reach as far up and back with your foot as possible.

HOW DOES A MUSCLE BECOME TIGHT?

Repeated high levels of exertion in practice and games can cause microtears in your muscles or tendons. In time, these tears heal and develop scar tissue. Scar tissue is strong but relatively inelastic. When you stretch, the previously injured muscles and tendons can't fully elongate because of the scar tissue and your muscles become stiff and tight.

Stretching

Stretching is a separate, planned, progressive program, just like running and strength training. It should come after your body is already warm, when your muscles are most elastic. Stretching will increase flexibility and range of motion. Inflexible muscles and joints limit movement and cause skills to be awkward and inefficient. Flexible muscles and joints, on the other hand, can resist muscle injury and soreness. A lack of flexibility limits performance and increases your risk of injury. Limited shoulder range of motion, for example, reduces arm speed. A tight back limits trunk rotation and restricts your ability to swing and throw. Tight hamstring and groin muscles are prone to pulls, and they shorten stride length and reduce speed. Stiff ankles limit push off, speed, power, lateral mobility, and first-step quickness.

You can improve your flexibility if you work at it. Sitting on the ground and talking to your teammates is counterproductive to successful injury-free performance. You don't get anything out of it, and you keep your teammates from getting better. Don't be selfish. If you don't care about getting better, don't stand in the way of your teammate. You wouldn't distract him while he was taking BP. Why would you want to keep him from getting ready to play?

Static Flexibility Stretches

These exercises develop flexibility in the legs, hips, trunk, shoulder, and arm. They improve flexibility but don't always prevent muscle pulls resulting from dynamic movements used in running, hitting, and throwing. Use proper form throughout each stretch. Stretch only until you feel mild tension. Stop just before you begin to feel pain. Forget about "no pain, no gain." More is not always better. If you exert too much pressure on the muscle, it will tear. Don't bounce and don't try to do too much at one time.

Daily Dozen

Do two sets of each of the following daily dozen stretches (see table 6.1). Hold each stretch for 10 to 15 seconds.

Standing Quadriceps Stretch

Lean against a partner or wall with your right hand. Reach behind you and grasp your right foot near the toes with your left hand. Pull your heel toward your buttocks and hold. Switch legs and repeat. If you have knee problems, do this drill while lying on one side with the top leg bent at the knee and the bottom leg out straight. Reach behind and grab the ankle of the top leg and pull your heel to your buttocks and hold. Switch legs and repeat.

Seated Back Twist (Hook and Look)

Sit up tall with one leg extended straight out in front of your body. Cross the other leg over top of the extended leg and place your foot flat on the ground. Turn away from the extended leg and place your elbow behind the knee crossed over the extended leg. Twist your trunk and look over your shoulder. Repeat in the other direction.

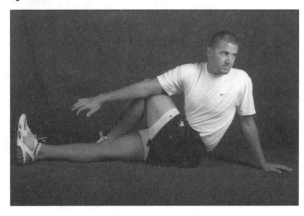

Buttocks (Piriformis) Stretch

Lie on your back. Cross your left leg over your right knee. The ankle of your left leg should touch your right knee. Keeping your head and shoulders on the floor, grab your right leg, behind the knee, with both hands and pull it slowly toward your chest. Pull until you feel your left hip stretch. Switch legs and repeat.

Back Stretch

Lie on your back and slowly pull both knees toward your chest until you feel a good stretch. Relax and extend your right leg out straight until it rests on the ground. Pull your left knee up and across your chest toward your right shoulder and hold. Switch legs and repeat.

Standing Calf Stretch

Stand in a forward lunge position with your right leg forward. Support yourself by placing your hands on a wall. Lean forward into the wall and press the heel of your back (left) leg toward the floor while keeping your left leg straight. Hold, relax and bend the left knee slightly. Press the heel into the floor while keeping the left slightly bent. Switch legs and repeat.

Butterfly Groin

Sit up tall in a butterfly position, with the soles of your feet together, chest up. Grasp your ankles and push your knees toward the floor with your elbows. Stretch until you feel tension in the inner thigh (groin).

Hip Flexor Stretch

From a standing position, lunge forward on your right foot. Make sure that the front knee does not move beyond the ball of your front foot. Push your right hip forward as you keep your left (back) leg straight. From the lunge position, kneel on your left knee. Place both hands on the your right knee and keep your head and trunk upright. Slowly slide the left knee backward and hold. Switch legs and repeat.

Lying Hamstring Stretch

Lie on your back with your left leg out straight. Bend your right knee and bring your right thigh toward your chest. Place both hands behind your right knee and hold. Slowly extend your right knee and point your toes as you pull your right thigh toward your chest. Switch legs and repeat.

Seated Hamstring Stretch

Sit with your right leg extended straight in front. Bend the knee of the left leg and place the sole of the left foot against the inside thigh of the right leg. Keep your head up and trunk straight. Bend forward at the waist, grab your right ankle and hold. Switch legs and repeat.

Inclined (Inchworm) Calf Stretch

From a push-up position, keep your heels flat on the ground as you slowly walk your feet to your hands, one step at a time.

Arm Stretch

Stand with one arm folded across your chest. Grab your elbow with the opposite hand and pull your arm across the chest and hold. Repeat with the arm across the face and down the back. Repeat with the other arm.

Forearm Stretch

Extend your left arm out straight, palm up. Grab the fingers of the left hand with your right hand (palm down) and slowly pull downward and hold. Turn the palm down and pull back on the fingers with your right hand and hold. Repeat on the opposite arm.

Cooling Down

This is a 5- to 10-minute period of light aerobic activity and static stretching that occurs immediately after a workout or game. The primary purposes of cool-down exercises are to return the body gradually to a resting state and reduce the chances of postexercise residual muscle soreness. Walk or jog for 5 minutes. When your heart rate is down and you're breathing at a normal rate, do two sets of the daily dozen.

Core Strength Training

You lift weights to improve performance and reduce the risk of injury. All gains developed in the weight room must be functional. If your training program doesn't help you move quicker, throw faster, swing harder, and avoid injury, it's not functional. Don't train just for the sake of getting bigger or stronger. Strength and size without a functional purpose are worthless.

Baseball players don't need to bench press 300 pounds or squat 400 pounds to be successful. The ball weighs only 5-1/2 ounces, and most bats weigh 34 ounces or less. Functional strength and muscle symmetry are more important than absolute strength. Strength is functional if you can swing the bat with authority, throw with zip, and move your body efficiently. Symmetry improves function and helps protect you from injury. Work to achieve a balance between the muscles on opposing sides of the body and between the opposing muscle groups.

How you train, what exercises you do, the order you do them, how often you work out, how much you lift, how long your rest between sets, and how long you recover between workouts determine whether your training will be useful. Training should be specific to baseball. Even strength training should closely mimic what occurs in game situations. The body functions as a whole, not as the sum of its parts. There is no valid reason to give each muscle group equal training in number of exercises, frequency, volume, or intensity. Muscles that participate most in the performance of the sport need the most attention. In baseball, the "power zone" includes the hips, legs, trunk, and back. Sport-specific movements (lunges, step-ups, leg curls, calf raises, sit-ups, lat pulls, and rowing) should be trained more often. Supporting muscle groups like the chest, shoulders, and arms can be trained once or twice per week without reducing the effectiveness of the workout.

Training Systems

Choosing among different training systems or routines can help you find the most appropriate workouts for various seasons and stages of your training. The routine you choose affects the frequency and intensity with which you'll work, the duration of rest and recovery between exercises, sets and reps, and results. Using a variety of strength-training routines can help you get the gains you want when you need them—and avoid boredom.

Circuit Weight Training (CWT)

Circuit training is an excellent way to develop fitness in a brief period. It's ideal for the postseason and early off-season when you are trying to develop a general fitness base, and it can add variety to in-season workouts. Use your body's weight as resistance in the postseason and choose exercises that work the muscle groups that provide balance and support (see table 7.1). Do one set of each exercise in the circuit, one after the other, resting 15 to 30 seconds between exercises. Rest one to two minutes and do another circuit.

Start off-season training with a two- or three-week CWT program using dumbbells, free weights, and machines. Select 10 to 15 lifts that train the total body. Do one set of each exercise in the circuit, one after the other. Rest and repeat the circuit three times. Table 7.2 contains a sample off-season CWT program.

Table 7.1 Sample Postseason CWT Program Using Body Weight as Resistance

Muscle group	Exercise	Circuit 1	Circuit 2
		Sets × reps	Sets × reps
Hip and leg	Step-up	1 × 10-12	1 × 10-12
Trunk	Sit-up	1 × 10-12	1 × 10-12
Chest and arms	Push-up	1 × 10-12	1 × 10-12
Legs	Walking lunge	1 × 10-12	1 × 10-12
Back and biceps	Modified pull-up	1 × 10-12	1 × 10-12
Shoulder	Push-up plus	1 × 10-12	1 × 10-12
Rotator cuff	Jobe series	1 × 10-12	1 × 10-12

Table 7.2 Sample Early Off-Season CWT Program

Circuit	Muscle group	Exercise	Sets × reps × % max
Core	Hip and leg	Squat	3 × 10-12 × 60-70
	Chest	DB bench	3 × 10-12 × 60-70
	Back	Seated long row	3 × 10-12 × 60-70
	Shoulder	DB shrug	3 × 10-12 × 60-70
	Back	Lat pull	3 × 10-12 × 60-70

Table 7.2 Sample Early Off-Season CWT Program

Circuit	Muscle group	Exercise	Sets × reps × % max
Assist	Triceps	Triceps press-down	3 × 10-12 × 60-70
	Trunk	Sit-ups	3 × 25
	Biceps	DB curl	3 × 10-12 × 60-70
	Calf	Standing calf raise	3 × 20 × 60-70
	Trunk	MD ball twists	3 × 25
Special circuit	Forearm/hand	Wrist curl	3 × 20 × 60
		Wrist extension	3 × 20 × 60
		Rice drill	3 ×
		Wrist roller	3 × 10

Repeat the circuit 3 times.

Multiple-Set Training

With multiple-set training, you complete all sets of one exercise before doing the next. You can use multiple-set training with total-body workouts, pyramid loading, or split routines. Use it in the off-season, after you have completed two to three weeks of CWT, or during the season to maintain strength. Alternate upper- and lower-body exercises and do core exercises first, assist exercises second, and special exercises last. Table 7.3 contains a sample multiple-set program.

Table 7.3 Sample Multiple-Set Total Body Workout

Muscle group	Core	Assist	Special
Hip and leg	Squat	Leg curl Standing calf raise	Squat and touch
Chest	DB bench	DB incline fly	
Trunk	Sit-up	MD ball rotation	
Shoulder	DB shrug	DB row	Jobe series
Back	Seated long row Lat pull		
Triceps	Triceps press-down	DB kickback	
Biceps	DB curl	Hammer curl	
Forearm/hand			Wrist flexion/extension

Pyramid Training

With pyramid training, you increase the load and reduce the reps each set. This is an advanced form of multiple-set training for the preseason, one that only experienced athletes should use. Loads are usually based on a percentage of 1RM (see page 168). A sample pyramid is presented in table 7.4.

Four-Day Split Training

Another advanced form of training, the four-day split, breaks the workout into four segments so you can train different areas of the body on different days. Use it after you have established a sound base. It's appropriate during off-season and in-season training. Loads can be constant or set up in a pyramid from set to set. This approach allows you to devote more time to one area without having to spend all day in the weight room. Work the legs, back, and biceps on one day and the chest, shoulders, and triceps on the next. Take a day off and repeat the sequence. Do six to eight exercises per workout. Complete all sets of one exercise before doing the second and do core exercises first. A sample four-day split routine is presented in table 7.5.

Table 7.4 Sample Pyramid Workout

Lift	Set	Rep $\times$ % max
Squat	Warm-up	10 $\times$ 50
	1	8 $\times$ 80
	2	6 $\times$ 85
	3	4 $\times$ 90
	4	2 $\times$ 95

Table 7.5 Sample Four-Day Split Workout

Day	Muscle	Core	Assist	Special
1	Hip and leg	Squat	Leg curl Standing calf	Squat and touch
	Back	Lat pull	DB row	
	Biceps	EZ-bar arm curl	DB curl	
	Trunk	Sit-up		
	Forearm/hand			Wrist twist
2	Chest	Incline press	DB fly	
	Triceps	EZ-bar triceps press	DB kickback	
	Shoulder	Shrug		Jobe series
	Trunk		MD ball rotation MD ball sit-up	
	Forearm/hand			Ulnar flex Plantar flex

Note: Do some form of trunk, forearm/hand, and rotator cuff workout at least every other day.

Six-Day Split Training

This method is most effective in the preseason when you are using heavy weights to maximize strength, and it is not for inexperienced lifters! Increase (pyramid) the load from set to set but reduce the number of exercises to only four to six per workout. Do two or three core lifts, one or two assist lifts, and one or two special lifts each workout. Complete all sets of one exercise before doing the second. Work the legs one day, the chest, shoulders, and triceps the second day, and the back and biceps the third day. Take a day off and repeat the sequence. Table 7.6 gives a sample six-day split.

Exercise Types—Core, Assist, and Special Lifts

You'll be using three types of exercises: core exercises, assist exercises, and special lifts. Core exercises are multijoint movements that use a large muscle mass and relatively heavy loads. They involve complex, multijoint movements of the large muscles of the hips, back, chest, and shoulders to improve strength, joint stability, balance, skill, flexibility, and performance. Assist exercises are single or multijoint movements that use less muscle mass and lighter loads. They isolate

Table 7.6 Sample Six-Day Split Workout

Day	Muscle	Core	Assist	Special
1	Hip and leg	Squat	Leg curl	SAT
		Lunge	Standing calf	DB lat lunge
	Trunk	Sit-up		
	Forearm/hand			Wrist flex/ext
	Rotator cuff			Jobe series
2	Chest	DB bench	DB incline fly	
	Shoulder	Shrug		Scapula series
	Triceps	Triceps press-down	DB kickback	
	Trunk		MD ball rotation	
	Arm/hand			Wrist roller
3	Back	Lat pull		
		Seated long row		
	Biceps	DB curl	Hammer curl	
	Trunk	MD ball sit-up		
	Arms/hands			Wrist flex/ext

Note: Do some form of trunk, forearm/hand, and rotator cuff workout at least every other day.

the smaller muscles to strengthen specific areas and prevent injury. Special lifts are usually single-joint exercises that work weak or special areas of the body, such as the rotator cuff, scapula, wrist, and forearm. They mirror movements used in game situations and use light loads and many reps to strengthen the muscles and tendons most prone to injury. Table 7.7 presents categories and types of exercises by body region. For best results, use a blend of core, assist, and special lifts and choose a training intensity, volume, and tempo that will stress and enhance the specific energy delivery systems used in game situations.

Figuring the Components of Your Strength Training

A total-body workout should include at least one core exercise for each major muscle group. Supplement these with assist and special lifts.

Choose 8 to 10 exercises that work opposing muscle groups to develop symmetry between muscle groups. Do six to eight core lifts, two or three assist lifts, and one or two special lifts. In the preseason phase do a split routine with three or four core lifts, two or three assist lifts, and one or two special lifts each workout.

Do complex, multijoint exercises that require the most balance and coordination first, when you're fresh. Perform single-joint, small-muscle exercises last. Do squats and leg presses before leg extensions and leg curls. Work the chest, shoulders, and back before the arms and forearms. If you fatigue the smaller muscles, you can't generate maximum intensity in the larger muscles. Fatiguing the arms, for example, will limit the quality of your chest and back work. When possible, alternate exercises for the upper and lower body. Avoid doing two consecutive exercises for the same muscle group.

Use free weights and dumbbells to simulate the sport-specific movements, agility, balance, and coordination required in game situations. Use machines for exercises that you can't do with free weights. Most machines are easier to use than free weights—and some exercises that are standard on machines (such as lat pulls, triceps presses, and leg curls) are almost impossible to do with free weights. Free weights require more balance and coordination and more closely simulate the movements that occur in sport. Dumbbells are smart. They might not be high tech, but they're functional. For best results, use a combination of exercises using both free weights and machines. Use free weights to simulate sport-specific movements and machines to isolate a muscle or movement for special emphasis or rehabilitation.

The more reps you do per set, the fewer sets you do. How many sets you do depends also on the type of exercise, number of exercises you do in a given workout, and your training experience. Core exercises require more sets than assist or special exercises.

As a guideline, perform three to four sets when doing total-body workouts; go up to four to five sets when doing split routines. Table 7.8 shows the number of sets required for different types of exercise during each training phase.

The number of times, or repetitions, that you can do an exercise without resting is a function of load. The heavier the load, the lower the number of reps and vice versa. With your maximum load, by definition you lift only once. With

Table 7.7 Categories and Examples of Exercises

Muscle group	Core	Assist	Special
Hip and Leg	Squat	DB squat	Squat and touch
	Lunge	DB lunge	Split-squat
	Step-up	Leg extension	DB lateral lunge
	Leg press	Leg curl	DB crossover lunge
		Hip abd/add	Step-down
		Standing calf	Cowboy squat
		Seated calf	
		Straight-leg dead lift	
Trunk	Sit-up	MD ball rotations	
	Leg drop	MD ball sit-up	
Chest	Bench press	DB fly or push-up	
	Incline press	DB incline fly	
	DB bench press	Pec dec	
	DB incline press	Incline push-up	
Shoulders	Shrug	Lateral DB raise	Jobe (rotator cuff)
	DB shrug	Reverse DB raise	Scarecrow
	Pullover	Reverse pec dec	
Back	Lat pull	DB row	Tubing row
	Seated long row	Seated row	Good morning
	Bent-over row	Pull-up or modified pull-up	Hyperextension
Triceps	EZ-bar tri press	DB kickback	Tubing tri press
	Tri press-down	Dips	
	Close-grip bench	Reverse tri press-down	
Biceps	EZ-bar arm curl	DB hammer curl	Tubing arm curl
	DB curl	DB reverse curl	
	Bar curl	Machine curl	
Forearm/hand		Wrist roller	
		Wrist flexion	
		Wrist extension	
		Wrist twists	
		Ulnar flex	
		Radial flexion	
		Rice drills	
		Towel pull-up	
		Hand gripper	

Table 7.8 Number of Sets During Training Phases

Exercise type	Postseason	Off-season	Preseason	In-season
Core	3-5	4-6	4-6	3-4
Assist	2-3	3-4	3-4	2-3
Special	2-3	2-3	2-3	2-3

94 percent of the maximum, you might lift 3 times; with 74 percent you might lift 10 times. Reps can be used as a tool for achieving different training effects. Doing high reps (15 to 20 reps) with lighter loads increases muscular endurance, doing fewer reps (8-10 reps) with heavier loads increases strength, and performing fewer reps yet (2-4 reps) increases power.

Volume is the total work done in a given exercise or workout. It is determined by multiplying sets by reps. The higher the volume, the lower the intensity and vice versa. Use high-volume work in the off-season to build a sound training base. Reduce the volume as the season approaches.

Lift and lower the weight at a controlled, slow speed in phases 1 and 2. Take one to two seconds to lift and two to three seconds to lower in the off-season. Work more explosively in the pre- and in-season.

Do all exercises through a full range of motion (ROM) to ensure complete muscular development and enhance flexibility. It's better to lift a lighter load through a full ROM than to lift a heavier load through a partial ROM.

Vary the program from month to month and week to week to prevent monotony and avoid strength plateaus. The best way to promote improvement is to keep the body guessing about what is coming up next. Change the number of reps, sets, load, exercise type, or speed of exercise. Alter one variable at a time. Never increase intensity (load) and volume (sets times reps) at the same time.

Rest is the amount of inactivity between sets of a given workout or between consecutive workouts. You must include short rest periods (30 seconds) to increase muscular endurance and produce moderate strength gains. Longer rest periods (two to five minutes) are needed to increase strength and power. Rest two to five minutes between heavy sets of core exercises for the same muscle group and one to two minutes between sets of assist and special exercises, but don't sit down. Stand, stretch, walk around, or get a drink. Keep moving. Staying active keeps your heart rate elevated and helps prevent your muscles from tightening up between sets and exercises. Allow at least 48 hours of recovery between workouts of similar body parts. Insert three to five days of active rest between training phases.

Determining Intensity (Load)

Intensity is the most important factor in strength training. High-intensity work builds strength and power; low-intensity work increases muscular endurance.

The amount of weight you can lift for a single rep is called the one-repetition max (1RM). The amount you can lift five times is your 5RM. Intensity and reps are related. The higher the intensity (heavier the load), the fewer reps you can do and vice versa. Intensity is usually expressed as a percentage of your 1RM.

Core exercises require a higher intensity (heavier load and fewer reps) than assist and special exercises. Limit assist exercises to loads that you can lift at least 6 to 12 times. Do special exercises with loads that you can lift for 10 to 20 reps.

Start the off-season training phase with higher reps and lighter loads to build a good strength-endurance base. Increase load and decrease reps from phase to phase to develop strength and power. The minimal threshold for the development of muscular strength is 60 percent. Loads below 60 percent of your maximum strength (about 15 reps) are good for warm-up, but they won't stimulate an increase in strength.

How to Find and Adjust Your Training Load

If you have less than one year of supervised strength-training experience, you should use the required repetitions method. It's easier and quicker to learn. Resistance is determined by your ability to complete a specified number of repetitions of each exercise. The training load depends on the goal that you're trying to achieve (endurance, strength, or power). You don't do the same thing all year around. If you're working on endurance, in which the volume of training (number of reps) is the critical factor, load is determined by how many reps you can do in all sets of a particular exercise. For strength and power, in which intensity is more important, load is determined by how may reps you can do in the first set. For example, if you're building a strength-endurance base and the workout calls for 4 × 10, select a load that allows you to do the full number of reps (10) in each set.

We emphasize two training programs in this book—one using reps (for high school players) and the other using a percentage of maximum (for college and pro players). Finding the right training load for each exercise requires some trial and error. You can *estimate* your 10RM load by lifting a percentage of your body weight. Table 7.9 shows how to use body weight to determine starting loads for both machines and free weights. Most people can use more resistance when they're working on machines than when they're doing the same exercise with free weights. Sometimes training load will vary depending on the type (brand) of machine you're using.

Using body weight to predict starting loads works well for beginners or someone just starting to work out after a long layoff. Adjust the values downward by 5 to 10 percent if you are under 140 pounds. To use the program, first warm up. Then, go to table 7.9 and multiply your body weight by the appropriate percentage to determine a starting weight for each lift. For example, if you're a 200-pounder doing squats with free weights, multiply your weight in pounds by .70 to get a starting load of 140 pounds. If you're doing triceps work, multiply your body weight by .15 to get a training load of 30 pounds. Round up or down to the nearest 5-pound increment.

Strength-Endurance. The training load is too light if you can do all reps in each set. Increase the load by 3 to 5 percent in the next workout. It's too heavy, on the other hand, if you're more than 1 rep away from the target in the first set. If, for example, you can do only 8 reps of a 4 × 10 workout on the first set, the load is too heavy. Reduce it by 3 to 5 percent and continue the workout. If you're within 1 rep of the target on the first set, keep using this load until you can do 10 reps in all sets. The load is adequate if you're within 1 rep of the target on the first set but can't do all reps in each set. Examples of when to keep or change the load when working on strength and endurance are presented in table 7.10a.

Speed-Power. The training load is too light if you can do all reps in the *first* set. Increase the load by 3 to 5 percent in the next workout. For example, if you do sets of 6, 5, 4, and 3 reps in a 4 × 6 workout, increase the load in the next workout because you did the target number of reps (six) in the first set. The load is too heavy if you fail to get within 1 rep of the target on the first set. Reduce the load by 3 to 5 percent and continue the workout. If you did 5 reps in the first set, continue to use the same load in subsequent workouts until you can do 6 reps in the first set. Examples of when to keep or change the load when working on speed and power are presented in table 7.10b.

Basing training loads on reps is quicker than the 1RM method and reduces the need for frequent testing. It also lets you adjust the load as needed, from day to day, based on your performance in the previous workout and accounts for variation in daily ability. If you feel tired or strong, the load can be adjusted to optimize the workout. This method encourages progress. You add more weight when you lift the target load for the specified number of sets and reps.

Table 7.9 Selecting Training Loads on Percentage of Total Body Weight (TBW)

Machines	% TBW	Free weight	% TBW
Leg press	80	Squats	70
Incline press	40	Incline press	40
Leg curl	25	DB bench press	15
Lat pull	45	DB incline press	15
Leg extension	40	Lunge	30
Bench press	40	Bench press	40
Arm curls	15	Arm curls	15
Triceps press	15	Triceps press	15
Fly	20	DB fly	15
Incline fly	20	DB incline fly	15
Seated row	45	DB row	20
Standing calf raise	50	Standing calf raise	50

Adapted from Ward et al., 1991.

Table 7.10a Adjusting Training Load When Training for Strength-Endurance

Example 1:	**Goal**	4 × 10 × 100 lb
	Results	8 × 100, 7 × 100, 6 × 100, 6 × 100 lb
	Comment	Did only 8 reps in first set—load was too heavy
	Rationale	More than 1 rep away from target (10) in first set
	Adjustment	Reduce load by 3-5% on next workout
Example 2:	**Goal**	4 × 10 × 100 lb
	Results	10 × 100, 10 × 100, 8 × 100, 7 × 100 lb
	Comment	Did 2 × 10, 1 × 8, and 1 × 7—load was adequate
	Rationale	Did not complete all reps in all sets
	Adjustment	Use same load in next workout

Table 7.10b Adjusting Training Load When Training for Speed-Power

Example 1:	**Goal**	4 × 6 × 100 lb
	Results	4 × 100, 4 × 100, 3 × 100, 3 × 100 lb
	Comment	Did only 4 reps in first set—load was too heavy
	Rationale	More than 1 rep away from target (6 reps) in first set
	Adjustment	Reduce load by 3-5% on next workout
Example 2:	**Goal**	4 × 6 × 100 lb
	Results	5 × 100, 5 × 100, 4 × 100, 4 × 100 lb
	Comment	Did 2 × 5, and 2 × 4—load was adequate
	Rationale	Within 1 rep of target (6 reps) in first set
		Did not complete all reps in first set
	Adjustment	Use same load in next workout

Training Loads for Advanced Athletes

The system most commonly used to decide training loads for advanced athletes is the 1RM method. Although this method is popular among football, track, and power-lifting athletes, baseball players, especially those with less than one year of supervised strength-training experience, should not attempt a 1 RM test. You can get a fast, safe, accurate estimate of your maximum strength in most lifts with a submaximum test. Done properly, submaximum tests will take less time and provide values within 5 percent of those achieved with maximum efforts. This book *uses the 5RM test to estimate 1RM values,* but you can use the information in table 7.11 to predict maximum values for any rep range between 2RM and 10RM.

Warm up and use a spotter. Start easy and progress slowly. This is not a max-out or power-lifting session. Don't cheat. Bad form and cheating movements are unsafe and can cause you to overestimate your training loads. Start with a weight light enough that you know you can do 10 to 12 reps with good form. It's always better to start with a weight that is too light than one that is too heavy. Do 12 to 15 reps and then rest for two minutes. Increase the weight by 2 to 20 percent. Use more weight if the last set was easy and less if it was too hard. Do 6 to 8 reps with the new weight and then rest for three minutes. Increase the duration of the rest interval as you increase the weight load. Raise the weight by an additional 2 to 20 percent and do as many reps as you can. If you follow the procedures as outlined, you should end up with a weight that you can lift with good form for five times maximum (5RM).

Enter your 5RM value into table 7.11 to estimate your 1RM. Assume, for example, that you were able to bench press a 200-pound load five times. Go to the top of the chart and choose the column headed *5* for the number of reps done. Find the row with *200* on the left to match the weight lifted. The intersection of the column headed *5* and the row beginning with *200* gives the number *229,* which is your estimated 1RM. Round up to achieve an estimated 1RM of 230 pounds. Had you been able to do six reps with 200 pounds, your predicted 1RM would be 235 pounds. If you had been able to do four reps, your maximum would be 222 pounds. The examples in table 7.12 on page 172 illustrate how to administer a 5RM test and estimate your 1RM for an incline press and a leg press.

How to Use Your 1RM to Find Your Training Percentage

Multiply the estimated 1RM value for each lift by the percentage given in the workout prescription to determine training loads. Assume, for example, that your predicted 1RM in the bench press is 230 pounds and that you are to do a 5 × 5 × 75 percent workout. Multiply your 1RM by .75 (230 pounds × .75 = 172 pounds) and then round up or down to the nearest 5 pounds to achieve a training load of 170 pounds.

To make your work easier, table 7.13 on page 173 provides various percentages of different maximum values. The values in the column on the left side of the table represent 1RM values. The column across the top lists percentages from 45 to 95. To find a workout load, begin by finding your 1RM in the left column. Next, find the percentage you want on the top. The intersection of these two lines is your weight load for the 1RM value and percentage used. Find the appropriate percentage for each lift in your program. Table 7.14 on page 174 illustrates how to find the training percentages for the 1RM values calculated in the examples in table 7.12.

Loads for Core Lifts

The training load determined from table 7.13 is the amount of weight you should lift in the last set. If, for example, your maximum in the bench press is 200 pounds and the workout calls for 5 × 5 × 75 percent of maximum, the load in the last set (fifth set) is 150 pounds. Loads in other sets are less than 75 percent. See table 7.15 on page 175 to determine training loads for the first four sets. Read backward from the intersection of the column headed *Set 5* and the row in which the fifth set was 150 pounds to determine the loads for the first four sets. Table 7.16 on page 176 shows the training loads for each set in a 5 × 5 × 75 percent workout. This stair-step approach provides a good warm-up and yields better results than those achieved by doing all five sets with the same load.

Table 7.11 Estimate of 1RM from Submax Test Data

Pounds	10	9	8	7	6	5	4	3	2
5	7	6	6	6	6	6	6	5	5
10	13	13	12	12	11	11	11	11	11
15	20	19	19	18	18	17	17	16	16
20	27	26	25	24	24	23	22	22	21
25	33	32	31	30	29	29	28	27	26
30	40	39	38	36	35	34	33	32	32
35	47	45	44	42	41	40	39	38	37
40	53	52	50	48	47	46	44	43	42
45	60	58	56	55	53	51	50	49	47
50	67	65	63	61	59	57	56	54	53
55	73	71	69	67	65	63	61	59	58
60	80	77	75	73	71	69	67	65	63
65	87	84	81	79	76	74	72	70	68
70	93	90	88	85	82	80	78	76	74
75	100	97	94	91	88	86	83	81	79
80	107	103	100	97	94	91	89	86	84
85	113	110	106	103	100	97	94	92	89
90	120	116	113	109	106	103	100	97	95
95	127	123	119	115	112	109	106	103	100
100	133	129	125	121	118	114	111	108	105
105	140	135	131	127	124	120	117	114	111
110	147	142	138	133	129	126	122	119	116
115	153	148	144	139	135	131	128	124	121
120	160	155	150	145	141	137	133	130	126
125	167	161	156	153	147	143	139	135	132
130	173	168	163	158	153	149	144	141	137
135	180	174	169	164	159	154	150	146	142
140	187	181	175	170	165	160	156	151	147
145	193	187	181	176	171	166	161	157	153
150	200	194	188	182	176	171	167	162	158
155	207	200	194	188	182	177	172	168	163
160	213	206	200	194	188	183	178	173	168

(continued)

Table 7.11 *(continued)*

Pounds	10	9	8	7	6	5	4	3	2
165	220	213	206	200	194	189	183	178	174
170	227	119	213	206	200	194	189	184	179
175	233	226	219	212	206	200	194	189	184
180	240	232	225	218	212	206	200	195	189
185	247	239	231	224	218	211	206	200	195
190	253	245	238	230	224	217	211	205	200
195	260	252	244	236	229	223	217	211	205
200	267	258	250	242	235	229	222	216	211
205	273	265	256	248	241	234	228	222	216
210	280	271	263	255	247	240	233	227	221
215	287	277	269	261	253	246	239	232	226
220	293	284	275	267	259	251	244	238	232
225	300	290	281	273	265	257	250	243	237
230	307	297	288	279	271	263	256	249	242
235	313	303	294	285	276	269	261	254	247
240	320	310	300	291	282	274	267	259	253
245	327	316	306	297	288	280	272	265	258
250	333	232	313	303	294	286	278	270	263
255	340	329	319	309	300	291	283	276	268
260	347	335	325	315	306	297	289	281	274
265	353	342	331	321	312	303	294	286	279
270	360	348	338	327	318	309	300	292	284
275	367	355	344	333	324	314	306	297	289
280	373	361	350	339	329	320	311	303	295
285	380	368	356	345	335	326	317	308	300
290	387	374	363	352	341	331	322	314	305
295	393	381	369	358	347	337	328	319	311
300	400	487	375	364	353	343	333	324	316
305	407	394	381	370	359	349	339	330	321
310	413	400	388	376	365	354	344	335	326
315	420	406	394	382	371	360	350	341	332
320	427	413	400	388	376	366	356	346	337
325	433	419	406	394	382	371	361	351	342
330	440	426	413	400	388	377	367	357	347

Pounds	10	9	8	7	6	5	4	3	2
335	447	432	419	406	394	383	372	362	353
340	453	439	425	412	400	389	378	368	358
345	460	445	431	418	406	394	383	373	363
350	467	452	438	424	412	400	389	378	368
355	473	458	444	430	418	406	394	384	374
360	480	465	450	436	424	411	400	389	379
365	487	471	456	442	429	417	406	395	384
370	493	477	463	448	435	423	411	400	389
375	500	484	469	455	441	429	417	405	395
380	507	490	475	461	447	434	422	411	400
385	513	497	481	467	453	440	428	416	405
390	520	503	488	473	459	446	433	422	411
395	527	510	494	479	465	451	439	427	416
400	533	516	500	485	471	457	444	432	421
405	540	523	506	491	476	463	450	438	426
410	547	529	513	497	482	469	456	443	432
415	553	535	519	503	488	474	461	449	437
420		542	525	509	494	480	467	454	442
425		548	531	515	500	486	472	459	447
430		555	538	521	506	491	478	465	453
435		561	544	527	512	497	483	470	458
440		568	550	533	518	503	489	476	463
445		574	556	539	524	509	494	481	468
450		581	563	545	529	514	500	486	474
455		587	569	552	535	520	506	492	479
460		594	575	558	541	526	511	497	484
465		600	581	564	547	531	517	505	489
470		606	588	570	553	537	522	508	495
475		613	595	576	559	543	528	514	500
480		619	600	582	565	549	533	519	505
485		626	606	588	571	554	539	524	511
490		632	613	594	576	560	544	530	516
495		639	619	600	582	566	550	535	521
500		645	625	606	588	571	556	541	526

Adapted from Strength Tech, Inc.

Table 7.12   How to Administer a 5RM Test and Estimate a 1RM From a Bench and Leg Press

Warm up and proceed through the following three steps. Repeat the testing pattern for the remaining exercises in your program.

Incline press			Leg press		
Step one:		Warm up	**Step one:**		Warm up
		12-15 reps at 85 lb			12-15 reps at 200 lb
Step two:		Take the 5RM test	**Step two:**		Take the 5RM test
	Set 1:	12-15 reps at 115 lb		**Set 1:**	12-15 reps at 250 lb
		2-min rest			2-min rest
	Set 2:	10-12 reps at 125 lb		**Set 2:**	10-12 reps at 275 lb
		2-min rest			2-min rest
	Set 3:	6-8 reps at 140 lb		**Set 3:**	6-8 reps at 300 lb
		3-min rest			3-min rest
	Set 4:	5 reps at 170 lb		**Set 4:**	5 reps at 325 lb
		record result			record result
Step three:		See table 7.11	**Step three:**		See table 7.11
		1RM = 195 lb			1RM = 370 lb

Loads for Assist Lifts

As with core lifts, the training load is the amount of resistance to be used in the last set. Assume, for example, that your predicted 1RM for dumbbell curls is 40 pounds and that you are doing a percent workout. Multiply your estimated 1RM value by 70 percent to achieve a training load of 30 pounds. This is your load in the last set. Your load in set one is 20 pounds and your load in set two is 25 pounds (table 7.17 on page 178). Calculate loads for all assist lifts in your program. Table 7.18 on page 179 illustrates the loads for three sets of a $3 \times 5 \times 75$ percent workout.

Adjusting the Sequence to the Season

Postseason

Use the first two to three weeks to learn how to do each exercise correctly. Do a circuit training program three times per week for two to three weeks and do a total-body workout each day. Start with three circuits of 10 to 12 basic exercises. Alternate exercises for opposing muscle groups and place core exercises first in the exercise circuit. Start light and increase the load each circuit. When you can do all reps in each circuit for a given exercise, increase the load by 3 to 5 percent. Table 7.19 on page 179 illustrates the progression for a three-week, off-season CWT program.

Table 7.13 Percentage Table (Rounded to Nearest 5 Pounds)

Weight	45%	50%	55%	60%	65%	70%	75%	80%	85%	90%	95%
100	45	50	55	60	65	70	75	80	85	90	95
110	50	55	60	65	70	75	85	90	95	100	105
120	55	60	65	70	80	85	90	95	100	110	115
130	60	65	70	80	85	90	100	105	110	115	125
140	65	70	75	85	90	100	105	110	120	125	135
150	70	75	85	90	100	105	115	120	130	135	145
160	75	80	90	95	105	110	120	130	135	145	150
170	80	85	95	100	110	120	125	135	145	155	160
180	80	90	100	110	115	125	135	145	155	160	170
190	85	90	105	115	125	135	145	150	160	170	180
200	90	100	110	120	130	140	150	160	170	180	190
210	100	105	115	125	135	145	155	170	180	190	200
220	100	110	120	130	145	155	165	175	185	200	210
230	105	115	125	140	150	160	175	185	195	205	220
240	110	120	130	145	155	170	180	190	205	215	230
250	115	125	140	150	165	175	190	200	215	225	240
260	120	130	145	155	170	180	195	210	220	235	245
270	125	135	150	160	175	190	200	215	230	245	255
280	125	140	155	170	180	195	210	225	240	250	265
290	130	145	160	175	190	205	220	230	245	260	275
300	135	150	165	180	195	210	225	240	255	270	285
310	140	155	170	185	200	215	230	250	265	280	295
320	145	160	175	190	210	225	240	255	270	290	305
330	150	165	180	200	215	230	250	265	280	300	315
340	155	170	190	205	220	240	255	270	290	305	325
350	160	175	195	210	230	245	265	280	300	315	335
360	160	180	200	220	230	250	270	290	310	320	340
370	165	175	205	225	240	260	280	295	315	330	350
380	170	180	210	230	250	270	290	300	320	340	360
390	175	190	215	235	240	275	295	310	330	250	270
400	180	200	220	240	260	280	300	320	340	360	380
410	190	205	225	245	265	285	305	330	355	370	390

(continued)

Table 7.13 *(continued)*

Weight	45%	50%	55%	60%	65%	70%	75%	80%	85%	90%	95%
430	205	215	235	255	280	300	320	355	365	390	410
440	200	220	240	260	290	310	330	370	370	400	420
450	205	215	245	270	295	315	340	370	380	405	430
460	210	230	250	280	300	320	350	375	390	410	440
470	215	235	255	285	305	330	355	375	400	420	450
480	220	240	260	290	310	340	360	380	410	430	460
490	225	245	270	295	320	345	370	390	420	440	470
500	230	250	280	300	330	350	380	400	430	450	480

Table 7.14 How to Find the Training Percentage for a 5 × 5 × 75% Workout

Incline press:	Leg press:
1RM = 190	1RM = 370
75% = 145	75% = 280

Off-Season

Switch to a multiple-set program and do a total-body workout three times per week on alternate days. Start with four to five sets of core exercises and two to three sets of assist exercises. See the tables in chapter 2 for off-season fitness training programs.

Preseason

Switch to a four-day split routine. Work the lower body one day and the upper body the next. Take a day off and repeat the sequence. Follow the program outlined in the tables in chapter 3.

Spring Training

Your training goal is to convert sport-specific strength into baseball-specific strength, speed, and power. Use a four- or six-day split. Work the lower and upper body on alternate days (four-day split) or work chest and triceps on one day, legs on the second day, and back and biceps on the third day (six-day split).

Reduce the number of exercises to three to five per day to conserve energy for hitting, fielding, and throwing. Do large-muscle, multijoint exercises quickly and explosively to recruit the greatest number of fibers at the highest rate possible. Work smaller muscle groups at a slower rate. Beginners use a load that lets them do all reps in the first set. Follow the program outlined in the tables in chapter 4.

Table 7.15 Determining Training Loads for Major Muscle Groups

Set 1	Set 2	Set 3	Set 4	Set 5	Set 6
75	85	95	105	115	125
75	85	95	110	120	130
75	90	105	115	125	135
75	90	105	120	130	140
85	95	110	125	135	145
85	105	115	135	145	155
85	105	115	135	150	160
95	110	125	140	155	165
95	110	125	140	155	170
95	115	130	145	160	175
95	115	130	150	165	180
95	125	140	155	170	185
95	125	140	160	175	190
95	135	150	165	180	195
95	135	150	170	185	200
135	145	160	175	190	205
135	145	160	180	195	210
135	155	170	185	200	215
135	155	170	190	205	220
135	155	180	195	210	225
135	155	180	200	215	230
135	155	185	200	215	235
135	155	185	205	220	240
135	155	185	205	225	245
135	155	185	210	230	250
135	155	185	215	235	255
135	155	185	220	240	260
135	155	185	225	245	265
135	155	185	230	250	270
135	155	195	235	255	275
135	155	195	240	260	280
135	185	225	245	265	285

(continued)

Table 7.15 *(continued)*

Set 1	Set 2	Set 3	Set 4	Set 5	Set 6
135	185	225	250	270	290
135	185	225	255	275	295
135	185	225	260	280	300
135	185	225	265	285	305
135	185	225	270	290	310
135	185	225	275	295	315
135	185	225	280	300	320
135	185	225	285	305	325
135	185	225	290	310	330
135	185	225	295	315	335
135	185	225	300	320	340
135	185	225	290	310	330
135	185	225	290	310	330

Adapted from Pauletto, 1991.

Table 7.16 Example of Training Load in Each Set of a 5 × 5 × 75% Program for a Core Exercise

Incline press:		Leg press:	
1RM = 190		1RM = 370	
75% = 145—load in last (5th) set		75% = 280—load in last (5th) set	
Set	Reps × weight	Set	Reps × weight
1	5 × 85	1	5 × 135
2	5 × 105	2	5 × 185
3	5 × 115	3	5 × 225
4	5 × 135	4	5 × 260
5	5 × 145	5	5 × 280

In-Season

Work to maintain at least 90 percent of the strength, speed, and power gained in off-season and preseason workouts. Lift for 15 to 20 minutes per workout. Use a four- or six-day split-routine. Follow the program outlined in the tables in chapter 5. All players use alternate days of heavy and moderate workloads with core lifts.

Program for the Trunk

The trunk comprises the second largest muscle mass in the body. Hitting and throwing a baseball is sequential, beginning at the toes and ending in the fingers.

Each segment contributes at the instant of impact or release. How far or fast the ball travels is the sum effect of the different body segments.

A strong trunk lets you transfer all or most of the force generated by the hips and legs to the shoulder, arm, wrist, and hand, and reduces the stress on the arm, shoulder, and low back. It also helps you absorb forces associated with check swings, headfirst slides, and collisions. A weak midsection limits force potential, reduces arm and bat speed, increases the risk of injury, and makes you look bad in the lobby.

HIT, RUN, AND THROW

To throw harder, hit with power, get out of the box quicker, and run faster, work on your stomach. Fifty percent of the force used in swinging a bat and throwing a ball comes from trunk rotation. And once you make contact or release the ball, the trunk continues to work, providing nearly 50 percent of the force used in running. The abs perform three essential functions in baseball. They stabilize the spine in running, transfer forces in hitting and throwing, and protect the back in diving, sliding, and jumping. They also help maintain the strong upright posture needed for proper running form.

Dos and Don'ts of Crunches

Sit-ups don't selectively burn fat and take off love handles deposited around the waist, and they don't burn many calories. You would have to do about twenty thousand continuous sit-ups to burn a pound of fat. Sit-ups strengthen your abs only if you do them right. For a strong, functional trunk, follow 10 sit-up rules:

1. Work the lower abs first and then work your oblique muscles. Finish with your upper abs. Your upper abs support the actions of the obliques, and if you fatigue them first, they won't be able to help the obliques.

2. Do some form of ab work every day. Your abs are involved in all aspects of baseball, as well as all aspects of daily life.

3. Do crunches. Curl only your head, shoulders, and upper back off the floor, not your entire torso. Crunches work the abs. Full sit-ups work the hip flexors.

4. Bend your knees. Straight-leg sit-ups cause your back to arch, which in turn can strain your low back. Bend your knees and keep your low back pressed into the floor during lifting and lowering phases.

5. Keep your elbows back. Lock your fingers behind your head and keep your elbows back even with your shoulders. You should never see your elbows when you come up. If you do, then you're using the momentum of your arms, not your abs, to get you up.

6. Exhale as you come up, as your abs contract. This will ensure that you use the deeper muscles. If you inhale as you come up, your abdomen will protrude, causing you to overarch and possibly strain your lower back.

7. Inhale as you go back, as your back and shoulders approach the ground.

8. Go slowly and easily! When you work fast, momentum takes over, you bounce up and down, and your abs don't get much work. Crunch and hold for two to three seconds and return slowly. Let your head and shoulders touch the ground after each rep to ensure that you work the abs through a full ROM.

Table 7.17 Determining Training Loads for Assist Exercises

Set 1	Set 2	Set 3
5	10	10
5	10	10
10	15	20
15	20	25
20	25	30
25	30	35
30	35	40
30	40	45
35	45	50
40	50	55
40	50	60
45	55	65
50	60	70
55	65	75
60	70	80
65	75	85
70	80	90
75	85	95
80	90	100
85	95	105
85	100	110
85	100	115
90	105	120
95	110	125
100	115	130
105	120	135
110	125	140
115	130	145
120	135	150

Adapted from Pauletto, 1991.

Table 7.18   Sample of Training Load in Each Set of a 3 × 5 × 75% Workout for an Assist Exercise

Triceps press-down:	Leg curl:
1RM = 60	1RM = 100
75% = 45—load in last (3rd) set	75% = 75—load in last (3rd) set
Set Reps × weight	**Set Reps × weight**
1 5 × 30	1 5 × 55
2 5 × 40	2 5 × 65
3 5 × 45	3 5 × 75

Table 7.19   Sample Three-Week CWT Program

		Circuit 1	Circuit 2	Circuit 3
Week	**Day**	**(rep × load)**	**(rep × load)**	**(rep × load)**
1	1	15 × 50%	12 × 55%	10 × 60%
1	2	15 × 55%	12 × 55%	10 × 60%
1	3	15 × 55%	12 × 60%	10 × 60%
2	1	15 × 50%	12 × 60%	10 × 65%
2	2	15 × 55%	12 × 60%	10 × 65%
2	3	15 × 60%	12 × 60%	10 × 65%
3	1	15 × 55%	12 × 65%	10 × 70%
3	2	15 × 60%	12 × 65%	10 × 70%
3	3	15 × 65%	12 × 65%	10 × 70%

Rest: 0:15-0:30 between exercises
        1:00-2:00 between circuits

9. Don't hook your feet. Hooking your feet under a pad lets your legs and hip flexors do most of the work. Your abs won't get much work.

10. Don't overdo it. Stop when you feel your form breaking down. Stop if you feel discomfort in your lower back.

Crunches

The following exercises will strengthen the abdomen and trunk, prevent back problems, and help transfer forces from the legs to the arms and shoulders. Do them with the knees bent. Start with the daily core outlined below and do them year-round. Supplement these with exercises from the drop, 4 × 4, 50, or 100 series.

Daily Core

Do at least 10 reps of each of the following daily core exercises. Do them every day and do at least 100 reps each day.

Knee-Ups

Lie down with both feet on the ground and knees bent. Use your lower abs to pull both knees to the chest. Pause, return, and repeat.

Seated Leg Tucks

Lean back about 45 degrees with your legs straight and arms back. Use your lower abs to pull both knees to chest. Pause, return, and repeat. Always keep your feet off the ground.

V-Ups

With hands behind your head and elbows back, pull your shoulders and knees up at same time to meet in the middle. Pause, return, repeat.

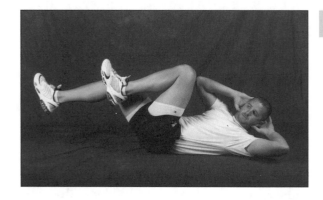

Pump Sit-Ups (Bicycle)

Lie on your back with both knees bent and hands behind your head. Pull your left knee into your chest and extend your right leg out straight. Twist left and touch your right elbow to your left knee. Pause and then extend your left leg out straight and pull your right knee into your chest. Twist right and touch your left elbow to your right knee. Alternate touching the opposite elbow to the opposite knee while extending (cycling) the other leg. Do two or three sets of 10 reps.

Crunches

Lie down with your knees bent, your feet flat, and your hands behind your head. Contract your abs and press your low back and feet into the floor. Come up no more than 6 to 12 inches and tense your ab muscles. Hold this position for two or three seconds, then slowly lower your back to the floor.

Lateral Crunch With Knees Bent

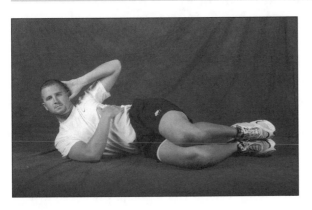

Lie on your right side with both knees bent and one leg on top of the other. Place your left hand behind your head and your right hand just below the ribs on your left side. Crunch up and pull your left elbow toward your left hip. Return and repeat. Do 10 reps on each side.

Side-to-Side

With arms straight, and hands by your hips, bend to the right and touch the outside of your right ankle with your right hand. Return and bend left. Alternate bending right and left. Do 10 reps on each side.

Drop Series

These exercises work the muscles used in twisting the trunk when hitting and throwing. Start with one set of 10 reps of each. Build to 3 × 20.

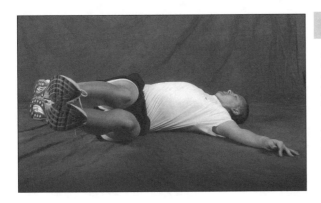

Side Leg Drops

Lie down with arms straight out at the sides and palms down. Raise both legs straight up over your hips. Keep your feet and legs together and drop your legs side to side. Stop just before your feet touch the ground and reverse directions. Drop legs side to side.

Seal

Stretch your ab muscles after each abdominal workout with the seal. From a push-up position, push up with your arms while keeping your hips on the ground and hold for 10 to 15 seconds to stretch your abs. Twist right, look over your right shoulder, and hold for 10 to 15 seconds. Relax, then push up, twist left, look over your left shoulder, and hold.

4 × 4 Series

These exercises involve pump (cycling) movements. Do four sets of four reps of each of these two movements for a total of 32 reps.

Basic 4 × 4

Lie down with both feet on the floor and hands behind your head. Bring your right knee into your chest and extend your left leg out straight, as in the photo of pump sit-ups. Crunch both elbows to your right knee four times. Pull your left knee toward your chest and extend your right leg out straight and repeat. Repeat the cycle four times for 32 total reps.

50 Series

Each exercise in this series has five parts, or movements. Do 10 reps of each part in sequence for a total of 50 reps per exercise.

Part 1—Crunch and Twist With Feet Down

Start with both hands behind your head, knees bent, and feet on the ground. Follow this sequence:

crunch	10 ×
twist left	10 ×
crunch	10 ×
twist right	10 ×
crunch	10 ×

Part 2—Crunch and Twist With Ankles Crossed

Cross your legs at the ankles and lift both feet off the ground until your hips and knees form right angles. Follow the sequence from part 1.

Part 3—Same-Side Crunch With Feet Down

Start on your back with hands behind your head and feet on the ground. Follow this sequence:

crunch	10 ×
crunch right elbow to right knee	10 ×
crunch left elbow to left knee	10 ×
crunch right elbow to right knee	10 ×
crunch left elbow to left knee	10 ×

Part 4—Same-Side Crunch With Ankles Crossed

Repeat part 3 with your legs crossed at the ankles and lift both feet off the ground until your hips and knees form right angles.

Part 5—Ins, Outs, Overs, Ups, and Side-to-Sides

Lie on your back with your arms forward and your elbows straight.

curl up and reach inside both knees	10 ×
curl up and touch outside both knees	10 ×
curl up and touch top of both knees	10 ×
bend side to side and touch outside of each ankle	20 ×

100 Series

Each exercise in this series has five parts that you repeat on each leg for a total of 100 reps. Do 10 reps of each part in each sequence.

Part 1—Cross-Knee Crunch and Twist

Lie on your back and cross your left knee over your right.

crunch	10 ×
twist left	10 ×
crunch	10 ×
twist right	10 ×
crunch	10 ×
repeat with left leg	50 ×

Part 2—Cross-Knee Crunch With Foot Up and Down

Lie on your back and cross your left knee over your right.

crunch	10 ×
lift right foot two inches off the ground and crunch	10 ×
extend right leg out straight and crunch	10 ×
return to position 2 and crunch	10 ×
return to position 1 and crunch	10 ×
repeat with left leg	50 ×

Part 3—Cross-Knee Twist With Foot Up and Down

Repeat part 2 and twist to one side when you come up.

Medicine-Ball Exercises for the Trunk

Do medicine ball exercises to develop the body's core—the abs, low back, and hip. A strong core is essential for balance, stabilization, force production, force reduction, and the transfer of power. Do drills described below three to five times per week to build strength, endurance, range of motion, and power in the core muscles of the body. Use a four- to six-pound MD ball if available. If not, use a five-pound DB.

Trunk—Medicine Ball

Rocky Twist

Sit with your knees bent, feet on the ground, and trunk inclined backward about 45 degrees. Receive a pass from a partner standing two to three feet in front of you. Hold the ball in front of you at full arm extension. Twist your upper body and move the ball side to side. Pause and pass it back without moving your trunk forward or backward. Repeat the drill with your partner standing farther away. Also repeat with your feet off the ground.

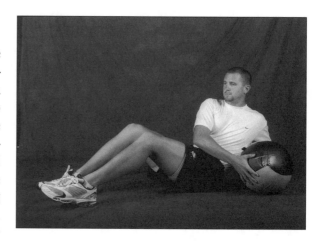

North Carolina

Sit with your knees bent, feet on the ground, and trunk inclined backward about 45 degrees. Receive a pass to your right hand and shoulder from a partner standing two to three feet in front of you. Twist as far as you can to your right and then twist back and pass it back across your body to your partner's right hand using a right-handed push pass without moving your trunk forward or backward. Repeat the drill on the opposite side. Repeat the drill with your partner standing farther away and with your feet up.

Lateral Twist and Pass With Feet Down

Sit with your knees bent, feet on the ground, and trunk inclined backward about 45 degrees. Receive a pass from a partner standing two to three feet to your left. Twist as far as you can to your right and then twist back and pass it back across your body using both hands without moving your trunk forward or backward. Repeat the drill with your partner standing farther away or, for more difficulty, twist 2 to 10 times before passing the ball back. Also repeat with your feet up.

Lower-Body Strength-Training Exercises

Doing squats with a bar increases absolute strength, while doing single-leg squats and squats and touches (SAT) with body weight increases functional strength. A 200-pounder, for example, who squats 200 pounds lifts a total of 400 pounds (body weight plus 200 pounds of iron). Because this weight is distributed over both legs, each leg receives a load of 200 pounds. If he does a one-leg squat or SAT without any external weight, the load on the support leg is 200 pounds. Working against body weight is effective and functional. It produces about the same load per leg, improves balance, and increases joint stability without putting stress on the back.

STRENGTH TIP: SQUATS OR STEP-UPS?

Step-ups increase functional strength, speed, and power and help protect against knee injury. Most strength and conditioning coaches advocate the squat for building strong, powerful legs and hips, but the step-up is actually more effective and functional for baseball players who need to improve acceleration, first-step quickness, and speed in a limited time. Step-ups simultaneously use all the muscles of the lower extremity in movement patterns similar to those used in running and jumping.

Stand one to two feet away from a 15- to 18-inch box or bench. Maintain an upright posture from start to finish with hips under the shoulders, chin slightly up, and eyes focused on a point slightly higher than eye level. Place the nondominant leg on the box first, with toes pointed straight ahead or slightly outward. Exhale, keep the entire foot in contact with the box, and extend the lead leg until the knee is just short of lockout. Pause for second, keep the back foot off the bench, exhale, and slowly bend the support leg until the back foot touches the ground. Flex the knee as the foot touches the ground to minimize pressure on the low back. Return the lead foot to the ground, pause, and repeat. Do one set with the nondominant leg before working the dominant leg.

You can vary the load by changing the height of the box. In general, the higher the box, the greater the hamstring recruitment. For explosive strength, do pop-ups. Walk into the box, moving your arms opposite to your legs. Step up on the box with the right foot and drive the left knee and right arm up with enough force to pull (pop) the right foot two or three inches off the box. Step down with the left foot and do all reps with the right leg before doing the left.

Lower Body

Squats and Dumbbell Squats

Stand with your feet parallel and about shoulder-width apart, with toes pointed outward between 35 and 45 degrees. Lift the bar from the supports and rest it across the upper back or hold a DB in each hand at arm's length with hands down the side of the legs. Lower the buttocks until thighs are parallel to the floor, pause, and return to the starting position. To maintain proper position, pick a spot to look at that will cause you to keep your head slightly up and your back straight. Inhale while lowering the bar and exhale while lifting.

Lunges and DB Lunges

Stand with feet parallel and about shoulder-width apart, with toes forward. Hold a bar across the upper back or a DB in each hand at arm's length. Step forward and support the body in a split-leg position. The front leg should be bent approximately 90 degrees at the knee. Push back up with the lead leg to the starting position and repeat. Repeat the drill on the other leg.

Walking Lunges

Hold a DB in each hand or a bar across your shoulders. Lunge forward on the right foot. Immediately step over the right knee with the left foot and lunge forward with the left foot. Repeat the sequence for 10 to 12 steps with each foot.

Lateral Lunges

Hold a dumbbell in each hand or a bar across your shoulders. Lunge out with the left leg at a 45-degree angle. Push back. Repeat on the right leg.

HAMSTRINGS

The hamstrings cross both the hip and the knee and perform two related functions. They extend the hip and flex the knee. In sports, the hamstrings' primary function is to extend the hip, not to flex the knee. Failure to adequately condition the hams to extend the hip can increase your risk of injury. Leg curls, although an excellent exercise for the lower portion of the hamstrings, do little for the upper hams. For maximum effectiveness, do leg curls for the lower portion and hip extension exercises for the upper hams. Leg presses work the hip extensor muscles but do little for the hamstrings. The best exercises for the upper hamstrings are step-ups, lunges, split-squats, and SATs. They work the hamstrings in movement patterns similar to those required in starting, stopping, running, and throwing. Train one leg at a time and use free weights to develop agility, balance, and body control.

Crossover Lunges

Stand with a dumbbell in each hand or a bar across your shoulders. Use a crossover step with your left foot and lunge across your body to the right. Push back and cross over to the left on your right leg.

Leg Curls

Lie on your stomach on a leg-curl machine with ankles under a roller pad. Curl one leg at a time. Curl lower legs to the buttocks, pause, and return.

Calf Raise

Stand erect with bar on shoulders or DBs in hands with arms extended. Place both feet on a 2-by-4 with toes forward. Slowly raise up on the toes as high as possible, pause, return, and repeat. Use a seated calf machine for variety.

Squat and Touch (SAT)

These exercises strengthen the muscles that stabilize the hip, knee, and ankle joints and develop the balance and coordination you need to field your position and run the bases. Stand on your right leg with your upper body erect. Bend your left leg at the knee and extend it behind you for balance. Squat on your right leg by bending at the hip, knee, and ankle. With your left hand, touch the floor directly in front of your right foot. Extend your right leg, stand up, and repeat. Repeat on the left leg and then step in these seven different directions:

- Forward SAT—Step forward with the right leg, SAT, return, and repeat with other leg.
- Backward SAT—Step backward with the right leg, SAT, return, and repeat with other leg.
- Forward-backward SAT—Step forward with the right leg, SAT, and return. Step backward on the left leg. Repeat by stepping forward with the left leg and backward on the right leg.
- Lateral SAT—Step to the right on the right leg, SAT, return, and repeat. Do both legs.
- Side-to-side SAT—Step to the right on the right leg, SAT, and return. Step to the left on the left leg, SAT, and return. Continue stepping side to side.
- Diagonal SAT—Step forward and to the right on the right leg, SAT, return, and repeat. Do both legs.
- Forward-backward diagonal SAT—Step forward and to the right on the right leg, SAT and return. Step backward and to the left on the left leg, SAT, and return. Continue stepping front and back.

Cowboy Squats

For the inner thighs, stand with your feet about shoulder-width apart with toes pointed way out. Squat to parallel and return. Keep your knees in direct line over the middle of your foot throughout the movement. For variety, repeat the movement with a weight vest or holding a DB in each hand.

Split Squats

Stand in stride position in front of a flat bench or box with your right foot forward and your hands at your side. Place the instep of your left foot on top of the bench or box. Keep your head and shoulders up and squat down until your right thigh is parallel to the ground. Check the position of your right knee relative to your right foot. In the down position, your right knee should be behind the end of your toes. If it goes over your right foot, slide your right foot forward. Pause, return, and repeat. Repeat on the left leg. Use DBs for more resistance.

Leg Press

Lie or sit down on a leg-press machine with your back flat against the support pad. Bend hips and knees to right angles and keep feet secure against the platform. Extend (press) both legs until they are straight. Pause, return, and repeat.

Multihip

This exercise has four movements. Adjust the foot platform so that your hip joint lines up with the axis of the resistance as your side faces the machine. Keep your body erect and do one leg at a time. Use the following variations:

Hip Flexion

Adjust the resistance pad so that it is at five o'clock position. Hold the handles and place your right leg behind the pad. Keep your knee bent and trunk erect. Pull your thigh forward to horizontal or slightly higher. Pause, return, and repeat.

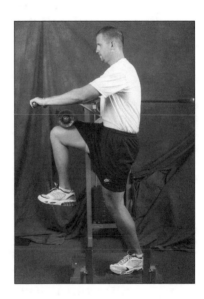

Hip Extension

Adjust the resistance roller to the eight or nine o'clock position when exercising the right leg. Place the right leg on top of the roller so that it is in a maximally hip-flexed position. Hold onto the handles for support. Push down on the lever arm until your leg is slightly behind your body. Pause, return, and repeat. Bend the knee on the way up and straighten it on the way down.

Hip Abduction

Stand facing the machine. Place the resistance pad at the seven o'clock position. Put your right leg behind the pad so that it crosses over the left (support) leg. Raise the leg out to the side (abduct) as far as is comfortable. Pause, return, and repeat.

Hip Adduction

Stand facing the machine. Place the resistance pad at the four o'clock position. Put your right leg over the pad. Pull the leg to the middle (adduct) as far as is comfortable. Pause, return, and repeat.

Upper-Body Strength-Training Exercises

You don't have to bench press 300 pounds to hit .300 or win 300 games. Hitting and throwing occur while you are standing, not lying on your back. As the saying goes, "The only athletes who play on their backs are bad wrestlers and bad football players." You don't have to train on your back to play on your feet.

Grip strength is important, but don't get so carried away with it that you neglect the rest of your body. Your forearms and hands make up only 2 or 3 percent of your total muscle mass and come into action only after you have started the bat and ball moving with your legs, hips, trunk, shoulders, and arms.

Upper Body

Bench Press or DB Bench Press

Lie on a flat bench with knees bent and feet flat on the floor. Keep buttocks and shoulder blades in contact with the bench. Lower the bar to chest level, pause, and press it straight up over the chest. When using DBs, lower them to shoulder level and then press the DBs upward and inward, forming the tip of a triangle at the top. Pause and slowly return. Do not arch the back. Pitchers and players with arm or shoulder problems may want to substitute push-ups for this exercise.

Incline Press or DB Incline Press

Sit on an inclined bench with knees bent and feet flat on the floor. Keep buttocks and shoulder blades in contact with the bench. Do not arch the back. Hold the bar at shoulder height. Press the bar straight up in the air, pause, return, and repeat. When using DBs, hold them with the arms flexed and hands even with shoulders. Press the DBs upward and inward, pause, slowly return, and repeat. Pitchers and players with arm or shoulder problems may want to substitute push-ups for this exercise.

Push-Up

For the chest, shoulders, and arms, lie on the ground with your hands flat on the floor just under your shoulders, fingers pointing forward, and toes curled under. Push up until your weight is supported by your hands and toes, pause, and return. Do these from a kneeling position if you lack arm strength or are recovering from an injury.

Push-Up Plus

To strengthen the muscles that stabilize the scapula, do this exercise at the top end of a standard push-up. Push up to the top, pause for two to three seconds to stabilize the shoulder, and then continue to push from the shoulders until the upper back is rounded and the shoulder blades move forward and away from the body (shoulder protraction). Hold this position for two to three seconds and then slowly relax the shoulders until the back is parallel to the ground (shoulder retraction). Return to the starting position and repeat.

DB Fly

Lie on a flat bench with both feet flat on the floor. Hold a DB in each hand at arm's length directly in front of the shoulders with palms forward. Keep a slight bend in the elbow and lower the DBs to the sides. Pause, return, and repeat. Try to visualize doing this exercise with an imaginary barrel on your chest. Bring the DBs up and around the barrel to the point where they almost touch.

DB Incline Fly

Repeat the previous exercise while sitting on an incline bench.

Lat Pull—Overhand

Sit with knees under the pad with arms extended with a wide overhand grip on bar. Slowly pull the bar to the front of your chest, pause, and return. Never pull behind the head. Substitute DB rows with palm in or back for this exercise.

Lat Pull—Underhand

Repeat the previous exercise with a narrow, underhand grip on bar. Pull with the arms, not the hands. Substitute DB rows with palm in or back for this exercise.

DB Row—Palm In

Stand next to a flat bench. Place your left hand and left knee on the bench for support. Bend forward at the waist until your back is parallel to the floor. Let your right arm hang straight down from your shoulder joint, palm facing inward. Grasp a DB with your right hand and slowly pull it directly upward until it touches the side of your torso. Keep your right elbow relatively close to your body when lifting and lowering. Pause, return, and repeat. Repeat with the other arm.

Seated Long Row

Sit on a rowing machine with head up, back straight, legs extended, and knees slightly bent. Grasp the handles with palms facing inward and pull (row) the hands to the chest area. Straighten the back, pause, return, and repeat. For variety, repeat the exercise on a seated row machine. Do one set with the palms facing in and one with the palms facing down.

DB Row—Palm Back

This is similar to previous exercise, but the grip is with the palm facing back, and the DB is held away from the body. Keep the elbow up and out and the forearm straight down throughout the exercise. Raise the DB until the triceps are parallel to the floor. Pause, return, and repeat. Repeat with the other arm.

DB Protraction/Retraction

Do this exercise to help stabilize the shoulder. Lie on a flat bench with a DB in each hand, palms forward. Extend (press) the DBs to arm's length. Keep the elbows straight, relax the chest, and allow the shoulders and scapula to move toward the floor (retraction). Pause, contract the chest, and pull the shoulders and scapula forward (protraction; see photo). This is not a chest exercise. Always keep the arms extended. For variety, repeat the exercise on a chest-press machine.

Triceps Kickback

Place your left knee and left hand on a bench so that your back is about parallel to the floor. Grasp a DB with the right hand and hold it just under the right shoulder with the right elbow against your side and palm facing the body. Extend the elbow backward until the forearm is parallel to the floor. Pause, return, and repeat. After several reps, repeat with the other arm.

Triceps Press-Down

Stand in front of a high-pulley machine, with feet shoulder-width apart. Grasp a v-bar with an overhand grip. Keeping the elbows tight to the body, extend the arms and press (push) the bar straight down until both arms are straight. Pause, return, and repeat. Don't lock the elbows at the bottom of the movement and don't let the forearms come up higher than parallel to the floor at the top. For variety, repeat the exercise with a flat bar and the palms down and up (reverse triceps press).

Rope Triceps Press

Repeat the previous exercise using a rope. Grasp the rope with both hands, palms inward. Extend the arms and pull the rope straight down until both arms are straight. Flare the rope out to the sides as you near the end of the movement. Pause, return, and repeat. Don't lock the elbows at the bottom and don't let the forearms come up higher than parallel to the floor at the top.

EZ Triceps Press

Lie on your back on a flat bench, with both feet flat on the floor. With hands about shoulder-width apart, hold an EZ-curl bar at arm's length directly over your chest. Keeping the elbows stationary, slowly bend the elbows and lower the bar to the top of your forehead. Pause, extend the elbows, and return. Don't lock the elbows.

DB Arm Curl

Sit or stand with knees slightly bent and feet flat on the ground. Hold a DB in each hand with arms extended and palms facing forward (underhand grip). Curl (raise) one DB (palm up) to the shoulder. Pause, roll (turn the palm down), and return to starting position. Alternate using right and left arms.

DB Hammer Curl

Repeat the previous drill with the knuckles facing inward.

21s ARE NOT FUNCTIONAL

The guys in the gym with biggest biceps swear that the best routine for building biceps is 21s. But these train only the part that is working and develop strength only in the first or last half of the ROM. There's no transfer of strength to other points in the ROM. For peak performance, work the muscle through its full ROM. Skip the 21s. Do curls through a full ROM.

EZ-Bar Curl

Stand holding an EZ bar in both hands, with arms extended down. Curl both arms and pull the bar to chest height. Pause, return, and repeat.

Bar Curl

Repeat the previous exercise with a straight bar.

Machine Curl

Sit on an arm-curl machine. Adjust the seat lever until your elbows are in line with the machine's axis of rotation. Grasp the handgrips, with palms facing upward. Maintain an erect posture as you flex the elbows and pull the hands toward the shoulders. Pause, return, and repeat.

DB Shrug

Stand with arms extended downward at your sides. Hold DB in each hand with overhand grip, palms facing the body. Keep your feet shoulder-width apart. Bring your shoulders up to your ears, pause, pull shoulder blades together, pause, return, and repeat.

Back Extension (Raise)

Lie in a prone position over the seat of a back extension device with your feet secured between the rear pads and your pelvic girdle resting on the seat. Hang your upper trunk over the seat, keeping your spinal muscles relaxed. Place your hands behind your low back and keep your legs fully extended and straight. Raise your head and chest first and then raise your trunk. Stop when your upper trunk is parallel to the floor. Pause, return, and repeat.

Shoulder, Elbow, Forearm, and Hand

Few players give adequate attention in the gym to the smaller muscles of the rotator cuff, scapula, wrist, and hand. Many position players know that a strong rotator cuff, stable shoulder, and healthy elbow are important for pitchers but fail to see how important they are to their own game. Likewise, some pitchers fail to see how a strong wrist and hand strength can improve performance on the mound. Although these muscles are not the primary movers for throwing and swinging, they are extremely important.

Pitchers Aren't the Only Ones Using Arms

Pitchers are not the only ballplayers with shoulder problems. The shoulder is the body part most likely to be injured in both pitchers and infielders. Although shoulder injuries are more likely to occur in pitchers than in infielders or outfielders, infielders seek medical attention as often as pitchers and require as many surgical procedures. Why? Because they often throw off balance at a variety of angles, which places added stress on the shoulder and elbow. In addition, many infielders were pitchers in high school, which could have predisposed them to shoulder problems.

Rotator Cuff

All throwing athletes, not just pitchers, need a strong, healthy rotator cuff. The cuff consists of four small muscles that run from the shoulder blade (scapula) to the top of the upper arm (humerus). As a group, these muscles stabilize the upper arm in the shoulder socket and allow its range of motion. If, for some reason, one or more of the rotator cuff muscles can't help stabilize the shoulder, most major motions of the shoulder become impossible. An unstable shoulder can lead to impingement, tendinitis, bursitis, tears, joint wear, and pain. If you have an unstable shoulder, you can forget throwing, swinging, lifting weights, or even reaching overhead.

The cuff muscles work as a group to perform four basic functions: (1) counterbalance the upward pull of the deltoid on the humerus, (2) externally rotate the shoulder, (3) provide a stable base from which the prime and secondary movers at the shoulder can act, and (4) decelerate the arm when you throw. When you take the ball out of your glove, the deltoid muscles contract to bring your arm out to the side. Because the fibers of the deltoid run vertically from the top of the shoulder to the middle of the humerus, they pull almost straight up on the humerus. Without the cuff muscles, every time you lift your arm out to the side the deltoids would bang the head of the humerus up into the roof of the shoulder. In time, this impact of bone against bone would destroy the shoulder joint. Fortunately, this doesn't happen because the cuff muscles pull down on the humerus just enough to counterbalance the upward pull of the deltoids and prevent the head of the humerus from striking the roof of the shoulder.

When you throw (pitch), the cuff prevents impingement or restriction by rotating your arm outward (external rotation) as you approach the cocking position. To get a better idea of what impingement feels like, try the following exercise. First, raise your arms straight out to the side with your palm facing upward (external rotation). See how you bring both hands directly overhead without restriction? Now, turn the palms down (internal rotation) and bring the hands overhead as high as you can. Notice how you can't get them much higher than parallel. Motion stops when the site on the humerus (greater tuberosity) where the cuff muscles attach to the arm makes contact with the roof of the shoulder (acromion process) and impinges the tendons of the rotator cuff muscles and the subacromion bursa. Next, turn the arms inward until the palms are back and the thumbs are pointing down and raise the arms. How high can you go before it's uncomfortable for you to raise your arm? About 60 degrees? The cuff muscles help externally rotate the arm to reduce or prevent impingement in the throwing motion.

The last action of the cuff muscles is to decelerate the arm during throwing. The external rotators (infraspinatus and teres minor) contract eccentrically to put on the brakes at the end of the motion. They check forward movement to keep you from throwing your arm away from your body at release and slow down the rate of internal rotation during the follow-through.

EXERCISES THAT CAN HURT YOUR SHOULDER

Because the cuff muscles naturally rotate the arm outward to let you to raise your arm overhead, internal rotation is usually not a problem when you throw. It is, however, a problem when you work out. Lifts that call for you to raise your arm forward (forward raises), pull your hands to your chin (upright row), or pull your hands to the side (lateral raises) with the shoulder internally rotated (thumb down) can cause impingement. Supraspinatus flys with the thumb down are an excellent exercise for the rotator cuff, but don't go beyond 60 degrees or you will increase the risk of impingement. Also avoid overhead lifts in which the arm is abducted and externally rotated. Behind-the-neck presses, straight-arm forward raises with the palms up, and lat pulls behind the neck are unsound, put undue stress on your cuff, and increase the risk of developing shoulder instability.

Scapula

A stable shoulder is essential for proper throwing mechanics. By design, the shoulder joint is mobile and unstable. It consists of the head of the humerus (upper-arm bone), which is big and round, and the glenoid fossa of the scapula (shoulder blade), which is flat and shallow. The junction of these two bones has been compared to placing a volleyball in a saucer—you get a lot of mobility and a lot of instability. Injuries to the shoulder joint occur when the head of the humerus is allowed to move or wobble too much in the glenoid fossa. The cuff and scapular muscles help prevent this from happening. The cuff helps keep the head of the humerus in contact with the shoulder blade (glenoid fossa), and the scapular muscles, in turn, help keep the scapula in line with the humeral head throughout the throwing motion. If you don't adequately train the muscle of the shoulder blade, it will become weak as you fatigue. Weak muscles fatigue sooner than strong muscles, and fatigue disrupts the normal rhythm between the upper arm and shoulder blade. This abnormal rhythm changes your throwing mechanics and places more stress on your shoulder complex. Inadequate scapular strength-endurance will, in time, disrupt throwing mechanics, increase the risk of injury, and reduce velocity and accuracy.

Elbow

Elbow injuries tend to occur more often on the medial side (inner arm) than on the lateral side (outer arm). Stress on the medial collateral ligament and ulnar nerve is usually what causes pain. Sidearm pitchers, those who throw with poor mechanics, and players with weak cuff and scapular muscles are especially at risk. Although strength is important, the keys to preventing elbow pain are a healthy shoulder and proper throwing mechanics.

Forearm and Hand

Strong hands are important for hitting and pitching. Your hands are your last link with the bat and ball. How hard you swing is determined, in part, by how much force you apply to the bat. Hitters need grip strength to pull the inside pitch, drive the ball the opposite way, and muscle a jam shot over the infield. Pitchers need it to impart spin on the ball. A pitcher with good grip strength will throw a four-seamer harder and impart more spin to breaking pitches. Power hitters and power pitchers tend to score higher on tests of grip strength.

Rotator Cuff Program

Train the rotator cuff muscles three or four times per week year-round. Do the Jobe-type exercises depicted in table 8.1 with three- to five-pound dumbbells or surgical tubing. Start with one set of 10 and gradually build to three sets of 20 (see page 208).

Shoulders

Forward Raise

Stand with arms at the sides and palms facing back. Keeping your arms straight, slowly raise your hands forward to shoulder height with palms down.

Lateral Raise

Stand with your arms at the sides and palms toward the body. Keeping your arms straight and palms down, slowly raise your hands to shoulder height.

Shrug

Stand with your arms at your sides and palms toward the body. Keeping your arms straight, slowly raise (shrug) the shoulders to about ear level. May be performed with DBs.

Fly

Lie on your back with your arms straight up in the air about shoulder-width apart. With palms facing each other and a slight bend at the elbows, slowly lower your hands straight out to the sides.

Reverse Fly

Lie prone on a bench or flex your knees slightly and bend forward at the waist until your chest is parallel to the floor. Let your arms hang down straight down with your palms forward and thumbs pointing away from your body. Slowly raise both hands out to the side until they are even with your shoulders.

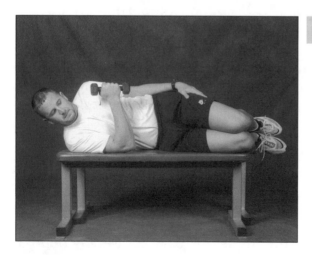

Internal Rotation

Lie on your back with arms down by your sides. Flex (bend) your right elbow to 90 degrees and hold your elbow against your right side. Keeping your elbow against your side, slowly lower (externally rotate) your hand away from your side as far as you can. Pause and bring it back across the chest.

External Rotation

Lie on one side with your knees bent. Bend the elbow of the top arm to 90 degrees and let your forearm and hand rest across your stomach. Keeping your elbow against your side, rotate your forearms outward until the thumb is pointing up, then slowly raise (externally rotate) the forearm until the hand is straight up in the air.

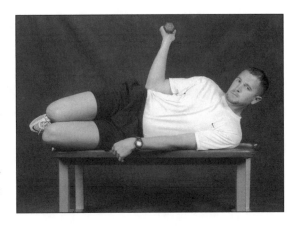

Supraspinatus Fly (Empty Can)

Stand with both arms down by your sides and hands rotated inward as far as possible with thumbs pointing down. Keeping your arms straight, slowly raise your hands forward and slightly out to the sides, as if pouring water out of a can. Do not lift higher than 60 degrees.

Upward Rotation

Lie prone on a bench or flex your knees slightly and bend forward at the waist until your chest is parallel to the floor. Pull your elbows back until your upper arms are even with your back. Bend your elbows and let your hands hang straight toward the ground with palms facing each other and thumbs up. Slowly raise both hands straight up (upward rotation) until they are even with your shoulders.

Shoulder Extension

Lie prone on a bench or flex your knees slightly and bend forward at the waist until your chest is parallel to the floor. Pull your elbows back until your upper arms are even with your back. Rotate your arms outward as far as you can (palms forward and thumbs away from your body) and slowly pull (extend) your hands back as far as possible.

Scapula Program

Do these exercises (table 8.1, page 208) three or four times per week, year-round.

Scapula

Scarecrow

Stand with a DB in each hand and hold both arms straight out from the sides at shoulder height. Bend each elbow to a right angle with palms forward and fingers pointing up. Keep your elbow up and rotate your right arm downward at the shoulder until your hand is pointing downward. From this position, rotate your right arm up as you rotate your left arm down.

Reach Back

From the top of a push-up, shift your weight to your right hand and slowly raise your left hand straight out to the side as you rotate away from the support hand. Continue to raise and rotate the trunk until the left hand is straight up over your body. Slowly return to a two-hand support position and reach back with the right hand.

Scapular Dip

Do this exercise either on a dip bar or off the edge of a bench. Use your scapula, not your triceps. From a normal dip position, with your chest up and elbows straight, lower your body toward the floor. Don't lean forward. Pause and then raise your body upward by pushing toward the floor.

Push-Up Plus

Assume a standard push-up position with hands about shoulder-width apart and fingers pointing forward. From the up position, retract (pull) the shoulder blades toward the spine and hold. Then protract (push) them as far away from the spine as possible. This is a scapula exercise, not a chest and triceps exercise. Work from a bent-knee position or while leaning into a wall if you lack sufficient strength to do a regular push-up.

Modified Pull-Up

Place a bar on the lowest rung of a squat rack. Lie down under the bar with your feet together. Reach up and grab the bar with an underhand grip. With your weight supported by your heels and hands, pull your chest up toward the bar.

Forearm and Hand Program

Train your forearms at the end of the workout. Otherwise you won't have the grip strength you need for your other exercises. Use light to moderate weight. Important as they are, these muscles are relatively small, and you can easily train them. Work these three or four times per week using a superset format. Pair wrist flexion with wrist extension, radial flexion with ulnar flexion, and wrist rollers with wrist twists. Hold the weight in your hands, not your fingers. Your finger muscles are small and weak. Don't fatigue them too soon. Work your forearms first.

Forearm

Wrist Radial Flexion

Stand up straight, with your arm extended and palm toward your body. Hold one end of a DB or hammer in your hand with your wrist straight. Using only the wrist, curl the weight up toward your thumb.

Wrist Flexion

Sit with your forearms resting on a bench, palms up, and elbows about six inches apart. Hold a bar or DB. Slowly flex your wrist and curl the bar or DB.

Wrist Extension

Sit with your forearms resting on a bench, palms down and elbows about six inches apart. Hold a bar or DB with your wrists and fingers flexed. Slowly extend your wrists. Because you have less muscle mass in your wrist extensors, you can't use the same load in flexion and extension.

Wrist Ulnar Flexion

Stand up straight, with your arm extended and palm toward your body. Hold one end of a DB or hammer in your hand with your wrist straight. Using only the wrist, curl the weight up toward your little finger.

Wrist Twist (Pronation/Supination)

Sit with your elbow against your knee holding one end of a DB or hammer in your hand so that it is pointing straight up. Brace your elbow with your other hand. Rotate the forearm as far as you can in one direction. Hold this position and then slowly rotate it in the other direction.

Wrist Roller

Stand with your elbows bent and down against your sides with your forearms parallel to the ground. Hold a bar in each hand using an overhand (palm-down) grip. Slowly roll the bar forward until the weight rises up to meet the bar. Pause briefly and then slowly roll the bar backward until the weight reaches the end of the rope. Keeping your elbows bent puts most of the stress on your forearms. Holding your arms out straight puts most of the stress on your shoulders.

Rice Drill #1—Pronation/Supination

Fill a five-gallon bucket with uncooked rice kernels. Sit with your right arm straight, palm inward, and fingers together and pointing down. Keeping your fingers and arm straight, rotate your arm clockwise (pronate) and counterclockwise (supinate) until your fingers touch the bottom.

Rice Drill #2—Stick Twist

Place an 8- to 10-inch-long stick about the thickness of a ruler or paint stirrer at the bottom of a bucket. Hold the stick in one hand. Twist your hand side to side.

Hand

Wrist flexion, wrist extension, wrist twist, and so forth are good for building forearm strength but not so good for the hands and fingers. The following exercises target the hand and fingers (see table 8.2). Start slowly. It's easy to overtrain these small muscles.

Rice Drill #3—Grip

From the position in drill #1, open and close your fingers as you work your fingers down to the bottom of the bucket.

Hand Grip

Hold a hand-grip device with your arm extended straight down by your side or use a blaster-type grip device.

Towel Pull-up

Wrap a towel around a pull-up bar and let both ends drop toward the ground. Grab one end of the towel with the right hand and the other with the left hand. Do not wrap the towel around the hands. Using your hands, do a pull up. This exercise works the weakest link in the chain (shoulders, arms and hands), the hands. You won't be able to do as many pull-ups as with the conventional method, but it will increase the strength of the hands and forearms better than most other methods.

Plate Squeeze

Hold a 25-pound weight plate in your fingers. Flex your fingers and pull the plate into the palm of your hand. Pause one second and slowly return to the starting position.

Table 8.1 Exercises for the Shoulder

Function	Exercise	Set × rep
Rotator cuff	Forward raise	1 × 10-20
	Lateral raise	1 × 10-20
	Shrug	1 × 10-20
	Fly	1 × 10-20
	Reverse fly	1 × 10-20
	Internal rotation	1 × 10-20
	External rotation	1 × 10-20
	Supraspinatus	1 × 10-20
	Upward rotation	1 × 10-20
	Shoulder extension	1 × 10-20
Scapula	Scarecrow	1 × 10-20
	Push-up plus	1 × 10-20
	Reach back	1 × 10-20
	Scapular dip	1 × 10-20
	Modified pull-up	1 × 10-20

Table 8.2 Exercises for the Forearm and Hand

Function	Exercise	Set × rep
Forearm	Wrist flexion/extension	3 × 10-20
	Radial flexion/ulnar flexion	3 × 10-20
	Wrist twist (pronation/supination)	3 × 10-20
	Wrist roller (forward/backward)	3 × 10-20
	Rice drill #1 pronation/supination	3 × 10-20
	Rice drill #2 stick drill	3 × 10-20
Superset these exercises. Start with 1 set of 10 and build to 3 × 20.		
Hand	Rice drill #3 grip*	1-5 ×
	Hand grip^	1-5 × 10-25
	Plate squeeze^	1-5 × 10-25

*Start with 1 set and build to 5 sets with 60 sec rest between sets.

^Start with 1 × 10 and build to 5 × 25 with 60 sec rest between sets. Increase weight as needed.

Chapter

9

Speed

You can cut up to a tenth of a second off your time from home to first in six weeks. With proper training, you can learn to run faster and reach your genetic potential for speed. You may not make the track team, but that shouldn't be your primary goal. Your goal should be to run faster in game situations.

You don't need an extremely high aerobic capacity to be successful in baseball. Baseball is an anaerobic game that requires mostly short bursts of all-out activity, not sustained submaximal effort. As a rule, if you can run a mile in 7 minutes or 1.5 miles in 10.5 minutes, your aerobic fitness should be sufficient for baseball.

Most runs in game situations are less than five seconds in duration, which means that quickness and acceleration are more important than pure speed. The average major-league player can run 60 yards in about 7.0 seconds, with the best in the game, Kenny Lofton, Deion Sanders, and Brian Hunter, running the distance in 6.2 or 6.3 seconds. Managers once believed that, no matter what they did, they couldn't make a slow athlete fast. They were right if *fast* is an arbitrary standard. The reality is, however, that good training can make any athlete faster and more efficient. How much faster is determined by genetics, but regardless of your genetic potential, you can get faster or you can get slower. Speed is an asset, but it's not the sole requisite for success. You can compensate for a lack of speed if you can react and start quickly, accelerate, stop under control, change direction, and avoid slowing down.

FIVE KEY COMPONENTS OF SPEED

Mechanics

Quickness

Acceleration

Agility

Speed-Endurance

You can take three steps to running faster: improve your running mechanics, improve your quickness, and improve your acceleration. You'll find the exercises and explanations in this chapter organized around those three steps. Start by noting your strengths and weaknesses. Use the drills outlined in this chapter to correct deficiencies and achieve your speed potential (see table 9.1 on page 213).

How much and when you work on each component will vary by position and where you are in the training year. Use the early off-season to develop a strong strength and aerobic base from which to launch an effective speed training program. Make your drills more sport-specific and position-specific as the season approaches. Pitchers, for example, need more aerobic and interval work, and position players require more speed-quickness. If you improve just one key component, you'll get faster. Improve them all and you'll achieve your speed potential.

You've run sprints for years without any measurable improvement? Don't continue to run meaningless sprints. Work on each of the key components of speed and you will get faster. Start with mechanics to develop good running technique. Then do speed intervals, quick starts, and sprints for acceleration. Run short shuttles for agility and long shuttles for speed-endurance. Lift for speed-strength and do plyometrics (see chapter 10) for speed-power. Don't forget to warm up, stretch, and cool down to avoid injury.

Improving Running Mechanics

The first step to running faster is to improve mechanics. Regardless of how much you run, how strong you get, or how much you stretch, you'll run only as fast as your mechanics permit. Develop good mechanics and spend three to five minutes on them every day. Don't take speed for granted.

Components of Running Mechanics: PAL

Robin Roberts, on being told that he could get to first base one step faster if he worked on running mechanics: "A lot of good that will do. I'm getting thrown out by three steps now."

The three basic components of good mechanics are posture, arm action, and leg action, or PAL (also see chapter 2).

Learn one component at a time. Work on the first component (posture) at half speed. Walk back and run again. Do five reps over 30 yards at half speed, rest one to two minutes, and then do five more reps at three-quarters speed. Rest and repeat the component at full speed. Then, try the next component (arm action). After learning each component in isolation, put them together in a single 30-yard run at half speed. Walk back and run again. Do five reps at half speed. Rest and do five reps at three-quarters speed. Rest and repeat at full speed. Stop when you become tired and start to slow down. When you run slow, you practice being slow. You have to run fast to be fast. Allow 24 to 36 hours of recovery between speed workouts.

COMPONENTS OF RUNNING MECHANICS

$$\left.\begin{array}{l}\text{Posture}\\ \text{Arm action}\\ \text{Leg action}\end{array}\right\} = \textbf{PAL}$$

Posture

Posture describes the alignment of the body, especially the head and trunk. Your head weighs about 10 pounds, and where it goes, the rest of your body follows. Look down and you lean forward. Look up and you lean back. Excessive lean in either direction reduces speed. Turning your head side to side or cocking it to one side keeps you from running in a straight line.

Body lean comes from the ankles, not the waist. To find proper body lean, stand tall and shift your weight toward your toes until the heels just leave the ground. The point at which your heels leave the ground is your proper body lean. Run the same way you walk, tall and relaxed, not hunched over. Keep your body tall and straight, as you would if looking over a fence.

Arm Action

Arm action involves the position and rate of movement of the arms and hands. Your arm pivots about the shoulder with the elbow locked at about 90 degrees. Assume that you have a rod through your shoulders and that each elbow is in a right-angle cast. The only movements possible at the shoulder are flexion and extension. Your elbows can't bend or open. If they open and close, most of your force goes up and down, not forward. Keep your elbows close to your sides. If they move away from your body, your trunk rotates side to side and you lose speed. Keep motions directly upward and backward from the shoulders.

Run cheek to cheek. Bring your hand forward to cheek level and then back past your pockets with your palms toward the body, thumbs on top of your hands, and hands relaxed. Bring your hand up to chest height on the front swing and down past your pocket on the down swing. Your arms and legs work together. The driving action of your hand past your buttocks coincides with the triple extension of the opposite leg to help propel you forward.

Your arms, not your legs, control speed. Don't believe it? Try this: jog slowly and check your arm action. Is it short and slow? Do your arms swing side to side across your body? Look at your stride. Is it slow and choppy? Now, pump your hands from cheek to cheek and watch your stride length increase. Want more speed? Pump your arms faster. Your arms and legs work together. Your legs move longer and faster to keep up with your arms. Pumping your arms from cheek to cheek makes you take faster, longer steps, which in turn increases speed.

SPEED TIP—SMOOTH AND EFFORTLESS

Accelerate without thinking about it. If you try to run harder, you'll tighten up and slow down. How many times have you tried to move your legs faster to beat out an infield hit or tried to kick it in after rounding third only to tighten up and slow down? Have you ever tried harder but failed to get to the ball? Speed is not about trying harder or forcing your legs to move faster. Use your arms, and your legs will automatically move faster.

Leg Action

Leg action focuses on the foot, ankle, knee, and hip. Lift your knee *forward, not up,* and let your lower leg relax and hang down. Keep your toe up and snap the foot down and back to drive you forward. Your foot should strike the ground directly under your center of gravity and push you forward. Ankle flexion occurs when you lift your toes toward your shin. Extension occurs when you push off or extend your foot. You have to load the ankle (flex it) before you can push off (extend it). Make sure that you pull the toe up toward the shin as your lead, or nonsupport, leg comes forward during recovery to load the ankle just before the foot strikes the ground. An unloaded ankle can't explode quickly on ground contact. You have to flex it while it's on the ground before you can get it in position for explosive movements. Loading the ankle while it's on the ground wastes time and slows you down.

Don't worry about stride length now. Reaching out causes you to overstride and slows you down. Also, forget high knee lifts. When your foot strikes the ground, the rebound will drive you forward and push your knee up. Punch the knee forward and let the rebound push it up.

Push the body forward! Place your foot on the ground and push away from the direction you want to go. Don't reach and pull. Push down and back to create an angle from the head to the foot that will move you forward.

Each component of running mechanics (posture, arm action, and leg action) affects the other two. If one is off, compensation of some form will always occur in the other two. The first area to break down is usually posture. Most athletes lose their eye focus or stand up too straight too soon. Both conditions disrupt normal arm action, reduce stride rate, and decrease stride length.

■ **D**rills for Running Posture

Eye Focus

Run 20 to 30 yards at half speed, keeping your head still. Look straight ahead and focus on an object at eye level near the point to which you are running. Walk back and repeat at three-quarters and full speed.

Table 9.1 Running Drills

Mechanics	Posture	Arm action	Leg action
	Eye focus	Seated arm runs	Leg cycles
	Cheek to cheek	Ins and outs	"A" skip
	Rise, fall, and run	Arm runs	
Quickness	First step	Reaction	Quick feet
	Wheel drill	Ball drops	Dot drill
	Get-ups	Reaction ball	X-jumps and hops
			Down-the-line drills
			Cone jumps/hops
			Supported jump-ups
			Rope jumping
			Quicks
			Wall runs
			Ladder drills
Acceleration	Start	Accelerate	Resisted/assisted runs
	5-yard starts	Build-up runs	Parachute runs
	Sprints	Acceleration sprints	Towing runs
	Jump/hop into a run		Hill runs
			Water running
Agility	First step	LSA	Resisted movements
	Box crossover	5-10-5 drills	Shuffle
		Microhurdles	Crossover
		Ball pick-ups	Backpedal
			Over the shoulder
			W drills
Speed-endurance	Gassers		Speed-aerobics
	200-400 shuttles		Repeat 100s
	Down/back in 15 sec		10 × 100 in 10 min
	30:30s		100-yd pick-ups
			60s and pick-ups
			Pole sprints
			Hollow sprints

Cheek to Cheek

Jog slowly with your elbows close to your sides and fixed at a right angle. Accelerate to half speed by bringing your hand forward to cheek level and then back past your pockets. Run for 20 to 30 yards keeping your elbow fixed and all movements at the shoulder. Walk back and run at three-quarters and full speed.

Rise, Fall, and Run

For proper body lean, stand with your feet parallel and about shoulder-width apart. With one arm forward and the other back, keep your body straight and rise up on your toes until you have to step forward to catch yourself and then sprint 10 to 15 yards.

Drills for Arm Action

Seated Arm Runs

Sit with your legs extended out straight. Keep your head up and arms relaxed with elbows fixed at a 90-degree angle and close to the sides. Move your left hand back past your pocket as your right hand comes up to your shoulder. As the hand passes the hip, turn the palm out slightly so the thumb brushes the hip to help keep your hands relaxed. Gradually increase arm speed as you pump your arms for 10 seconds. Do three sets and increase arm speed each set.

Ins and Outs

Stand with one arm forward and the other back. Keep your trunk erect, knees bent, head still, and eyes focused straight ahead. With your elbows fixed and arms and hands relaxed, slowly and rhythmically move your hands from cheek to cheek for 5 seconds. When your rhythm is good, use quick, pistonlike actions to accelerate to three-quarters speed for 5 seconds. Slow down to half speed for 5 seconds and then accelerate to maximum speed for 5 seconds. Repeat the drill three to five times going from half to three-quarters to full speed with a 10- to 15-second rest between sets. Then go from half to full speed and from zero to full speed. Gradually increase the duration of the drill to 10 seconds to simulate taking an extra base. Once you reach top speed (after about 5 seconds), let your arm action smooth out and become less pistonlike.

Arm Runs

Jog 30 yards at half speed moving your arms slowly. After 30 yards, keep your arm speed about the same but increase the length of your swing by moving your hands from cheek to cheek. Notice how your stride length increases as you get up on your toes. Keep this pace for 30 yards and then pump your arms as fast as you can and keep moving your hands from cheek to cheek. Did you get faster?

You had to. Your arms and legs work together. If you increase the range of motion and rate at which your arms move, your legs automatically move farther and faster to keep pace with your arms. Using your arms lets you speed up without having to think about it. It happens automatically.

Drills for Leg Action

Leg Cycles

Lean against a wall or rail. Cycle one leg through in a sprinting action. Emphasize keeping the leg from extending behind the body and having the foot kick the butt during recovery. Paw the ground with your foot to end the action. Dorsiflex the foot (pull the toes up) as the leg comes forward. Start slowly and gradually increase speed.

"A" Skip

Skip forward moving your arms opposite your legs. When you have established a good rhythm, lift the knee to waist height, keeping the toe up, and then forcefully extend the hip, knee, and ankle to drive the foot into the ground. Alternate right and left leg skips for 20 to 30 yards. Repeat the drill three to five times and gradually increase speed each set.

Improving Quickness

Speed is what you achieve after five or six steps. Quickness is what you get after the first one or two steps. You can learn to be quicker. You may never become lightning quick, especially if you're weak and your speed is mediocre, but you can become quicker. Small improvements can make a big difference. A fraction of a second can be the difference between a game-saving play and a run-scoring hit. To improve quickness, learn proper starting mechanics, improve reaction time, and develop quick feet. Incorporate starting and foot speed into your daily training routine. Give maximum effort on each rep. Limit drills to 10 to 30 seconds' duration in the early off-season to build a quickness base. Shorten the time to 10 seconds or less as the season approaches.

Starting Mechanics

Quickness begins with your starting position and first step. Start from a relatively low body position with the joints at a right angle and 75 percent of your body weight on your forefoot and 25 percent on your heel. Your first step determines where you're going and how fast you'll get there. Move only in the direction you want to go. Never give a step. Go directly to the ball or base, not up or down. Keep your center of gravity low for the first three steps to maximize leg drive. Gradually increase the length of each succeeding step. Throw your hands in the direction that you want to go to help start your arms pumping. Practice starting from different positions.

First Step

Your hips always move first. Practice being quick in all directions and practice all four types of first steps when going in different directions. Use a crossover step when moving a relatively long distance, as you would when stealing a base or going into the hole to field a ball. Use an open step when you need to move a relatively short distance. Use a drop step when going backward or diagonally backward to catch a fly ball. Do a turn and run to get to a ball that's over your head.

First Step Drills

Crossover Power Step

Turn your hips, throw your arms, cross over with the back foot, and drive off the ball of the foot of the front leg. Push off the right foot when going right and off the left foot when going left. Rotate your trunk and shoulders as you cross over, not before.

Open Step

Step out with the lead foot and push off with the back foot. Step quickly in the direction you want to go. Step with the right foot when going right and the left foot when going left. Move your hips and drive off the lead foot. Make your first step short and powerful.

Drop Step

Turn your hips and step out and back with the right foot when going right and with the left foot when going left. When going right, for example, start by turning your hips. Then move your right foot back 6 to 12 inches, throw your arms, and drive off the right foot.

Turn and Run

Open your hips in the direction of the run, take a drop step, pivot on the back foot, and drive off the lead foot. When going to your right, for example, turn your hips to the right, throw your arms, drop back a step with your right foot, pivot on your left foot, and drive off your right foot.

Wheel Drill

This drill helps develop a quick first step for all game situations. Begin with straight-ahead movements from a ready position using an open step. Go forward with your feet parallel. Then change your stance and go forward with your right foot forward and left foot back, and vice versa. When you can go forward, work on diagonal, lateral, and backward movements using crossover steps, drop steps, and turn-and-run techniques.

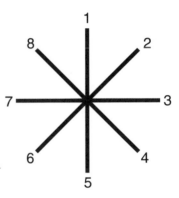

Stabilization

Learn how to stop on one foot. Start from a ready position in the middle of the wheel. Take one quick step and hold it for three to five seconds for balance. Stay low and return to the starting position. Then drive out low and fast for three to five steps. Break down and hold.

Get-Ups

Use the following drills to learn how to get up off the ground quickly when running the bases.

Head-first

Lie down as if you just slid head first into a base. There's an overthrow—get up quickly and sprint to the next base.

Feet-first

Lie down as if you just slid feet first into a base. Get up quickly and sprint to the next base.

Dive Back

Lie down as if you just dove back into a base. There's an overthrow—get up quickly, turn around, and sprint to the next base.

Reaction Time Drills

Reaction time is the interval between the stimulus and first movement. Reactions are much slower than reflexes. Reflexes (pulling your hand back after touching a hot stove) are involuntary actions that occur below the conscious level. Because you don't think about them, you can't control or train them. Reactions (getting a jump on the pitcher) are *conscious, voluntary* actions that you can think about, control, and train. Reaction drills require you to recognize a stimulus and quickly execute the right movement. Quick reactions start with being in the right place at the right time. Game-saving plays are the result of alertness, anticipation, focus, position, and training. Reactions are explosive. Do drills when you're rested and alert—fatigue makes you slower.

MAKE THE PLAY IN A HALF-SECOND OR LESS

Line drives and one hoppers through the infield are often clocked at 100 to 120 miles per hour. At these velocities, most balls will be on a first or third baseman standing even with the bag in a half-second. A pitcher standing about 56 feet away at release has less than three-tenths of a second to make the play or get out of the way.

Ball Drops

A partner stands about six feet in front of you and drops a tennis ball from head height. From a ready position, explode forward and catch the ball, without diving, before it bounces twice. Move up or back as needed. Make the drill more difficult by moving back or by dropping the ball from a lower height. Change the starting position and difficulty by using a crossover step before moving to the ball. Repeat in both directions. Change the drill by using two balls. A partner holds one ball in each hand and drops one or the other. Decide which ball is dropped, sprint forward or laterally, and catch it before it bounces twice. Make the drill more challenging by turning your back to the ball. Stand in a ready position with your back to a partner. On the command "drop," take a drop step with your right foot, turn right, find the ball, explode forward, and catch it before it bounces twice. Repeat turning left and repeat using two balls.

Reaction Ball

Stand in a ready position. A partner throws a Z-Ball to you on one bounce. Catch it before it bounces twice.

Quick-Foot Drills

Quickness starts with the first step, ends with the last step, and is controlled by the central nervous system (CNS). It begins in the brain and ends in the muscles. For maximum quickness, you have to reprogram the CNS to transmit faster signals, generate rapid contractions, and produce coordinated movements. Work on technique first and speed second. Learn how to do each drill correctly before adding speed. Keep the drills short and quick (five seconds or less). In time, you won't have to think about what's happening. You'll react automatically and take quicker, more powerful steps.

Dot Drill

Draw a two-foot-by-three-foot rectangle on the floor. Put a three-inch dot in each corner and in the middle of the rectangle. This drill has five parts. Do five reps of the first part as fast as you can and then, without resting, do five reps of each of the other parts.

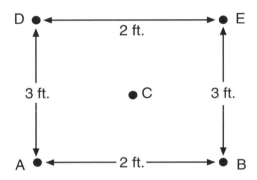

Up and Back

Stand at one end of the rectangle with the left foot on dot A and the right foot on dot B. Jump off both feet and land in the middle dot (C) with both feet at the same time. Immediately jump off both feet and land with the left foot on dot D and the right foot on dot E. Jump backward and come back in the same way.

Right Foot

Finish the up-and-back drill by landing with the left foot on dot A and right foot on dot B. Jump to dot C on the right foot and then, in order, jump to dots D, E, C, A, B.

Left Foot

End the right-foot drill with the right foot on dot B. Jump to dot C on the left foot and then, in order, jump to dots D, E, C, A, and B.

Both Feet

End the left-foot drill with the left foot on dot B. Jump to dot C and land on both feet. Now, jump in order to dots D, E, C, A, and B on both feet.

Turn Around

End the both-feet drill on dot B. Jump to dot C and land on both feet. Jump forward and land with the left foot on dot D and right foot on dot E. Quickly jump up and turn 180 degrees, face the other way, and land with the right foot on dot

D and left foot on dot E. Jump and land on dot C with both feet and then jump to dots A and B with feet split. Spin 180 degrees and repeat the drill.

X-Jumps and Hops

Stand on one side of an X. Jump from side to side 10 times on both feet. Keep your feet close to the ground and jump as fast as possible. Repeat the drill, jumping front to back and then jumping front to back and side to side. Repeat on one foot.

Down-the-Line Jumps and Hops

Stand to one side of a line five feet long. Move forward as you jump side to side as fast as you can. Jump to the end of the line. Rest and repeat moving backward. Repeat on one foot.

Down-the-Line Lateral Jumps and Lateral Hops

Stand with your toes on a line five feet long. Move to your right as you jump back and forth across the line as fast as you can. Jump to the end and come back moving to your left. Repeat on one foot.

Quicks

Stand facing a two-inch-high box with most of your weight on your left foot. Lightly place the ball of your right foot against the front edge of the box. Jump up quickly and cycle your feet so that most of your weight is on your right foot and your left foot is against the front edge of the box. Do 10 touches with each foot as quickly as you can.

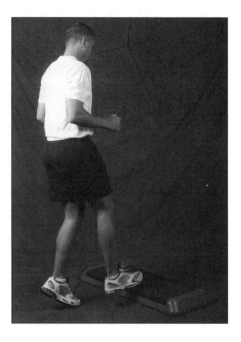

Wall Runs

Stand at arm's length from a wall. Place both hands on the wall for support. Lean into the wall and slowly run in place bringing your knees up. When you get into a good rhythm, sprint for 10 contacts with your foot. Slow down, stop, rest, and repeat.

Cone Jumps and Hops

Jump front to back over a six-inch cone as fast as you can. Repeat the drill jumping side to side and then jump front to back and side to side. Repeat on one foot.

Supported Jump-Ups

Place a 12-inch-by-12-inch square box that is 6 inches high next to a 30-inch box. Stand in front of the taller box and at arm's length away from the box. Place both hands on the box for support. Lean into the box and jump up on to and down off the box with both feet as quickly as possible. Make 10 jumps and rest. Repeat the drill with 12-inch, 18-inch, and 24-inch boxes.

Ladder Drills

Do ladder drills for foot speed and rhythm. Do a walk-through before you attempt to do each exercise with speed. Go as fast as you can, not as fast as you can't. Don't try to push speed to the point that you can't finish an exercise without goofing it up. Let your ability to complete all the steps be the limiting factor on your speed. Use the ladder to train movement quality, not just speed and quickness. Follow the word cues given below. Tell your feet what to do and they will obey. Don't stop at failure. Ladder exercises have a fast learning curve. Everyone looks and feels awkward the first few times through a new exercise. Relax, follow directions, and let learning happen.

Forward and Backward Wide Skip

Straddle the ladder. Skip forward down the ladder with your feet outside the ladder. Bring your knees up high and wide to increase range of motion. Repeat the drill going backward. Push your toes through the ends of your shoes to push your body backward. Push; don't reach back.

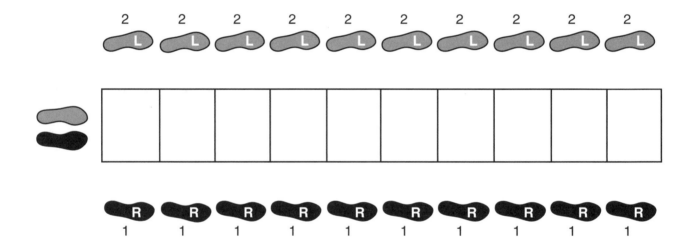

Skip and Crossover

Stand with both feet on the right side of the ladder. Skip across the ladder with your outside (right) foot. Land on the opposite side with your right foot outside the ladder. Skip back across with the outside (left) foot. Keep your head and chest facing straight ahead as your hip and knee cross over the ladder. Repeat the drill going backward.

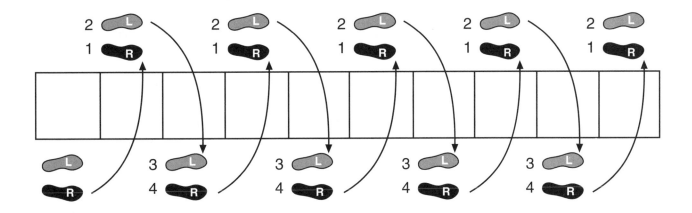

Icky Shuffle

Do this drill to develop a quick open or side step. Stand to the left of a ladder with both feet outside the first box. The drill starts with a side step and has three steps: in-in-out. Step into the first box with your right foot and then your left foot. Step across the ladder and outside with your right foot. Reverse the steps to the left, moving forward to the second box (left foot in, right foot in, left foot out).

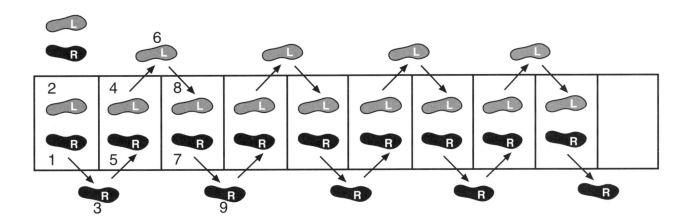

Always start with the foot nearest the ladder. Once you have the drill down pat, add a plyometric component to improve your ability to stop, balance, and cut back the other way. Start and increase the length of your third step as you leave the ladder (in-in-out). Push the outside step at least a yard or so beyond the outer edge of the ladder and then cut back as quickly as you can to the right. The increased length of the step forces you to lower your center of gravity as you prepare to change directions. Don't push the outside step too far out or you will have difficulty getting back to the ladder. Repeat going backward.

Crossover

Your word cues are "cross-out-out, cross-out-out." Start on the right side of the ladder, but this time cross your right (outside) foot over your left to land in square one. Then step outside the ladder with your left foot and then your right. Reverse the steps to the right (left foot in, right foot out, left foot out). Repeat going backward.

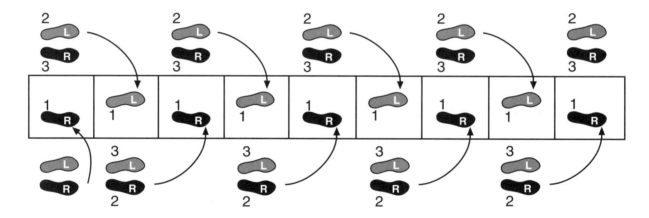

Two-Foot Hopscotch

Stand facing down the ladder with both feet together. Jump into the first square and land on both feet. Then jump up, spread your feet, and land with your feet straddling the second square. Continue going down the ladder, alternately placing two feet in and two feet outside each square. Repeat going backward.

One-Foot Hopscotch

Stand facing down the ladder with both feet together. Jump into the first square and land on the right foot. Then jump up, spread your feet, and land with your feet straddling the first square. Continue going down the ladder, alternately placing the right foot in and both feet outside each square. Repeat on the left foot.

Alternate One-Foot Hopscotch

Stand facing down the ladder with both feet together. Hop into the first square and land on the right foot. Then jump up, spread your feet, and land with your feet straddling the first square. Then hop into the second square and land on the left foot. Jump and straddle the second square. Continue going down the ladder, alternately placing the right foot and left foot in and both feet outside each square.

Rope Jumping

Short, fast jumps develop foot speed and improve your ability to make sudden changes in direction. Longer, slower jumps improve aerobic endurance. Jumping strengthens the ankles, knees, and shoulders and, because it requires constant shifting of body weight, improves balance and eye-foot coordination. Use a speed rope made of solid plastic PVC. Speed ropes are light and aerodynamically designed for speed and mobility. They are easy to handle, and you will progress more quickly than you would using leather, nylon, or heavy ropes. Wear cross-training shoes with good forefoot padding for shock absorption. Jump on softer surfaces (rubber flooring, gym mat, grass, or artificial turf) for aerobic endurance and harder surfaces (gym floor, carpet, or dirt for foot speed and quickness. Never jump on concrete. Always warm up with two or three minutes of shadow jumping (without a rope) and stretching.

Use the first two weeks of the off-season to learn proper technique and master the double leg and the stride jump. Jump only high enough to clear the rope. Land lightly on the balls of the feet. Stretch your calves during rest periods. Learn the basic jumps in table 9.2 and do a 10-minute circuit program using a mix of different types of jumps.

Table 9.2 Basic Jumps

Starting position	Feet together, body in line, eyes straight ahead, arms close to sides, and rope resting behind calves.
Rope measurement	Stand on center of rope with one foot. Pull handles along side to reach chest or underarm.
Double-leg jumps	Jump with feet together.
Stride jump	Jump and alternate feet, one forward and one back.
Skiers jump	Alternate jumping a few inches to the right and then to the left. Keep feet together and trunk straight ahead.
Crossover jump	Start with two-foot jump and cross one foot over the other on the second jump. Alternate crossing and uncrossing feet every other jump.
Single-leg jump	Jump on one foot.

Improving Acceleration

Acceleration gets you out of the box quickly and lets you steal bases, break up double plays, and get to balls in the gap. It helps you reach maximum speed in the shortest possible time. Although pure speed is good, acceleration is essential. Most plays cover 5 to 10 feet and rarely do you have to run longer than 30 yards, so success depends more on how much ground you can cover in the first 5 or 10 steps than how fast you can run 100 yards. Acceleration starts with the first step. Focus on starting mechanics, stay low, and make your first 5 or 6 steps explosive.

Starting Drills

Use these drills to achieve maximum speed quickly.

Five-Yard Starts

From a ready position, with your right foot slightly forward, sprint five yards. Walk back and repeat with the left foot forward. Repeat using a crossover step to the right and left.

Sprints

Sprint forward for 30 to 60 yards from a staggered stance. Repeat with a crossover step to the right and left.

Jump and Hop Into a Run

Jump forward three or four times on both feet. Land on one foot and sprint 20 yards. Repeat and land on the opposite foot. Repeat on one foot.

Acceleration Drills

Build-Up Runs (Jog, Stride, Sprint)

Jog 10 yards, stride 10 yards, and sprint 10 yards. Decelerate, walk back, and repeat. Gradually increase the distance to 15, 20, 25, and 30 yards.

Acceleration Sprints (Sprint, Jog, Sprint)

Sprint 10 yards, jog 10 yards, and sprint 10 yards. Slow down, walk back, and repeat. Gradually increase the distance to 15, 20, 25, and 30 yards.

Improving Agility

Baseball is a game of quick starts and stops, all of which you must make under control if you're to make the play and avoid injury. The ability to start, stop, and change direction is called lateral speed and agility (LSA). Success is related to how well you can start, stop, and change direction while keeping your body under control. On most plays, you'll take one or two steps sideways and then three or four steps straight ahead. Errors and injuries are often associated with plays involving an all-out change of direction.

Don't focus only on starting; you must also emphasize stopping. All movement involves both starts (force production) and stops (force reduction). Force production occurs when you break out of the box, go in the hole, or steal a base. Force reduction lets you stop under control, plant your foot, and make the throw.

LSA drills teach you to move quickly in all directions and control your body when moving at maximum speed.

First-Step Agility Drill

Box Crossover

Assume a ready position, with your right side next to a four-inch-high box. Use a crossover step and step onto the middle of the box with your left foot. Push off the box with your left foot and land in a ready position two to three feet on the opposite side of the box. Cross over onto the box with your right foot and drive your body back across the box. Make the drill more gamelike by doing ball pick-ups on each side of the box.

LSA Drills

5-10-5 Shuttles

Place three cones 5 yards apart. Start in the middle. Sprint to one end, stop, turn around, and sprint to the opposite end. Stop, turn around, and sprint to the middle. Repeat the drill using a mix of forward, backward, and shuttle movements. Then repeat the drill by sprinting 10 to 15 yards at the end.

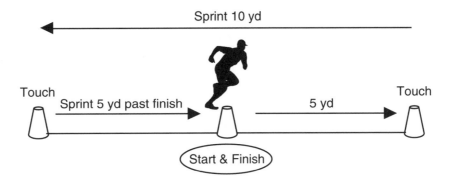

Sprint 10 yd

Touch   Sprint 5 yd past finish   5 yd   Touch

Start & Finish

Ball Pick-Ups

Assume a ready position three to four feet away from a partner. Shuffle five to six feet to the right as your partner rolls you a baseball. Squat down with good form (head up, back straight, and knees bent), pick up the ball, and toss it underhand back to your partner. Immediately shuffle to the left and field another ball.

Microhurdle Drills for LSA

High Steps

Set up four six-inch microhurdles three feet apart. Start by standing with both feet outside the end hurdle. Lift the inside foot (knee up, heel to buttocks, and toe up), push off with the outside foot, and step laterally over the first hurdle with first the inside foot and then the outside foot. Continue to move laterally over each hurdle (stepping first with the lead foot). When you

get to the end, stop with both feet outside the last hurdle. Then change direction and come back the other way. Increase speed when you get the rhythm down. Go over and back four times. Rest and repeat. For more speed, don't pause at each end. When you get to the end, place the lead foot outside the last hurdle and then quickly change direction and come back the other way. Repeat the drill with three hurdles for more speed and quicker changes of direction. For maximum speed, repeat the drill with two hurdles.

High Steps—Two-Hurdle Crossover

Stand with both feet outside the first hurdle. Cross over the first hurdle with the outside (left) foot. Then step over the second hurdle with the lead (right) and back (left) foot. Stop when both feet are outside the second hurdle. Go the other direction using a crossover step with the outside (right) foot. Go over and back four times. For maximum speed, don't pause at either end.

Resisted Movement Drills for LSA

Attach an eight-foot strip of tubing or bungee cord to a belt positioned at waist height. Have a partner hold a moderate amount of tension on the cord. From a ready position, move away from your partner using one of the following techniques. Walk back and repeat.

Lateral Shuffle

Shuffle five steps to the right, break down into a fielding position, and field a ground ball. Repeat to the left.

Crossover

Execute a crossover step and sprint five steps to the right. Break down and field a ground ball. Repeat to the left.

Backpedal

Backpedal five steps, break down, and catch a line drive.

Over the Shoulder

Pivot on your inside foot, turn, and break over the opposite shoulder. Run five steps and catch a fly ball. Repeat to the opposite side.

W

Inscribe a W as you move forward and backward five steps. Start with a backpedal, run forward, backpedal, and run forward. Stop and repeat the drill going the opposite way. Then do the drill by going forward on the first movement. Repeat the drill, moving a W laterally. Start with a shuffle to the right, shuffle back, shuffle right, and shuffle back. Stop and repeat the drill going the opposite way. Then do the drill by going left on the first movement.

Improving Speed-Endurance

Rarely will you run more than 30 yards in a game, but when you do, you can't slow down. Speed-endurance will give you the stamina to pitch into the late innings, take an extra base, and score without slowing down. Build general speed-endurance in the off-season using 200- to 400-yard interval sprints. Switch to sport-specific speed-endurance in the preseason with 30:30s and down-and-back runs.

Speed-Endurance "Gasser" Drills

200-, 300-, and 400-Yard Shuttles

Run 50 yards, stop, change directions, return, and repeat until you have run 200 total yards. Rest and repeat. Gradually build to 3 × 300 and 3 × 400.

30:30s

Start at one foul line. Stride around the warning track to the other foul line in 30 seconds or less. Rest 30 seconds and run again. If you can't make it in 30 seconds, run as fast as you can.

Down and Back (100 yards) in 15 Seconds

Start at one foul line. Sprint 50 yards, stop, change direction, and sprint back in 15 seconds or less. Rest 30 seconds and run again. If you can't go down and back in 15 seconds, run as fast as you can.

Interval Drills for Speed-Aerobics

Baseball is a game of speed, reaction, and power, not endurance. Although it's important to have an aerobic base, endurance training should not be the major focus of your training program. If you spend 80 percent of your time jogging, you'll spend 80 percent of your time practicing to be slow. Jog, cycle, or use the StairMaster early in the off-season to develop a base and then switch to interval sprints to improve speed, speed-endurance, power, and aerobic capacity in the same workout.

Repeat 100s

Stride 100 yards in 20 to 24 seconds. Rest 30 seconds and repeat. To make the drill more difficult, gradually reduce running time or rest.

100-Yard Pick-Ups

Place marks at 25-yard intervals on a 100-yard field. Start slowly and increase speed at each marker. Reach top speed at the 75-yard mark and hold it to the finish line. Run from start to finish in 15 to 20 seconds. Rest for 30 seconds and run again.

10 × 100 in 10 Minutes

Run ten 100-yard runs in 10 minutes. These are not continuous jogs. You have one minute in which to stride down and jog-walk back. Start your stopwatch and stride 100 yards at a comfortable pace (about 17 to 20 seconds), turn around, and jog back. Walk when you get within about 20 yards of the start. When one minute has elapsed, run again. Repeat the drill 10 times.

60s and Pick-Ups

Sprint 60 yards, walk back, and run again. After six sprints, do 20 to 25 ball pick-ups. Rest (30 seconds) and repeat.

Pole Sprints

Start at one foul line. Jog around the warning track to the opposite foul line, turn, and without stopping sprint straight across the outfield. Stop when you're about even with second base. Walk to the foul line and run again. Try to get even with second base in 45 seconds or less.

Hollow Sprints (Sprint, Jog, Sprint, Walk)

Sprint 60 yards, jog 60 yards, sprint 60 yards, walk 60 yards, then run again.

ADVANCED DRILL TECHNIQUES

Resisted running is running uphill on sand, with a weighted vest or body suit, up stadium stairs, or against a harness, sled, or parachute. These techniques can develop speed-specific strength and dynamic balance in the muscles used in sprinting. Attempting to achieve maximum speed against resistance will help you maintain a positive angle from the hip to the ground, achieve a strong leg drive, and generate maximum force from the ground up. With resisted running, the body recruits more muscle and nerve fibers and then transfers their effects to the task of sprinting. Running with ankle weights, however, has a negative effect on technique and stride length and should be avoided. For best results, observe the 10 percent rule when providing resistance and use a 10- to 15-yard running start on level ground before running uphill or against resistance. To keep mechanics and velocity as sport-specific as possible, limit resistance to no more than 10 percent of your body weight and make all runs at 90 percent of maximum speed or greater.

Assisted running is called overspeed training. With overspeed training, you run 10 to 15 percent faster than normal, develop the feel or sensation of overfast movement, and learn how to function under faster conditions. When these faster than normal conditions are removed, your body remembers the previous feeling of speed and applies it to normal conditions. Downhill running and towing are good methods of overspeed training.

The Speed Chute, developed for the 1988 Russian Olympic sprint team, is an effective aid to improving both running speed and running technique. These miniparachutes provide a drag as you run. The faster you run, the greater the resistance. Chutes can be used when running forward, backward, and around bases. By changing chute size and combining different sizes, you can vary the resistance, which is essential for breaking speed barriers.

Hydro, or water, running is used to maintain or improve fitness while avoiding the lower-extremity pounding that often comes with land-based running. Besides improving performance, there is evidence that water running can facilitate healing. There are two basic methods of water running. Deep-water running occurs in water that is over your head. A flotation device is used to keep your head and shoulders above water as you run. Shallow-water running occurs in waist-deep water at the shallow end of a swimming pool. Deep-water exercise is easy to do. All you need is a pool at least six feet deep and a flotation device like a ski vest or belt. The water provides resistance, and the vest keeps your head above water. For a more intense workout, try a scuba mask and snorkel. The mask will keep water out of your eyes, and the snorkel will allow you to breathe under water. Breathing under water increases the pressure on your thoracic cavity (makes it harder to raise and lower your ribs) and produces higher metabolic responses. First, you assume a vertical position in deep water and then run without touching the bottom. As you bring your thigh up, reach out and stride from your knee. Pull your leg down, under, and back, trying to kick yourself in the buttocks with your foot. Run tall with your hips under your shoulders. Don't let your buttocks drift backward. Keep your hands lower than your elbows. The hand of your lead arm should move no farther forward than the front of your chest and come back past your pocket on the back swing. Breathe naturally.

Slideboard training is excellent for burning calories and developing endurance as well as LSA, leg strength, coordination, and balance while moving laterally and without the impacts associated with running and jumping. You use a 12-foot-by-3-foot slippery board with adjustable, angled end stops and a pair of wool socks or booties. Shorten the board to 3 to 5 feet for rehabilitation drills and 7 to 9 feet when working on LSA and quickness. Place the booties over your shoes and assume a ready position at one end of the board with your head up, knees bent, back arched slightly, and arms bent to 90 degrees at the elbow. Stay low and push off with the back foot. Move the opposite leg and both arms in the direction you want to go to help overcome inertia. Glide to the opposite end, stop, and return. Beginners start with 10 to 12 reps (over and back is one rep) on a 9-foot board using 30-second work-rest intervals. Do 6 reps on day 2 with 60-second work-rest intervals and 10 reps with 15- to 30-second work-rest intervals on day 3. Work on LSA on day 4. Shorten the board to 8 feet and see how many times you can touch each end in 15 seconds. Rest 45 seconds and repeat the drill 10 times. Do an aerobic workout on day 5. Lengthen the board to 10 to 12 feet and slide continuously for 5 to 15 minutes.

10

Power

Strength is important, but power is the key to successful performance. Even if you're strong, you must also be able to apply strength quickly. Plyometric training develops functional, sport-specific power to help you run faster, jump higher, swing quicker, and throw harder. It bridges the gap between strength and speed. Plyometric exercises use explosive actions that mimic the movement patterns required in game situations.

In general, muscles respond relatively slowly—a contraction takes about five-tenths to seven-tenths of a second to develop maximum tension. But when you run, your foot is in contact with the ground for only about one-tenth of a second. You complete most movements, therefore, before you can develop maximal muscular force. Plyometric drills train both the muscles and the nervous system to help you generate maximum strength quickly.

Exactly how plyometric drills improve power is still unclear, but sport scientists think it's related to the stretch reflex. We know that muscles and tendons are elastic. We also know that if you stretch them immediately before asking them to contract they will contract with more speed and force. During the cocking phase of hitting, for example, a rapid stretch of the muscle fibers is responsible for producing the swing. Stretching these fibers activates the stretch reflex, which, in turn, sends a strong stimulus to the muscles causing them to contract with more speed and power. Plyometric training uses exercises that produce a rapid lengthening of a muscle quickly followed by a forceful shortening.

Working With Plyometrics

Plyometrics helps you integrate strength and speed. Use them in conjunction with speed and strength training, not as a substitute.

Safety

Because plyometric training is more stressful than weight lifting and sprinting, some risk is associated with its use. Injuries to the shin, knee, ankle, and lower back are not uncommon following plyometric training. In most cases, injuries are a direct result of too many workouts per week, too many reps per workout, improper form, hard surfaces, improper shoes, or failure to develop an adequate fitness base. The following 15 guidelines are crucial to reducing chances of injury:

1. Get in shape before you incorporate plyometrics in your training program to ensure that you have a minimal level of functional strength and balance.

2. Warm up before plyometrics and cool down afterward.

3. Wear good cross-training shoes to help absorb the impact on landing, stabilize the ankle, and protect the foot.

4. Do drills on a smooth, grass surface or gym mat to help dissipate the landing forces.

5. Use perfect form on all drills. Keep your head and trunk up. Bring your thumbs up and knees up on all jumps and hops. Land quietly on a full foot and bend the hips, knees, and ankles to absorb the shock of landing.

6. Start with simple, low-impact drills and progress to more complex, high-impact drills as skill and fitness level improve.

7. Start with horizontal movements because they are less stressful than vertical movements. Do drills (skips, jumps, and hops) for distance before doing them for height.

8. Consider your body weight when selecting drills. The stress associated with any drill increases with body weight. A low-stress drill for a 180-pound infielder could be a high-stress drill for a 220-pound pitcher. If you weigh more than 220 pounds, don't do many high-stress drills, especially if you have limited experience with plyometrics.

9. Start with drills that use two limbs. Single-support exercises are more stressful than double-support exercises. Do drills requiring two-leg jumps and landings first. Also do double-arm throws before single-arm throws.

10. Start slowly. The faster the rate of work, the greater the stress. Single-leg hops and bounding drills are more stressful than double-leg jumps. Start with slower exercises and gradually increase the speed of work.

11. Start with no external resistance. Doing a drill with added resistance increases the stress and slows the rate of movement. Avoid doing plyometrics with ankle weights, weighted vests, and so on.

12. Start with low-volume work. The more drills and reps you do, the greater the training demand. Volume and intensity are related. Do high-volume

work if the intensity is low and vice versa. Inexperienced athletes should do fewer exercises and reps than experienced athletes.

13. Start with low-intensity drills. The higher the intensity, the greater the training demand. Start with low-intensity exercises and gradually increase the effort as your skill and fitness improve. Advanced athletes have a greater tolerance for a given volume of high-intensity work.

14. Train two to three times per week. The more often you work out, the greater the stress. Avoid doing plyometrics more than three times per week.

15. Consider experience when selecting drills. Inexperienced athletes have a lower tolerance for plyometric work and should do mostly moderate-volume, low-intensity work involving noncomplex movements.

Progression

Do two- and one-foot standing long jumps in your first workout to learn how to land, stabilize, and jump up. These three techniques will be required in all subsequent plyometric workouts. In your second workout, review the skills developed in the first workout and learn how to jump and bounce in place to develop the quick-off-the-ground reactions needed to jump rope and jump high. Use workouts #3 through #5 to review the skills developed in the first two workouts and learn how to execute short, forward jumps to increase first-step quickness and acceleration. In workouts #6 through #24, learn how to increase horizontal velocity and make long, forward jumps to increase acceleration and top speed. Use a variety of drills to incorporate these skills into your weekly training program for the next four to five weeks and then learn how to do shock jumps to tax the neuromuscular system to its maximum. Beginners should avoid doing shock jumps until they have completed one full year of supervised training. Follow the outline in table 10.1 for the first five workouts. Do two sets of five reps of each drill with 30 to 60 seconds of rest between reps and drills.

Training Guidelines

There are four basic guidelines to using plyometrics:

1. The rate of stretch is more important than the length of stretch. When landing from a jump don't hesitate. Minimize the time between landing and takeoff. Intensity is also important. Be quick and give maximum effort on each rep.

2. Although using added resistance (such as ankle weights or weighted vests) can increase strength, too much weight can reduce speed and the ability to move explosively. For most drills, body weight is enough resistance. Don't do plyometric drills against external weight.

3. Proper technique is essential on every rep. In all jumping exercises, emphasize a knees-up-thumbs-up position to maintain balance and center the workload in the hips and legs. Emphasize proper follow-through and stress quality, not quantity, of effort.

4. Less is better. Start with two sets of 5 reps of the basic core exercises. Rest one to two minutes between sets and exercises. Add a third set after three weeks and build to three sets of 10. Do advanced drills no more than two or three times per week.

Table 10.1 Progression of Plyometric Skills and Drills for the First Five Workouts

Day	Skill	Drill
1	Landing	SLJ (standing long jump)—two-foot landing
		SLJ—one-foot landing
	Stabilization	SLJ—two-foot landing; hold 5 sec and jump again
		SLJ—one-foot landing; hold 5 sec and hop again
		SLJ—two-foot landing; hold 5-sec and jump again—repeat 3 times without rest
		SLJ—one-foot landing; hold 5 sec and hop again; repeat 3 times without rest
		Two-foot step off 6-inch box; hold 5 sec
		One-foot step off 6-inch box; hold 5 sec
	Jump-up	Jump up onto 12-inch box; hold 5 sec
2	Review	Do one set of five reps of each drill used in day 1
	Bouncing	Ankle flips
	In-Place	Tuck jump
		Split jump
		Scissors jump
3-5	Review	Do one set of five reps of each drill used in days 1 and 2
	Short jump	Three consecutive SLJ with two-foot takeoff and landing
		Five consecutive SLJ with two-foot takeoff and landing
		Five consecutive SLJ up stairs with two-foot takeoff and landing
		Single-leg hop—build to 10 consecutive hops off each leg

Plyometric Drills

"What kind of medicine is in medicine balls?"—**Yogi Berra**

Plyometric exercises are usually divided into five categories: (1) core drills, (2) trunk drills, (3) lower-body drills, (4) upper-body drills, and (5) total-body drills. Do core and trunk drills three or four times per week. Do upper-, lower-, and total-body drills once or twice per week on non-strength-training days (table 10.2). Use a medicine ball when indicated.

The ideal ball weight for speed and power is four to six pounds. Heavier balls can produce more strength but at a reduced speed of movement. The secret is the drill, not the ball. Substitute a basketball or volleyball if you don't have a medicine ball.

Table 10.2   Sample Plyometric Drills

Type of drill	Drill		
Core	Ankle bounce	Split jump	Standing long jump-hop
3 × weekly	Ice skater	Tuck jump	Lateral cone jump-hop
	Squat jump	Scissors jump	
Trunk (MD ball)	Twists	Good morning	Back-to-back (3 positions)
3 × weekly	Walking twists	Wood chopper	Figure-8 (3 positions)
	Backward toss-over	Rocker toss	Lateral pass (3 positions)
Lower body	Forward cone jump-hop	Box pop-up	Single-leg hop
1-2 × weekly	Side-to-side cone jump-hop	Box jump	MD donkey kick
	Bounds	Crossover jump	MD leg toss
Upper body	Chest pass (4 positions)		
(MD ball)	Two-hand overhead throw		
1-2 × weekly			
Total body	Squat and chest throw	Backward throw	Two jumps and throw
1-2 × weekly	Underhand throw	Discus throw	Cone jump and chest throw

Core Drills

These low-intensity drills develop balance, stability, and the ability to bounce and jump in place. Do these three times per week.

Ankle Bounce

Stand erect with knees locked. Bounce in place using only your ankles for force.

Ice Skater

Stand with feet flat on the ground, shoulder-width apart. Jump vertically and horizontally at the same time, going the greatest distance sideways. Explode back to the opposite side once your feet touch the ground.

Squat Jump

Stand with your feet shoulder-width apart. Interlock your fingers and place the palms of your hands against the back of your head to minimize the involvement of the arms and maximize the use of the legs. Quickly drop down to a half-squat position and immediately explode up as high as possible. Land quickly and jump up again. Try to achieve maximum height on each jump.

Tuck Jump

Stand with your feet shoulder-width apart and your hands palm down at chest height. Quickly drop to a quarter-squat level and immediately explode up. Drive your knees to your chest and attempt to touch them with the palms of your hands. Land and quickly jump up again. Concentrate on driving the knees up and tucking the feet under the body.

Split Jump

Start with your right foot forward, left foot back, and hands on your hips. Quickly drop until your right knee is flexed to 90 degrees. Then explode as high and straight up as possible. Swing the arms upward to gain additional lift. Land with legs in same place, bending the knee of the forward leg to absorb the shock. Regain stability and then quickly jump up again. Repeat with the left leg forward.

Scissors Jump

Start as before. Bounce up and down three times, then jump up and at the highest point of the jump, cycle your legs—kick the front leg back and bring the back leg forward. Land, bounce three more times, and then quickly jump up and reverse the position of the legs.

Standing Long Jump

Start with feet together, take a big arm swing, and jump forward as far as possible off both feet. Land on both feet and hold for five seconds. For variety, jump off both feet and land on one foot; jump off one foot and land on both feet; and jump, land, and sprint. You can also make three consecutive jumps and sprint.

Lateral Cone Jump-Hop

Stand to one side of a 12-inch cone. Jump side to side over the cone on both feet. Keep your chest up and emphasize keeping thumbs up and knees up. Repeat on one foot.

Trunk Drills

Before starting an intense plyometric program for your arms and legs, develop strength in the trunk. Why the trunk? Don't you run and throw with the legs and arms? Yes, but your trunk is the link between your arms and legs. Like most chains, your body is as strong as its weakest link. Regardless of how much you work your arms and legs, they're only as strong as your trunk. A weak trunk provides little support for your hard-working arms and legs. Do sit-ups and back extensions for the muscles that flex and extend the trunk and do exercises that combine diagonal and rotational patterns to mimic the actions of the spinal column in running, hitting, and throwing.

Twists

Hold a medicine ball at arms length and twist side to side 10 times while standing. Repeat from a kneeling and seated position.

Good Morning

Stand with knees slightly bent and a medicine ball behind your head. Bend at the waist. Stop when your chest is parallel to the floor and return.

Wood Chopper

Stand with feet shoulder-width apart and knees slightly bent. Hold a medicine ball at arm's length directly overhead. Bend forward at the waist with the knees bent. Swing the ball down between the legs as far as possible and return.

Back-to-Back Pass (Three Positions)

Stand back to back with a partner, arm's length apart. Hold a medicine ball at chest height with arms extended. Twist to your right as your partner twists to his left. Hand the ball to your partner and then, without pausing, twist to the left to receive the ball. Repeat in the opposite direction. Repeat to the opposite side. Repeat from a kneeling and seated position.

Figure-8 Pass (Three Positions)

Stand back to back with a partner, arm's length apart. Hold a medicine ball at chest height with arms extended. Twist to your left as your partner twists to his left. Hand the ball to your partner and then, without pausing, twist to the right to receive the ball. Repeat in the opposite direction. Repeat from a kneeling and seated position.

Off-Center Pass (Three Positions)

Stand with knees slightly bent. Have your partner face your back and stand about three feet behind you and three feet to your right. Twist to your right as your partner tosses you the ball and then twist to your left and toss the ball back. Repeat in the opposite direction and from a kneeling and seated position.

Back Extension

Lie face down on a back-extension device, with an MD ball against your chest and your head pointed to the floor. Extend your back until your trunk is parallel to the floor. Do not exceed parallel. Pause, slowly return, and repeat. Repeat by twisting right or left as you come up.

Lateral Pass (Three Positions)

Stand erect with your feet shoulder-width apart and knees slightly flexed. Hold a medicine ball with arms extended to chest height. Twist your trunk to the right and, without pausing, quickly rotate to the left and pass the ball across your body to a partner standing to your left side. Receive a return pass from your partner, let it twist your body back to the right, and then quickly pass the ball back. Repeat to the opposite side. Repeat from a kneeling and seated position.

Rocker Toss

Lie on your back with both legs up in the air and hold a medicine ball over your head at arm's length. Drop your legs, sit up, and toss the ball using an overhead throw to your partner standing 10 to 20 feet away. Once you release the ball, quickly hold your hands overhead so you can catch a return pass from your partner. Catch the ball and return to the starting position by letting your trunk go back to the floor and your legs go up.

Backward Toss-Over

Sit on the floor with your legs straight out in a V position. Bend forward at the waist and hold a medicine ball at arm's length between your feet. Raise your upper body, arms, and ball as a unit and toss the ball up and back over your head to a partner standing one to two feet behind you. Keep your arms straight and toss the ball with your body, not your arms. Finish with your arms straight up overhead to receive a return pass from your partner. Catch the ball, return to the starting position, and repeat. For variety, toss the ball over one shoulder. Bend forward and hold the ball at arm's length over your left foot. Rise up and toss the ball to a partner standing one to two feet behind your right shoulder. Repeat the drill tossing the ball over your left shoulder.

Lower-Body Drills

These drills will develop explosive force in the hips and legs. Use a combination of jumps (two-foot takeoff) and hops (one-foot takeoff) to develop power, coordination, and balance. Make the drills more sport specific by executing a quick 10- to 20-yard sprint immediately after your last jump or hop. Use medicine balls for added resistance.

Cone Jump-Hop (Forward)

Place 10 cones about three to five feet apart. Jump forward over each cone with feet together. Emphasize keeping chest up, thumbs up, and knees up. Repeat on one foot (hop). For variety, sprint forward or laterally for 20 yards immediately after the last jump or hop.

Cone Jump-Hop (Side to Side)

Stand to the left of a 12-inch cone with your feet together and pointing straight ahead. Jump back and forth across the cone 4 to 10 times as quickly as possible. Repeat on one foot. For variety, sprint forward or laterally for 20 yards immediately after the last jump or hop.

Single-Leg Hop

This drill is similar to running on one leg. Raise one knee, push off with your standing leg, hop forward, cycle your foot over your knee, and land on the same leg. Hop as far as possible on one leg for 10 consecutive hops. Do one set and switch legs. Measure the distance covered by each leg in the first set. Try to achieve an equal distance with each leg. Try to hop as far or farther in the second set.

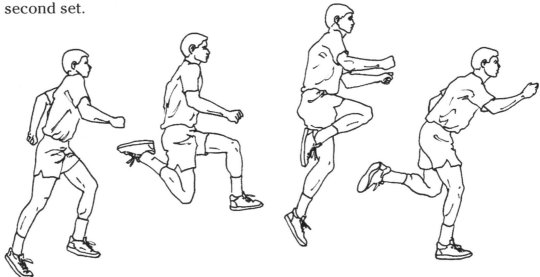

Bounds

This is an exaggerated running motion. Leg length and strength will determine how far you go. Jog easily for a few yards and then push off with the right foot. Bring your left leg forward while bending the knee and moving the right arm forward at the same time. As your left leg comes through, extend the right leg back. Hold this glide phase and then land on the right foot. Repeat the sequence immediately by pushing off on the left foot. Bound for 20 to 30 yards.

Box Jump

Stand about 18 to 20 inches in front of a stable 12- to 24-inch-high box. Dip slightly, swing your arms up, explode up, and land quietly on top of the box with your feet together. Remember to keep your knees and thumbs up when you jump and to land lightly, not with a thud. Step down and jump again. For variety, catch a ball immediately after landing or jump sideways on to the box.

Box Pop-Up

Stand with one foot on a 12- to 24-inch-high box. Forcefully extend the leg that is on the box and pop your body up in the air as high as possible. Land with the same leg on the box and gradually allow the other leg to contact the floor. Repeat with the other leg.

Crossover Jump

Stand two to three feet to the left of a 4- to 6-inch-high box. Step onto the center of the box with your right foot. Drive off the right foot and push your body to the opposite side of the box. Step onto the box with the left foot and drive your body back across the box. Gradually increase the force of the drive and push farther off the box. To make the drill more sport specific, have a partner roll a ball to you after each crossover.

MD Ball Leg Toss

Stand with a medicine ball held between your feet. Jump up and pull the ball up to your chest with your feet.

Donkey Kick

Lie on your back with both feet off the ground with hands under your buttocks for support. Have a partner toss a ball to the soles of your feet. Explode upward with both feet and kick the ball like a donkey. Repeat using one leg.

Upper-Body Medicine-Ball Drills

Do these drills to improve upper-body strength, range of motion, and power needed to improve arm and bat speed. Give maximum effort on each drill and pass or throw the ball to a partner standing 10 to 15 feet away.

Chest Pass (Four Positions)

Stand erect with feet shoulder-width apart and knees slightly flexed. Use a chest pass to throw the ball to a partner. Receive his return pass and immediately pass it back. For more arm and shoulder force, step forward when making the pass and step back after receiving a pass. For more trunk, hip, and leg strength, repeat the drill from a squat or lunge position.

Two-Hand Overhead Throw

Stand with feet about shoulder-width apart and the ball overhead in both hands. Step forward with one leg, extend the legs and hips, and throw the ball to a partner. Repeat with the opposite leg forward.

Total-Body Drills

Do these with a medicine ball to integrate the three links of the body (legs, trunk, and arms) in one explosive action. Give maximum effort on each rep to improve total-body speed and explosion. Pass the ball as far as you can on each rep. To make the drills more sport specific, sprint 10 to 20 yards after releasing the ball.

Squat and Chest Throw

Stand with feet about shoulder-width apart and the ball in front of the chest. Squat down and explode upward and forward with the legs as you make a two-hand chest throw (pass).

Underhand ("Granny") Throw

Stand with feet about shoulder-width apart and the ball hanging down as if attempting an underhand shot in basketball. Squat down and explode upward and forward as you make a two-hand underhand throw.

Backward Throw

Stand with feet about shoulder-width apart and the ball at waist level. Squat down and explode upward and forward with the legs as you throw the ball up and back over your head in the opposite direction.

Two Jumps and Throw

For more coordination and body control, repeat the three previous drills by jumping forward twice before making a throw.

Discus Throw

Stand with feet about shoulder-width apart and the ball at waist level. Bend the knees slightly and twist as far as you can to the right and touch the ball to the ground outside the right foot. From this position, twist back to the left and throw the ball up over your left shoulder. Repeat in the opposite direction.

Cone Jump and Chest Throw

Stand in front of a 12-inch cone with your feet together and pointing forward. Jump backward over the cone. Then jump forward, land, and make an all-out, forward chest throw (pass). Repeat, jumping side to side.

For More Information

Abrams, J.S. 1991. "Special Shoulder Problems in the Throwing Athlete—Pathology, Diagnosis and Nonoperative Management." *Clinics in Sports Medicine* 10:839.

Alter, M.J. 1990. *Sport Stretch.* Champaign, IL: Leisure Press.

"Androstenedion et al.: Nonprescription Steroids." Nov 1998. *Physician and Sportsmedicine* 26(11):15–18.

Anderson, B. 1980. *Stretching.* Bolinas, CA: Shelter.

Anderson, M.K., and S.J. Hall. 1995. *Sports Injury Management.* Media, PA: William and Wilkins.

Andrews, J.R., and K.E. Wilk. 1994. "Shoulder Injuries in Baseball" in *The Athlete's Shoulder,* ed. J.R. Andrews, B. Zarins, and K.E. Wilk. New York: Churchill Livingstone.

"Ask the Experts. Ginseng?" 1994. *Penn State Sports Medicine Newsletter* 2(9):8.

Axe, J.J. 1998. "Overview of the Principles of Conditioning and Training" in *Injuries in Baseball,* ed. J.R. Andrews, B. Zarins, and K.E. Wilk. Philadelphia: Lippencott-Raven.

Baechle, T. R. 1994. *Essentials of Strength and Conditioning.* Champaign, IL: Human Kinetics.

Balsom, P.D., B. Ekblom, K. Soderlund, B. Sjodin, and E. Hultman. 1993. "Creatine Supplementation and Dynamic High-Intensity Intermittent Exercise." *Scandinavian Journal of Medicine and Science in Sports* 3:143–149.

Balsom, P.D., K. Soderlund, and B. Ekblom. 1994. "Creatine in Humans With Special Reference to Creatine Supplementation." *Sports Medicine* 18:268–279.

Basmajian, J.V., and C.J. Deluca. 1979. *Muscles Alive—Their Functions Revealed by Electromyography.* Baltimore: Williams and Wilkins.

Beaulieu, J.E. 1981. *Stretching for All Sports.* Pasadena, CA: The Athletic Press.

Berning, J.R., and S.N. Steed. 1991. *Sports Nutrition for the 90s.* Gaithersburg, MD: Aspen.

Bickford, B. 1993. "Edible Energy Bars." *Training and Conditioning* 3(2):29–35.

Birch, R., D. Noble, and P.L. Greenhaff. 1994. "The Influence of Dietary Creatine Supplementation on Performance During Repeated Bouts of Maximal Isokinetic Cycling in Man." *European Journal of Applied Physiology and Occupational Therapy* 69:268–270.

Bisson, L.J., and J.R. Andrews. 1998. "Classification and Mechanisms of Shoulder Injuries in Throwers" in *Injuries in Baseball,* ed. J.R. Andrews, B. Zarins, and K.E. Wilk. Philadelphia: Lippencott-Raven.

Bloomfield, J., T.R. Ackland, and B.C. Elliott. 1994. *Applied Anatomy and Biomechanics in Sport.* Cambridge, MA: Blackwell Scientific.

Bompa, T. O. 1990. *Theory and Methodology of Training: The Key to Athletic Performance.* Dubuque, IA: Kendall/Hunt.

Bompa, T. O. 1993. *Power Training for Sport: Plyometrics for Maximum Power Development.* New York: Mosaic Press.

Bompa, T.O. 1993. *Periodization of Strength: The New Wave in Strength Training.* Toronto: Veritas.

Bradley, J.P., and J.E. Tibone. 1991. "Electromyographic Analysis of Muscle Action About the Shoulder." *Clinics in Sports Medicine* 10:789.

Bramhall, J. P. 1998. "Functional Anatomy of the Shoulder" in *Injuries in Baseball,* ed. J.R. Andrews, B. Zarins, and K.E. Wilk. Philadelphia: Lippencott-Raven.

Brunner, R., and B. Tabachnik. 1990. *Soviet Training and Recovery Methods.* Pleasant Hill, CA: Sport Focus.

Burke, E.R., and J.R. Berning. 1996. *Training Nutrition: The Diet and Nutrition Guide for Peak Performance.* Carmel, IN: Cooper.

Butts, N.K. 1993. "Effects of Body Position on Energy Cost During Stairmaster Exercise." *Medicine and Science in Sports and Exercise* 25(5s):S111.

Chu, D. 1989. *Plyometric Exercises With the Medicine Ball.* Livermore, CA: Bittersweet.

Chu, D. 1992. *Jumping Into Plyometrics.* Champaign, IL: Leisure Press.

Coleman, A. E. 1981. "Skinfold Estimates of Body Fat in Major League Baseball Players." *Physician and Sportsmedicine* 9:77–82.

Coleman, A.E. 1982. "In-Season Strength Training in Major League Baseball Players." *Physician and Sportsmedicine* 10:125–132.

Coleman, A.E. 1982. "Physiological Characteristics of Major League Baseball Players." *Physician and Sportsmedicine* 10:51–57.

Coleman, A.E. 1988. "A Baseball Conditioning Program for All Seasons" in *Injuries in Baseball,* ed. J.R. Andrews, B. Zarins, and K.E. Wilk. Philadelphia: Lippencott-Raven.

Coleman, A.E. 1989. *Astros Conditioning Manual.*

Coleman, A.E. 1991. *Player Performance During the Player's Strike.* Arlington, TX: Texas Rangers.

Coleman, A.E. 1991. *Total Fitness: A Physical Conditioning Program for Baseball.* Houston, TX: Houston Astros.

Coleman, A.E. 1993. *In-Season Speed.* Houston, TX: Houston Astros.

Coleman, A.E., and L. Laskey. 1992. "Assessing Running Speed and Body Composition in Professional Baseball Players." *Journal of Applied Sport Science Research* 6(4):192–197.

Coleman, A.E., M.J. Axe, and J.R. Andrews. 1987. "Performance Profile-Directed Simulated Game: An Objective Functional Evaluation for Baseball Pitchers." *Journal of Orthopaedic and Sports Phical Therapy* 9:101–105.

Coleman, E. 1996. "Nutrition Update: DHEA—an Anabolic Aid?" *Sportsmedicine Digest* 18(12):140–141.

Coleman, E. 1997. "Nutrition Update: Alcohol and Performance." *Sportsmedicine Digest* 18(12):140–141.

Coleman, E. 1997. "Nutrition Update: Herbal Harm and Invisible Ephedrine." *Sportsmedicine Digest* 19(5):57–58.

Coleman, E., and S.N. Steen. 1996. *The Ultimate Sports Nutrition Handbook.* Palo Alto, CA: Bull.

Colgan, M. 1993. *Optimum Sports Nutrition.* New York: Advanced Research Press.

Dillman, C.J., G.S. Fleisig, and J.R. Andrews. 1993. "Biomechanics of Pitching With Emphasis Upon Shoulder Kinematics." *Journal of Orthopaedic and Sports Physical Therapy* 18:402.

Dintiman, G., B. Ward, and T. Tellez. 1997. *Sport Speed.* Champaign, IL: Human Kinetics.

Dintiman, G., G. Coleman, and B. Ward. 1985. "Speed Improvement for Baseball." *Sports Fitness Magazine* 1:118–119.

Dintiman, G.B., R.D. Ward, and A.E. Coleman. 1985. "Good Ball Players Are Fast Ball Players." *Sports Fitness Magazine* 5:82–85, 118–119.

Egoscue, P. 1997. *The Egoscue Method Exercise Therapy Program* (VCR). San Diego, CA: Larry Magill Productions.

Eltzer, H., R. Evon, R. Lynn, and E. Kunkel. 1997. "Energy Bars and Gels: Do They Enhance Performance?" *Scan's Pulse,* Summer.

"Ephedrine: Does it work? Is it safe?" 1994. *Penn State Sports Medicine Newsletter* 3(4):1–2.

"Fads, Fictions, Frauds—and Facts. Unwanted Water." 1995. *Penn State Sports Medicine Newsletter* 3(7):8.

"Flat, Sexy Stomach in 5 Minutes Flat!, A" 1996. *Tufts University Diet & Nutrition Letter* 14(6):6–7.

Fleck, S.J., and W.J. Kraemer. 1988. *Designing Resistance Training Programs.* Champaign, IL: Human Kinetics.

Fleck, S.J., and W.J. Kraemer. 1996. *The Ultimate Truing System: Periodization Breakthrough.* New York: Advanced Research Press.

Fleisig, G.S., R.F. Escamilla, and S.W. Barrentine. 1998. "Biomechanics of Pitching: Mechanism and Motion Analysis" in *Injuries in Baseball,* ed. J.R. Andrews, B. Zarins, and K.E. Wilk. Philadelphia: Lippencott-Raven.

Frangolias, D.D., E.C. Rhodes, and J.E. Tauton. 1996. "The Effect of Familiarity With Deep Water Running on Maximal Oxygen Consumption." *Journal of Strength Conditioning Research* 10(4):215–219.

Galik, C. 1993. "Link by Link: Understanding the Closed Kinetic Chain." *Training and Conditioning* 3(2):4–11.

Gambetta, V. 1993. "A Test Slide: The Many Uses of the Simple Slide Board. *Training and Conditioning* 3(3):10–15.

Gambetta, V. 1993. "Leaps and Bounds." *Training and Conditioning* 3(4):7–14.

Gambetta, V. 1994. "In a Blur." *Training and Conditioning* 4(3):4–13.

Gambetta, V. 1994. "Speed Ways." *Training and Conditioning* 4(4):12–20.

Gambetta, V. 1995. "From the Core." *Training and Conditioning* 5(3):16, 19–22.

Gambetta, V. 1997. "Quick to the Ball." *Training and Conditioning* 7(6):31–35.

Gambetta, V. 1997. *Building the Complete Athlete.* Sarasota, FL: Optimum Sports Training.

Gamabetta, V. 1997. "Concepts of Baseball Conditioning: The White Sox Experience." *Strength and Conditioning* 19(4):7–9.

Gambetta, V., and S. Odgers. 1991 *The Complete Guide to Medicine Ball Training.* Sarasota, FL: Optimum Sports Training.

Gambetta, V., S. Odgers, A.E. Coleman, and T. Craig. 1988. "The Science, Philosophy and Objectives of Training and Conditioning for Baseball" in *Injuries in Baseball,* ed. J.R. Andrews, B. Zarins, and K.E. Wilk. Philadelphia: Lippencott-Raven.

Glass, B., D. Wilson, D. Blessing, and E. Miller. 1995. "A Physiological Comparison of Suspended Deep Water Running to Hard Surface Running." *Journal of Strength Conditioning Research* 9(1):17–21.

Greenhaff, P.L., A. Casey, A.H. Short, R. Harris, K. Soderlund, and E. Hultman. 1993. "Influence of Oral Creatine Supplementation on Muscle Torque During Repeated Bouts of Maximal Voluntary Exercise in Man." *Clinical Science* 84:565–571.

Greenhaff, P.O. 1995. "Creatine and Its Application as an Erogenic Aid." *International Journal of Sport Nutrition* 5:s100–s110.

Gross, M.L., S.L. Brenner, I. Esformes, and J.J. Sonzogni. 1993. "Anterior Shoulder Instability in Weight Lifters." *American Journal of Sports Medicine* 21(4):599–603.

Groves, R. and D.N. Camaione, 1983. *Concepts in Kinesiology, 2nd edition.* Philadelphia: Saunders.

Hagerman, F.C., L.M. Starr, and T.F. Murray. 1989. "Effects of a Long-Term Fitness Program on Professional Baseball Players. *Physician and Sportsmedicine* 17(4):101–119.

Halpern, A.A., and E.E. Bleck. 1979. "Sit-Up Exercises: An Electromyographic Study." *Clinical Orthopaedics and Related Research* 145:172–178.

Harris, R.C., K. Soderlund, and E. Hultman. 1992. "Elevation of Creatine in Resting and Exercised Muscle of Normal Subjects by Creatine Supplementation." *Clinical Science* 83:367–374.

Hay, J.G. 1993. *The Biomechanics of Sport Technique.* Englewood Cliffs, NJ: Prentice Hall.

Hendrick, A. 1995. "Your Soccer Personal Trainer—Determining How Much Weight You Should Use, Three Choices." *Performance Conditioning for Soccer* 2(6):2–3, 6.

Hinojosa, J.R. et al. 1997. "The Effects of an External Nasal Dilator Strip on Differentiated Ratings of Perceived Exertion." *Medicine and Science in Sports and Exercise,* 29(5s):s283.

"HMB: Proceed With Caution." 1996. *Penn State Sports Medicine Newsletter* 4(10):3.

Horrigan, J., and J. Robinson. 1991. *The 7-Minute Rotator Cuff Solution.* Los Angeles: Health for Life.

Hultman, E., K. Soderlund, J.A. Timmons, G. Cederblad, and P.L. Greenhaff. 1996. "Muscle Creatine Loading in Men." *Journal of Applied Physiology* 81:232–237.

Hurley, J., and B. Liebman. 1993. "Restaurant-Food Secrets Revealed." *Nutrition Action Health Letter* 21(1):1–19.

Hurley, J., and B. Liebman. 1995. "How to Pick a Cereal." *Nutrition Action Health Letter* 22(5):11–13.

Hurley, J., and B. Liebman. 1995. "Inside Sandwiches." *Nutrition Action Health Letter* 22(3):1, 10–14.

Hurley, J., and B. Liebman. 1997. "50s Restaurant Food: 'Happy Days' . . . or 'Grease'?" *Nutrition Action Health Letter* 24(4):1, 10–13.

Hurley, J., and B. Liebman. 1997. "Fast Food Follow-Up: What's Left to Eat?" *Nutrition Action Health Letter* 24(9):13–15.

Hurley, J. and B. Liebman. 1997. "What's at Steak?" *Nutrition Action Health Letter* 24(1); 1, 10–13.

Hurley, J., and L. Corcoran. 1998. "Meals to Go." *Nutrition Action Health Letter* 25(1):12–15.

Hurley, J., and S. Schmidt. 1995. "All Juiced Up." *Nutrition Action Health Letter* 22(6):11–13.

Hurley, J., and S. Schmidt. 1996. "Hard Artery Cafe?—Dinner House Make Fast Food Look Good." *Nutrition Action Health Letter* 23(8):1, 4–7.

Hurley, J., B. Liebman, and S. Schmidt. 1996. "Bad News Breakfast." *Nutrition Action Health Letter* 23(2):1, 8–11.

"Is It Real or Is It Met-Rx^tm?" 1995. *Penn State Sports Medicine Newsletter* 3(6):1–2.

Jobe, F.W. et al. 1984. An EMG Analysis of the Shoulder in Pitching. A Second Report. *American Journal of Sports Medicine* 12(3):218–220.

Jobe, F.W., J.E. Tibone, C.M. Jobe, et al. 1990. "The Shoulder in Sports" in *The Shoulder,* ed. Rockwood, C.A. Jr., and F.A. Matsen. Philadelphia: Saunders.

Jobe, F.W., J.E. Tibone, J. Perry et al. 1983. "An EMG Analysis of the Shoulder in the Throwing and Pitching: A Preliminary Report." *American Journal of Sports Medicine* 11:3–5.

Katch, F.I., P.M. Clarkson, W. Kroll, T. McBride, and A. Wilcox. 1984. "Effects of Sit Up Exercise Training on Adipose Cell Size and Adiposity." *Research Quarterly for Exercise and Sport* 55:242–247.

Kleiner, S. M. 1998. *Power Eating.* Champaign, IL: Human Kinetics.

Koch, F. 1994. *Strength Training for Sports.* Applied Futuristics.

Kraus, H. 1965. *Backache, Stress and Tension.* New York: Simon and Schuster.

Kurz, T. 1991. *Science of Sports Training.* Island Pond, VT: Stadion.

Lee, B. 1996. "Jump Into Top Conditioning and More Explosive Volleyball." *Performance Conditioning for Volleyball* 3(8)4–5.

Liebman, B. 1997. "Carbo-Phobia: Zoning Out on the New Diet Books." *Nutrition Action Health Letter* 23(6): 4–6.

Liebman, B. 1997. "Defending the Zone: Where's the Evidence?" *Nutrition Action Health Letter* 24(3): 10–11.

Liebman, B., and D. Schardt. 1997. "The Claim Game." *Nutrition Action Health Letter* 24(7): 10–11.

Loehr, J.E. 1994. *The New Toughness Training for Sports.* New York: Penguin Books.

Luketic, R, G.R. Hunter, and C. Feinstein. 1993. "Comparison of StairMaster and Treadmill Heart Rates and Oxygen Uptakes." *Journal of Strength Conditioning Research* 7(1):34–38.

Mastropaolo, J. 1975. *Kinesiology for the Public Schools.* CA: Paramount Academy.

McFarlane, B. 1988. *A Look Inside the Biomechanics and Dynamics of Speed, NSCA Strength Training and Conditioning for Speed Development: A Coaches Guide.* Lincoln, NE: NSCA.

Michaud, T.J., D.K. Brennan, R.P. Wilder, and N.W. Sherman. 1995. "Aquarunning and Gains in Cardiorespiratory Fitness." *Journal of Strength Conditioning Research* 9(2):78–84.

Nissen, S.L., and N.N. Abumrad. "Nutritional Role of the Leucine Metabolite Beta-Hydroxy-Beta-Methylbutyrate (HMB)." *Journal of Nutritional Biochemistry* 8:300–311.

Nissen, S.L., et al. 1996. "Effects of Leucine Metabolite Beta-Hydroxy-Beta-Methylbutyrate on Muscle Metabolism During Resistance Exercise Training." *Journal of Applied Physiology* 81(5):2095–2104.

Noden, M. 1997. "Give Me The Wide-Open Spaces." *Sports Illustrated* 86(25):110.

Nyland, John. 1997. "Static Hamstring Stretching for Knee Injury Prevention." *Performance Conditioning for Soccer* 3(8):6.

Odgers, S. and M.J. Axe. 1998. "The Baseball Catcher's Special Requirements" in *Injuries in Baseball,* ed. J.R. Andrews, B. Zarins, and K.E. Wilk. Philadelphia: Lippencott-Raven.

Parr, R.B., J.H. Wilmore, and R. Hoover. 1978. "Professional Basketball Players: Athletic Profiles." *Physician and Sportsmedicine* 6:77–84.

Pauletto, B. 1991. *Strength Training for Coaches.* Champaign, IL: Leisure Press.

Porcari, J.P., S.M. Pethan, K. Ward, D. Fater, and L. Terry. 1996. "Effects of Training in Strength Shoes on 40-Yard Dash Time, Jumping Ability and Calf Girth." *Journal of Strength Conditioning Research* 10(2):120–123.

Radcliffe, J.C., and R. C. Farentinos. 1985. *Plyometrics.* Champaign, IL: Human Kinetics.

Raven, P.B., Gettman, L.R., Pollock, M.L., et al. 1976. "A Physiological Evaluation of Professional Soccer Players." *British Journal of Sports Medicine* 10:209–216.

Royal, D. 1963. *Darrell Royal Talks Football.* Englewood Cliffs, NJ: Prentice Hall.

Ryan, N. 1992. *Miracle Man: Nolan Ryan, the Autobiography.* Dallas, TX: Word Publishing.

Ryan, N., and T. House. 1991. *Nolan Ryan's Pitcher's Bible.* New York: Simon and Schuster.

Schardt, D., and S. Schmidt. 1997. "DHEA: Not Ready for Prime Time." *Nutrition Action Health Letter* 24(2): 3–5.

Schlaadt, R.G., and P.T. Shannon. 1990. *Drugs.* Englewood Cliffs, NJ: Prentice Hall.

Schmidt. 1996. "Caffeine: The Inside Scoop." *Nutrition Action Health Letter* 23(10):1, 4–7.

Shadmehr, R., and H.H. Holcomb. 1997. "Neural Correlates of Motor Memory Consolidation." *Science* 277:821–825.

Shmock, P., and E. Swenson. 1990. *Weight Ball Training.* Seattle: Sound Publishing.

"Smokeless Performance." 1995. *Penn State Sports Medicine Newsletter* 3(5):6–7.

Smythe, R. 1988. *Speed Building* (VCR). Mountain View, CA: M-F Athletics.

Stanitski, C.L., et. al. 1977. "On the Nature of Stress Fractures." *American Journal of Sports Medicine* 7:391–396.

Thomas, J.A. 1988. *Drugs, Athletes, and Physical Performance.* New York: Plenum Press.

Toyoshima, S., T. Hoshikawa, M. Miyashita, and T. Oguri. 1974. "Contributions of the Body Parts of Throwing Performance" in *Biomechanics IV,* ed. R.C. Nelson, and C.A. Morehouse. Baltimore: University Park Press.

"Treadmills Make Best Indoor Calorie Burners." 1996. *Tufts University Diet & Nutrition Letter* 14(4):1.

Uram, P. 1980. *The Complete Stretching Book.* Mountin View, CA: Anderson World.

Volek, J.S, and W.J. Kraemer. 1996. "Creatine Supplementation: Its Effect on Human Muscular Performance And Body Composition." *Journal of Strength Conditioning Research* 10:200–210.

Ward, R., and P. Ward. 1991. *Encyclopedia of Weight Training.* Laguna Hills, CA: QPT.

Westcott, W. 1996. *Building Strength and Stamina: New Nautilus Training for Total Fitness.* Champaign, IL: Human Kinetics.

Williams, M.H. 1976. *Nutritional Aspects of Human Physical and Athletic Performance.* Springfield, IL: Charles C Thomas.

Williams, M.H. 1998. *Ergogenic Edge.* Champaign, IL: Human Kinetics.

Williford, H.N., M.R. Scharff-Olson, L.A. Richards, D.L. Blessing, and N. Wang. 1995. "Determinants of the Oxygen Cost of Slideboard Exercise." *Journal of Strength Conditioning Research* 9(2):90–94.

Wilmore, J.H., and D.L. Costill. 1994. *Physiology of Sport and Exercise.* Champaign, IL: Human Kinetics.

Wilmore, J.H., and W.L. Haskell. 1972. "Body Composition and Endurance Capacity of Professional Football Players." *Journal of Applied Physiology* 33:564–567.

Wisniewski, J.F. 1988. "Smokeless Tobacco" in *Injuries in Baseball,* ed. J.R. Andrews, B. Zarins, and K.E. Wilk. Philadelphia: Lippencott-Raven.

Yessis, M., and F. Hatfield. 1986. *Plyometric Training.* Canoga Park, CA: Fitness Systems.

Young, J.L., B.A. Casazza, J.M. Press, and S.A. Herring. 1988. "Biomechanical Aspects of the Spine in Pitching" in *Injuries in Baseball,* ed. J.R. Andrews, B. Zarins, and K.E. Wilk. Philadelphia: Lippencott-Raven.

Zarins, B., and S.R. Luallin. 1998. "Rotator Cuff and Impingement" in *Injuries in Baseball,* ed. J.R. Andrews, B. Zarins, and K.E. Wilk. Philadelphia: Lippencott-Raven.

Zatsiorsky, V.M. 1995. *Science and Practice of Strength Training.* Champaign, IL: Human Kinetics.

Zuti, W.B., and L.A. Golding. 1976. "Comparing Diet and Exercise as Weight Reduction Tools." *Physician and Sportsmedicine* 4:49.

About the Author

Gene Coleman has been a Major League Baseball (MLB) strength and conditioning coach for 22 years, working with the Houston Astros and Texas Rangers. One of the first strength and conditioning specialists hired in MLB, Coleman has worked with many of the game's stars, including Nolan Ryan, Jeff Bagwell, Craig Biggio, Ken Caminiti, Joe Morgan, Randy Johnson, and Moises Alou. He was the first to research the physical, physiological, and performance profiles of MLB players.

In addition to *52-Week Baseball Training*, Coleman has published 24 conditioning manuals for baseball teams, eight research articles on MLB players, and 50 other articles related to health and fitness. Coleman has worked as a strength and conditioning coach for the men's basketball team at the University of Texas at Austin, where he also worked on the football strength and conditioning staff. He has served as a consultant for several college athletic programs, as well as teams in the NFL, NHL, and NBA.

A college professor and strength and conditioning coach for 33 years at the University of Texas, Texas Tech, University of Houston, and Eastern Kentucky, Coleman received his EdD from the University of Texas at Austin, his MEd From Oklahoma University, and his bachelor's degree in physical education from Lamar University. Coleman has experience outside the sports arena as well, serving for six years as a member of the research team involved in astronaut selection for NASA. He received a Certificate of Recognition from NASA for writing the *Astronaut Training Manual* and helped design exercise protocols and evaluate exercise devices for space flight. Coleman is currently a full professor and chair of the program in fitness and human performance at the University of Houston at Clear Lake.

Coleman lives in League City, Texas with his wife, Barbara. They have two children, Jarrett and Ashlyn. In his spare time, he enjoys working out and watching baseball and college football.